Managing Responsibly

Corporate Social Responsibility Series

Series Editors:
Professor Güler Aras, Yildiz Technical University, Istanbul, Turkey
Professor David Crowther, DeMontfort University, Leicester, UK

Presenting applied research from an academic perspective on all aspects of corporate social responsibility, this global interdisciplinary series includes books for all those with an interest in ethics and governance, corporate behaviour and citizenship, regulation, protest, globalization, responsible marketing, social reporting and sustainability.

Recent titles in this series:

A Handbook of Corporate Governance and Social Responsibility
Edited by Güler Aras and David Crowther
ISBN: 978-0-566-08817-9

Making Ecopreneurs
Edited by Michael Schaper
ISBN: 978-0-566-08875-9

Ageing Populations and Changing Labour Markets
Edited by Stella Vettori
ISBN: 978-0-566-08910-7

Towards Ecological Taxation
David Russell
ISBN: 978-0-566-08979-4

Human Dignity and Managerial Responsibility
Edited by Ana Maria Davila Gomez and David Crowther
ISBN: 978-1-4094-2311-9

Territories of Social Responsibility
Edited by Patricia Almeida Ashley and David Crowther
ISBN: 978-1-4094-4852-5

Managing Responsibly

Alternative Approaches to Corporate Management and Governance

Edited by

JANE BUCKINGHAM and

VENKATARAMAN NILAKANT
University of Canterbury, New Zealand

Routledge
Taylor & Francis Group

LONDON AND NEW YORK

First published 2012 by Gower Publishing

Published 2016 by Routledge
2 Park Square, Milton Park, Abingdon, Oxfordshire OX14 4RN
711 Third Avenue, New York, NY 10017, USA

First issued in paperback 2016

Routledge is an imprint of the Taylor & Francis Group, an informa business

Gower Applied Business Research
Our programme provides leaders, practitioners, scholars and researchers with thought provoking, cutting edge books that combine conceptual insights, interdisciplinary rigour and practical relevance in key areas of business and management.

British Library Cataloguing in Publication Data
Managing responsibly: alternative approaches to corporate management and governance. – (Corporate social responsibility series)
    1. Social responsibility of business.
    I. Series II. Buckingham, Jane. III. Nilakant, V., 1952–
    658.4'08–dc23

Library of Congress Cataloging-in-Publication Data
Buckingham, Jane.
    Managing responsibly : alternative approaches to corporate management and governance / by Jane Buckingham and Venkataraman Nilakant.
        p. cm. – (Corporate social responsibility)
    Includes bibliographical references and index.
    ISBN 978-1-4094-2745-2 (hardback : alk. paper) – ISBN 978-1-4094-2746-9 (ebook)
    1. Industrial management. 2. Social responsibility of business. 3. Business ethics.
I. Nilakant, V., 1952– II. Title.

    HD31.B76945 2011
    658.4'08–dc23

                                                                    2012006148

ISBN 13: 978-1-138-27722-9 (pbk)
ISBN 13: 978-1-4094-2745-2 (hbk)

Contents

List of Figures and Tables

Figures

Tables

Notes on Contributors

John Alexander was born in Karaikudi, Tamil Nadu, India. He completed his doctorate in 2006 at the Institute of Philosophy, University of Leuven, Belgium, and is Professor of Business Ethics at Loyola Institute of Business Ethics, Chennai, south India. He is the author of *Capabilities and Social Justice* (2008) and many research articles in leading journals. He was a Visiting Research Fellow at Harvard University, under the guidance of Amartya Sen, and in 2010 was a Visiting Scholar at New Zealand South Asia Centre, University of Canterbury. His teaching areas include business ethics, sustainable development, theories of justice, and social and political philosophy.

Arindam Basu is an epidemiologist, ear nose and throat surgeon, and Director of the New Zealand South Asia Centre, University of Canterbury (2012). He is a Senior Lecturer in the Health Sciences Centre, University of Canterbury, where he teaches environmental health and related topics in health services research. His research interests are in the area of environmental and occupational epidemiology and associated models in health services research and delivery. He has served as a consultant to several organizations in designing epidemiological and fact-finding research on corporate environmental responsibility, and has authored over twenty book chapters and articles on various aspects of public and environmental health.

Jane Buckingham is a Senior Lecturer in History and former Director of the New Zealand South Asia Centre, University of Canterbury (2010–11). She is a specialist in South Asian history, with research interests in law, welfare, philanthropy, and the history of medicine and disability. She has published on disability, health and law, and her book *Leprosy in Colonial South India: Medicine and Confinement* (2002) was released as an e-book in 2008. Most recently, she has explored the philosophy and ethics of corporate management and governance. Her 2011 article, co-authored with John Alexander, on Indian traditions of 'common good leadership' was published in *Business Ethics: A European Review*.

Peter Cammock is the Director of Management Development at the University of Canterbury, and founder of the New Zealand Centre for Positive Leadership. His doctoral research explored the behaviours and characteristics of effective managerial leaders, and he has maintained an interest in leadership throughout his academic career. He was recently described by journalist Reg Birchfield of *Management Magazine* as 'one of the nation's best leadership writers', and has written a number of articles for international journals, as well as two books: *The Dance of Leadership* (2001, 2003) and *The Spirit of Leadership* (2008, 2009). He is particularly interested in the interplay of vision, emotionality, spirituality and character that is the necessary foundation of transformational leadership. These aspects of leadership are currently central to his academic and consulting activities.

Marjolein Lips-Wiersma is past Chair of the Management, Spirituality and Religion Interest Group of the Academy of Management, is Associate Editor of the *Journal of Management, Spirituality and Religion*, and has published numerous papers on meaningful work, existentialism, ethics and workplace spirituality in such journals as *Leadership Quarterly, Journal of Organizational Behavior, Journal of Management Inquiry* and *Journal of Business Ethics*. Her current research focuses on the antecedents and outcomes of meaningful work.

Colleen Mills is an Associate Professor of Organizational Development and Leadership at the University of Canterbury. Her research focuses on communication and sense-making during organizational change and development. Her work has been published in various journals, including the *Journal of Business Communication, International Journal of Entrepreneurial Behaviour and Research* and *Southern Review: Communication, Politics and Culture*. She has contributed to several edited publications, and recently co-authored, with Joanna Crossman and Sarbari Bordia, *Business Communication for the Global Age* (2011). She is a member of the editorial boards of *Group and Organization Management, Australian Journal of Communication* and *Communication Journal of New Zealand*, and is a past President of the Australian and New Zealand Communication Association.

Venkataraman Nilakant is an Associate Professor of Management at the University of Canterbury. He has published a number of papers in scholarly journals. He specializes in management of change, and has co-authored three books in this area: *Managing Organisational Change* (1998), *Change Management: Altering Mindsets in a Global Context* (2006) and *Changing Tracks: Reinventing the Spirit of Indian Railways* (2009).

Amal Sanyal is an Associate Professor of Economics at Lincoln University, New Zealand. He works on economic development, public policy, organization structure, incentives and corruption. He has published his work in a number of academic journals, including *The Indian Economy Review* and *Journal of the Korean Economy*, and in edited collections. He previously taught at Jawaharlal Nehru University, New Delhi, and held the State Bank of India Chair on Public Policy. For several years he was also economic adviser to the government of Mauritius.

Te Maire Tau is an Associate Professor of History at the Ngāi Tahu Research Centre, University of Canterbury. His interest is in Māori oral tradition, mythology and philosophy. He also has an ongoing interest in the philosophy of Karl Popper and tribal development. His publications include *Natanahira Waruwarutu: Kaiapoi Whare Pū-rākau* (2011). He has spoken and written widely on corporate and traditional management of water and electricity, and issues of cultural and natural sustainability for Māori in New Zealand.

Preface

Among the many wonderful innovations of the twenty-first century, is an on-line tool developed by Google called Books Ngram Viewer. This tool displays a graph that shows how selected phrases have occurred in a corpus of books over a specific period. Viewing the graph gives an indication of the frequency of use of those phrases in books. In other words, the graph indicates what ideas are dominant or in common currency. It thus offers an interesting snapshot of changing social trends. When you enter the phrases 'corporate social responsibility, shareholder value', the graph reveals some interesting results. The graph shows that, between 1950 and 1990, corporate social responsibility dominated shareholder value quite significantly. Around 1990, the idea of shareholder value became dominant, surpassing corporate social responsibility as an idea in common currency. Although corporate social responsibility has become increasingly significant since 2000, it has not challenged the dominance of shareholder value.

At the time of writing, the global financial crisis (GFC), largely brought about by irresponsible financial institutions in 2008, still threatens to unravel the global economy. Despite the official end to the recession triggered by the GFC, the weight of European and American debt continues to stifle recovery. The Head of the International Monetary Fund has warned that the global economy is entering a 'dangerous phase'. As Elizabeth Warren so eloquently points out: 'innovation in the market for physical products has led to more safety and cutting-edge features'. Innovation in financial products, however, has left consumers at the mercy of the creditors.

Admittedly, there are multiple causes for our current predicament. To financial collapse have been added the economic and human cost of massive climatic and seismic events. From late 2009, severe flooding in Pakistan, Australia and Brazil, and earthquakes in Chile, Samoa, Haiti, Christchurch, north India and Japan have brought devastation and misery. The economic costs of disaster management add further pressures to globalized economies already weakened by poor governance.

There is little doubt, however, that shareholder value enhancement in weakly regulated financial markets has been a major factor contributing to the ongoing economic crisis. While crises are deeply disturbing, they also force some re-examination of the ideas in common currency.

The idea for this book arose from a deep frustration with the evident inadequacy of current management and governance approaches to coping with economic crises. Moreover, business models which have been demonstrably ineffective in sustaining the economic welfare of both local communities and international economies are being applied, particularly by Western governments, to public institutions such as hospitals and universities. Although increasingly run on outmoded business models, these institutions are not direct producers of monetary wealth. Their value lies in providing a public good: supporting the social foundation of wealth creation, providing the education, values, corporeal care and skills needed for economic development in a stable civil society. While this book focuses on business ethics and governance, we suggest that its questioning of the narrow focus on maximization of shareholder interest in business practice is equally relevant to profit-driven models of governance and financial accountability now applied to hospitals and universities.

This book is an attempt to forge an alternative to the dominant idea of shareholder value enhancement. Drawing on multiple disciplines and perspectives, it offers alternative ways of viewing the profession of corporate management and governance. However, the diversity of views expressed here shares a single underlying assumption: wealth creation is a collective effort. No individual can become wealthy on his or her own. Unfettered pursuit of self-interest that underlies the idea of shareholder value enhancement misses this point. Free market capitalism has been at its best when the pursuit of self-interest has been moderated by an attention to other people's interests. Ignoring the social aspects of business distorts our view of management and governance.

We hope this book will stimulate debate on how we view and articulate ideas about management and governance. It emphasizes non-Western approaches to management and governance because: first, the ongoing global European and American debt crises underline the redundancy of the dominant Anglo-American shareholder model of profit-maximization for business success, and second, we are convinced that understanding non-Western traditions is crucial to developing alternative sustainable management approaches in a globalized corporate world. Managing responsibly is far more complex and challenging than enhancing the single metric of shareholder value. Our book sees corporate management responsibility to primary stakeholders – owners, employees, suppliers and consumers – as a core management principle rather than an optional extra. It also shows that balancing multiple interests, which is at the heart of modern corporate management, is an issue that humanity has grappled with throughout history.

This book is dedicated to the people of Christchurch. Several of the contributing authors lost their homes in the Canterbury earthquakes, others lost friends or neighbours, and all of us struggle with the challenge of rebuilding the city, universities and communities in which we live and work. Fortunately, community consultation is part of the governance culture in Christchurch. Although governance and financial management systems are far from perfect, there is a public acknowledgement that including the knowledge, capability and interests of a broad stakeholder base is the key to sustainable recovery. How well the Canterbury Earthquake Recovery Authority, local council, government, university, business, building and banking management convert this recognition into action will to a large extent determine the fate of our city.

Jane Buckingham and Venkataraman Nilakant

Acknowledgements

First, sincere thanks to the authors who – despite losses of home, office, library, computers and the strain of living with persistent earthquakes – all contributed the chapters they had committed to. Grateful thanks also to Catherine Hurley for her conscientious work as copyeditor, and to the College of Arts, University of Canterbury, for funding her work. The editors also wish to thank Güler Aras and David Crowther for the opportunity to contribute to Gower's Corporate Social Responsibility series, and Commissioning Editor Martin West for his patient and thoughtful guidance through the development of this publication.

The editors acknowledge and appreciate support provided by the Seriously Asia Fund, an initiative of New Zealand's Ministry of Foreign Affairs and Trade, which provided airfares for John Alexander's visit to the University of Canterbury. In 2010, as Visiting Scholar to the New Zealand South Asia Centre (NZSAC), John collaborated on the 'Success and the Selfless Manager' symposium which began the shaping of this book. Thanks also to the Indian Council for Cultural Relations Visiting Scholar program, which funded early development of the project during Jane Buckingham's affiliation with Loyola Institute of Business Administration in 2009.

Sincere thanks to University of Canterbury and to the NZSAC's patron, the Rt Hon. Sir Anand Satyanand GNZM, QSO, former Governor-General of New Zealand, for supporting our centre, the only interdisciplinary South Asia research centre in New Zealand. At the University of Canterbury, thanks also to our NZSAC and History Department colleagues for facilities and collegial support, and to Professor Jack Copeland, former Head of Humanities, for encouragement throughout the project.

Introduction: Globalizing Corporate Social Responsibility – Challenging Western Neo-liberal Management Theory

Jane Buckingham and Venkataraman Nilakant

The Context of Business

Theories of management and organization are rarely, if ever, neutral or value-free. Our ideas of how to manage and lead corporate organizations are heavily dependent on the nature of our context. In other words, time and place influence not only our ideas of the world, but also our models of management and governance. In particular, our institutional environment – the norms, values and myths – is particularly important to how we view management and leadership.

At the time of writing, the world faces multiple challenges. Four are particularly significant. First, economic growth in the developed countries has slowed down, thanks to the global financial crisis of 2009–10 that largely resulted from the irresponsible actions of financial institutions in the United States. In both the United States and Europe, soaring unemployment, increasing bankruptcies and the threat of depression have led to greater intervention by governments in the conduct of business. In the United States, the middle class, long held as the bastion of free market capitalism, now appears to be an endangered species. Second, our consumption-driven lifestyles have endangered the physical environment through increased carbon dioxide emissions that have contributed to global warming. Climate change has severely alarming consequences for multitudes of people across the world. Third, while deregulation and globalization have brought prosperity to many regions in the world, they have also deepened the divide between the rich and the poor. The world today is a very unequal place. Fourth, the rise of trans-national religious fundamentalism has resulted in the globalization of terror.

Paradigm Change or Business as Usual?

In these tumultuous times, these four challenges call into question our prevailing values and beliefs about the appropriate conduct of business. How relevant are our prevailing theories and models of corporate management in a changing world?

There are those who would argue that our prevailing models of management and leadership are robust and do not need any fundamental changes. There are others who view these models of management and leadership as part of the problem. This book is based on the premise that we need to re-examine our current models of management and leadership if we are to survive the present and enrich the future. First, let us examine the current model.

Persistence of Flawed Economic Theories

While there are multiple reasons for the global financial meltdown of 2009, our prevailing model of corporate management is also partly to blame. Ghoshal (2005) argues that bad economic theories of management are destroying good management practices. Referred to as 'the contractarian perspective' in this book, these economic theories view organizations, not as social arrangements, but as a nexus of contracts (Jensen and Meckling 1976). They assume that managers act solely to enhance their self-interest, which differs from the welfare of the shareholders. For that reason, managers cannot be trusted to act in the best interests of shareholders. Consequently, shareholders have a claim on the fiduciary duty of managers.

Ghoshal (2005) argues that the mindless adoption of these theories has led to bad management practices. Research has shown that using a set of good management practices characterizes high-performance organizations. Pfeffer (1998) identified the seven 'high performance management practices' that can lead to innovation, productivity and sustained profitability as follows: employment security, selective hiring, self-managed teams and decentralization, extensive training, reduction of status differences, sharing of information, and high and contingent compensation. However, there is little evidence of the widespread use of these practices in contemporary corporate organization (Pfeffer 2007).

The extreme case of Scott Paper illustrates the dysfunctional consequences of management practices based on the economic model. Corporate executive Albert (Al) Dunlap, who claimed that shareholders were the number one constituency, took over Scott Paper in the United States in 1994. Nicknamed 'Chainsaw Al', he promptly fired 11,000 employees and sold several businesses (Beer and Nohria 2000). By doing so, he tripled shareholder value as Scott Paper's market value rose from about US$3 billion in 1994 to about US$9 billion by the end of 1995. As Beer and Nohria note: 'The changes at Scott Paper unfolded like a military battle plan. Managers were instructed to achieve specific targets by specific dates. If they didn't adhere to Dunlap's tightly choreographed marching orders, they risked being fired' (Beer and Nohria 2000: 136). However, the short-term success had devastating long-term consequences: 'Dunlap trebled shareholder returns but failed to build the capabilities needed for sustained competitive advantage – commitment, coordination, communication, and creativity. In 1995, Dunlap sold Scott Paper to its long-time competitor Kimberly-Clark' (Beer and Nohria 2000: 137).

Ghoshal (2005) argues that the management practices that underlay Scott Paper are a direct consequence of flawed economic models of organization. He identifies agency theory and transaction cost economics as particularly damaging, yet these became the dominant theories of organization in the last two decades:

> *Combine agency theory with transaction costs economics, add in standard versions of game theory and negotiation analysis, and the picture of the manager that emerges is one that is now very familiar in practice: the ruthlessly hard-driving, strictly top-down, command-and-control focused, shareholder-value-obsessed, win-at-any-cost business leader of which Scott Paper's 'Chainsaw' Al Dunlap and Tyco's Dennis Kozlowski are only the most extreme examples.*
>
> *(Ghoshal 2005: 85)*

Despite overwhelming evidence that these economic theories are flawed, they have continued to persist in management education, research and practice. Why is this so? One reason could be that social science theories, even the positivist ones, are not value-neutral. They incorporate implicit assumptions about what the world is like or what it should be. One might argue that an ideology of neo-liberalism underlies present economic theories of organization.

There is little doubt that the rise of neo-liberalism in the 1980s and 1990s has strongly shaped our current theories of management and business. Neo-liberalism views individual freedom as the indicator and goal of human progress. In the neo-liberal perspective, individual liberty has priority over other concerns (Rawls 1971). However, neo-liberalism goes beyond Rawls'moderate formulations to assert that personal liberties, including property rights, should take precedence over all other goals (Nozick 1974). Taken together, neo-liberalism 'proposes that human well-being can best be advanced by liberating individual entrepreneurial freedoms and skills within an institutional framework characterized by strong private property rights, free markets, and free trade' (Harvey 2005: 2). Individual utilities and personal well-being are best served by pursuing self-interest – hence the ultimate goal of human action from a neo-liberal perspective is the pursuit self-interest. The philosophical foundation of neo-liberalism is more than two thousand years old. Its intellectual origins can be traced to the work of Plato, Hobbes, Mandeville, Bentham and Machiavelli (McCloskey 2006). However, in the last two hundred years, in the field of economics, it has led to a narrow view of self-interest maximization as the sole motivation of human conduct, leading to a neglect of other ethical issues that may also be important in explaining human conduct. Neo-liberalism is a major cause of economic deregulation and the diffusion of free market capitalism to different parts of the world.

The prevailing, yet relatively recent, model of corporate management is part of the neo-liberal revolution that has swept across the world since the early 1980s. In the 1980s, along with the rise of neo-liberalism, there was a transfer of power and control from corporate managers to shareholders (Useem 1993, Useem 1996). It has long been held that the purpose of business is to make a profit. Under shareholder capitalism, this was refined further. The purpose of business was redefined as the enhancement of shareholder value. In simple terms, the prevailing model of corporate management privileges shareholders over other stakeholders. This view is now so entrenched in the business psyche and in business schools that it is taken for granted (Sundaram and Inkpen 2004). Yet, not long ago, Peter Drucker, considered the father of modern management, argued that the purpose of business was to create a customer. He regarded the goal of making a profit as false and irrelevant (Drucker 2001).

Ideology of Neo-liberalism

An ideology of 'liberalism' underlies the economic model of corporate management (Friedman and Friedman 2002). The two main premises that shape theory within this ideology are: (a) a commitment to individual freedom, and (b) a belief in human failings (Ghoshal 2005). Taken together, these lead to a theory of management in which individual self-interest is seen as the driving force of human interactions. As this theory is based on an ideology of individual freedom, it avoids issues of morality and ethics, since these are seen to fall within the purview of individual liberty. The result is an economic model of corporate management where the notion of justice is the freedom to pursue individual self-interest as long as this does not disadvantage shareholders (Sen 1987, Boatright 1996, Stiglitz 2004). But, as Ghoshal reflects: Why should shareholders be privileged over other constituents?

> We also know that the value a company creates is produced through a combination of resources contributed by different constituencies: Employees, including managers, contribute their human capital, for example, while shareholders contribute financial capital. If the value creation is achieved by combining the resources of both employees and shareholders, why should the value distribution favor only the latter? Why must the mainstream of our theory be premised on maximizing the returns to just one of these various contributors?
>
> (Ghoshal 2005: 80)

The current economic theory of corporate management is based on the premise that a business firm is a nexus of contracts between different constituents such as shareholders, managers, employees, suppliers, customers and the community. Each constituent is expected to act rationally, which is defined as the pursuit of self-interest. Pursuit of self-interest is not only rational, but it also makes the system economically efficient. Economists argue that the shareholders, as investors, bear the most risk if the enterprise were to collapse. Therefore, the economic theory argues, it is the duty of managers to promote the interests of shareholders over others (Jensen and Meckling 1976, Boatright 1996).

This means that the starting point for any alternative model of corporate management would have to be based on different principles of justice. Clearly, shareholder value enhancement as the exclusive goal of corporate management needs to be re-examined. Corporate management has responsibilities that extend beyond shareholders. Yet to argue so without an economic basis would be to risk sermonizing. There are two main reasons to contest the exclusive attention to shareholder value in business firms. First, as discussed above, the idea of focusing exclusively on shareholder value is based on flawed economic theories. Second, as a practical goal, it is limiting and fails the test for a healthy business enterprise.

Efficiency, Fairness and Sustainability

As a human enterprise, the firm also needs to be fair. It must necessarily adhere to principles of justice that are part of its wider environment. In addition, it must endure beyond the short term. In other words, it needs to be sustainable. Therefore, any theory of corporate management must address three main issues: efficiency of the enterprise, the fairness of its dealings, and sustainability of its activities. If a business enterprise were not efficient, it would not be sustainable regardless of how fair it is. Similarly, if a business enterprise were not seen to be fair, it would find its legitimacy questioned and its long-term survival would be at risk.

Would an organization that is both efficient and fair necessarily be sustainable? This depends on our notion of fairness. As Rappaport notes: 'investment and corporate managers have a mutually reinforcing obsession with short-term performance, with earnings the most widely accepted metric' (Rappaport 2005: 65). If fairness is defined as exclusive attention to the short-term interests of a small group of investor-shareholders, the enterprise as an ongoing entity may not be sustainable in the long term. The case of Scott Paper, discussed above, attests to this notion. Therefore, for a business to be sustainable in the long term, it would have to redefine its goals, and particularly its notions of justice and fairness.

Fairness needs to be defined more broadly as the opportunity for stakeholders such as shareholders, employees, customers, suppliers and the community to enhance their welfare as long as their pursuit of their interests does not disadvantage others. Implicit in this understanding of fairness is an inclusive attention to the interests of a larger range of people recognized as stakeholders. This definition does not challenge the fundamental assertion of economic theory that people pursue their self-interest, but requires the firm to attend to the interests of stakeholders other than financial shareholders or those with a dominant role in the company's governance. Although limited access to wealth and corporate power may restrict the opportunities for the wider groupings of stakeholders to act in their own interests, fairness would require that their self-interest be taken into account in company activity. Sustainability requires the capacity to manage the tensions between fairness and efficiency likely to arise in the long term as a firm pursues profit. Broadening the stakeholder base and adopting a notion of fairness, which includes the interests of a wider range of stakeholders, can provide social and intangible resources such as loyalty and flexibility, which will support the firm in a complex economic environment. It is relatively easy for an organization to be both efficient and fair in the short term when the notion of fairness is limited to attention to the needs of a circumscribed group of stakeholders. However, in the long term, such a limited notion of fairness may be incompatible with efficiency. Allowing a broader stakeholder base to pursue self-interest in ways that support company efficiency but are not detrimental to others' welfare builds a broader-based social capital investment into the firm's ongoing efficiency. Recognition of the interests of stakeholders, such as employees, customers and the community, gives the firm an investment base with deeper economic and social roots, and so gives it a wider range of resources for dealing with possible competition between the self-interests of various stakeholder groups and economic challenges.

Adopting a notion of fairness broader than the one that exists in current economic theory renders both theory-building and practical action inherently complex. But it also encourages management thinking that is more nuanced, relevant and rich. Taking this one step allows for a more truly libertarian interpretation of the 'self-interest' basis of economic theory than the current neo-liberal approach. Current theory views shareholder welfare in terms of resources. The company is required to provide increasing resources to shareholders in terms of dividends. At the same time, majority shareholders are of greatest value to the company, and the company is inclined to work harder to both attract and retain high capital investing shareholders (Young and O'Byrne 2001: 5–8). As Booth notes: 'It is a normative statement that creating shareholder value (CSV) is the correct goal of the firm' (Booth 1998: 1). Even while retaining the current neo-liberal understanding of justice as primarily an aspect of individual liberty, expanding the notion of fairness to include

the interests of broader, less well-resourced groups of stakeholders begins to
challenge existing corporate practice.

In addition to limiting the firm's practice of fairness, exclusive focus on
shareholder wealth creates organizations typically characterized by a culture
of compliance and control. While there is movement towards developing
more integrated and consultative business models which recognize the 'self-
organizing' character of employee interactions within firms and which break
up internal hierarchies, command-and-control hierarchies remain dominant
in both the private and public sector (Woods 1996, Olson and Eoyang 2001,
Seddon 2005). Focus on shareholder wealth tends to create firms with a
command-and-control hierarchy, where employees, including managers, are
expected to do what they are told in the pursuit of a single goal. In this context,
the opportunity to develop sustainability in terms of the firm's human capital
and its capacity to inspire and support research and development are severely
limited. Employees, particularly those with high aspirations, are likely to find
the culture highly constraining, and the culture itself tends to stifle innovative
thinking from the lower ranks (Manz and Simms 1993). The organizational
culture in such firms is not oriented towards personal growth and development,
despite often having substantial human resource procedures in place. As a
manager at Scott Paper during Al Dunlap's tenure observed: 'I have a [profit]
goal of $176 million this year, and there's no time to involve others or develop
organizational capability' (Beer and Nohria 2000: 136).

The critiquing of the position taken by Scott Paper is implicit in corporate
social responsibility (CSR) arguments, which emphasize the importance of
integrating community into the functional orientation of the company. As
Joseph argues: 'CSR in reality is the alignment of business operations with
social values' (Joseph 2009: 403). When the company's goal of serving the
interests of the shareholder is widened to include the interests of multiple
stakeholders – including employees, suppliers, customers and the community –
the limited capacity of command-and-control hierarchies in discovering and
answering to these broader interests becomes evident. The broader stakeholder
approach to the firm cannot ensure that groups other than shareholders will be
treated more justly, or that the firm will be socially responsible in its practices.
However, it does allow for conditions of engagement both within the firm and
with others affected by its activities which support exploring ethical options as
legitimate aspects of business practice. In general, a broader stakeholder model
of business allows more flexibility in engaging with relationships between
CSR interests and activities and other corporate markers of success, such as

profitability and return on investments. To be really effective in leveraging CSR initiatives, stakeholder approaches need to replace as normative, shareholder focused command-and-control company models (Banerjee 2007: 25–8). Only in such circumstances can approaches to business management and business ethics be reconfigured to become more genuinely just.

Managing Responsibly

Management of corporate organizations in the twenty-first century is a profession, and corporate managers are professionals. While the profession of management may not be as developed as that of doctors, lawyers, engineers or scientists, it is nevertheless established as a distinct and widely recognized profession. As professionals, corporate managers have responsibilities. As Drucker argues, managers must adhere to the Hippocratic oath: 'Primum non nocere' ('First do no harm'). According to Drucker, the first rule of professional management ethics is 'not knowingly to do harm' – which is the basic rule of an ethics of public responsibility (Drucker 2001: 66). Merely exhorting managers to do no harm, however, is not enough. An institutional framework that lays out appropriate models for corporate governance must support it. As Aras and Crowther argue, there is a close relationship between good corporate governance and responsible business activity (Aras and Crowther 2009: 33–7). However, there remains a tension between the importance placed on social responsibility and the requirement for company profit. If the first goal of the company is profit and the second social accountability, then there is a risk that CSR will remain a 'luxury' rather than an essential element in business practice. Even when a company is committed to socially responsible practices, defining what that means in each context of business and service exchange is complex. To establish mechanisms that measure a corporation's actual practice of social responsibility is similarly difficult, particularly when massive discrepancies between statements of CSR practices and their delivery are common and notions of a company's 'value' tend to remain predominantly economically based (Aras and Crowther 2009: 30–33).

There is no simple or comprehensive means of instilling ethical values or practice into management and business activity. This book insists, however, that despite the difficulties of implementation, ethical practice can no longer be seen as a luxury. The massive international impact of the global financial crisis and the chronic European and American debt crises show that unless business is done justly and management is oriented towards wider stakeholder welfare, business will be socially, environmentally, morally and economically unsustainable. While we cannot offer absolute solutions, the authors of this book hope that our contributions will open debate and stimulate genuine interest in adopting alternative approaches to management, which will maximize not only narrow shareholder self-interest and profit, but also the welfare of all stakeholders.

This book does not propose a full-blown alternative theory of corporate management. It does, however, suggest that such a theory would have to address three issues: efficiency, fairness and sustainability. All chapters deal with one or more of these issues. Some point out the inherent defects in the exclusive pursuit of self-interest. Others offer alternatives to the current model of corporate management. These alternatives are based in contemporary and historical management models from India, New Zealand and the Pacific. The globalized nature of the current market, supply and labour economy makes such integration of non-Western historical and contemporary cultural practices into management essential for economic and ethical sustainability (Aras and Crowther 2009: 37–9, Hilimoniuk 2011). In some chapters, non-Western and indigenous traditions are discussed as offering alternative models to 'self-interest maximization'. Others explore the practical implications of Māori and Pacific Islander challenges to dominant management models. Taken together, these chapters aim to challenge the prevailing economic model of corporate management and suggest alternatives that are also fair and sustainable.

Part I of this book deals with the institutional framework for managing responsibly. The professional ethics of doing no harm needs to be operationalized by alerting managers to the dangers of relying on self-interest as the basis for corporate growth. Managers need to be provided with alternative frameworks and models of management that can work. Part II discusses the limitations of self-interest maximization as an organizing principle and lays out alternative frameworks and models. The book then explores how and why the professional ethics of doing no harm requires corporations to develop leadership capacities for the current global environment. Finally, the book suggests ways in which such capacities can be developed.

Part I: Making Managers Responsible

Part I deals with how to make managers more responsible to other stakeholders. Economic theories of organization focus on managerial incentives to align the interests of managers with those of the shareholders. Sanyal's chapter, 'Selfish Managers: Can We Eliminate Perverse Incentives?', deals with the dysfunctional effects of aligning managerial incentives too tightly with shareholders' interests. Capitalism works with incentives targeted at individuals. Hence the expectation that managerial decisions will be closely related to incentives detailed in the managers' appointment contracts. Sanyal argues that such incentives, which prioritize profit to the extent that they function without any broader ethical guidelines, can be termed 'perverse'. According to Sanyal, these 'perverse incentives' have led to two types of disastrous behaviour. The first leads managers to falsely signal a healthy company. Such signalling involves criminal acts – such as false accounting – and eventually brings both the manager and company to crisis. The second provokes managers to run down the interests of other business stakeholders in the quest for shareholder value. This pushes corporations to neglect environmental concerns, human rights, and product and worker safety, which impacts negatively on the wider communities, both local and global, connected with the company. Sanyal argues that a change in corporate governance, to make managers responsible to the wider body of stakeholders, can reduce the problem of perverse incentives. He gives examples of existing organizations that serve multiple stakeholders, and suggests practical ways to launch these ideas into the business mainstream.

The next chapter deals with the complex inter-relationships between corporate governance, business practice, the environment and human health. Management practices have the potential to cause harm to both the physical environment and human health. In his chapter, 'Corporate Environmental Responsibility: Whose Business, Whose Health?', Basu gives an overview of such relationships, provides a framework to evaluate them, and outlines the steps needed to better prevent the environmental and health damage caused by poor business decisions. Basu argues that the industrial activities and associated business processes of large corporations directly impact on the environment, which in turn can have deep and lasting impacts on public health. He reviews examples of the way such activities have affected environmental health in both India and New Zealand, and in the light of these proposes alternative business strategies which will foster environmental sustainability. One approach is embedded in the enactment of laws, framing of policy and governance – a top-down approach to regulate the industrial processes so that environmental damage is minimized. Complementing this is a grassroots corporate initiative to assume environmental responsibility, whereby corporations become self-regulatory in their commitment to protect the local and global climate and natural environment. Basu argues for the need to develop a framework based on both strategies that best optimizes sustainability and minimizes harm to the environment. Drawing on Indian and New Zealand experience, he contends that such a framework would be beneficial to environmental health provided it is grounded in the emergent paradigms of ecological modernization.

Part II: Traditional Values and Ethical Management

Part II draws on traditional non-Western value systems to propose alternatives to the current paradigm of exclusive self-interest maximization. In their chapter, 'The Duty of Corporate Management: From the Perspective of Dharma', Nilakant and Lips-Wiersma examine the role of corporate management through the lens of *dharma* – a Hindu concept that refers to both appropriate conduct and one's duty. First, they discuss the notion of dharma and examine the evolution of the role of corporate management. They argue that contemporary business practices are strongly influenced by a particular stream of economic theory, which they refer to as 'the contractarian perspective'. They identify the notion of dharma within the contractarian perspective as being to enhance shareholder value, and discuss its dysfunctional consequences. They then propose an alternative notion of the dharma of corporate management to mitigate the negative consequences of the contemporary business practice of exclusively focusing on the interests of shareholders. Nilakant and Lips-Wiersma argue that the dharma of managers cannot be to pay exclusive attention to shareholder value enhancement. Instead, they propose that the appropriate duty of managers in corporate organizations is to balance the interests of the various stakeholders. They suggest four tensions that need to be balanced in corporations: the tension between empowerment and autonomy, between the image of an organization and its character, the tension between stakeholder management and stakeholder inclusion, and between advancing business interests and leaving a legacy. Finding a balance between and within these tensions requires balancing self-interest with concern for others. According to Nilakant and Lips-Wiersma, any alternative conception of managerial work must acknowledge the tension or contradiction between pursuing self-interest and concern for others. They suggest that it may not be possible for managers to easily reconcile these and arrive at 'win–win' situations. Challenging the current prioritizing of shareholder value, Nilakant and Lips-Wiersma argue that according to the dharma model, managerial and shareholder interests may have to be sacrificed if they are inconsistent with an ethical circumstance that requires putting other stakeholders' interests above their own.

The next chapter in Part II deals with how business organizations in ancient India integrated Indian value systems into their business practice. In 'Guilds and Governance in Ancient India: Historical Practices of Corporate Social Responsibility', Buckingham argues that even though there are increasing assertions of commitment to CSR in contemporary company practice, there is little understanding of what CSR actually means. There is a need to look to historical models to develop notions of social responsibility relevant in a globalized corporate world. Despite recent business scandals, doing business ethically has a long history in India. Guilds in pre-modern India offer examples of business organizations which are deeply connected with their local communities, which mediate their business activities through the Buddhist and Hindu cultural practices of the time. Further, they act as both self-regulatory systems and as part of the broader government regulatory frameworks of the ancient Indian economy. Guilds not only play a role in maintaining ethical business standards, but also participate in philanthropic activities as part of their religio-social responsibility. Buckingham concludes that an exploration of India's ancient guild formations suggests ways that companies can be committed both to profit and to constructive functioning in relationship with government and community for the common good.

In the last chapter of Part II – 'Tribal Economies?' – Tau provides an indigenous Māori perspective on Crown settlements with Māori under the Treaty of Waitangi. The Treaty of Waitangi, a pact between Māori tribes and the British Empire in 1840, guaranteed the tribes *tino-rangatiratanga* (chieftainship/ownership) over the fisheries, estates, properties and all other *taonga* (prized possessions). However, the Māori were gradually dispossessed of their land and impoverished. For instance, in the South Island in 1848, settlers bought 20 million acres from the Māori for £2,000. Tau argues that for much of the nineteenth and early twentieth centuries, Māori were stripped not only of their possessions, but also of their identity. In 1975, the New Zealand government enacted the Treaty of Waitangi Act, under which a tribunal was set up to make recommendations on claims brought by Māori relating to actions or omissions of the Crown in breach of the promises made in the Treaty of Waitangi. In 1998, acting on the recommendations of the Waitangi Tribunal, the New Zealand government transferred NZ$170 million in cash and about NZ$270 million in assets to Ngāi Tahu, the largest tribal group in the South Island of New Zealand. As a result, Ngāi Tahu became the largest private land owner in the South Island, as well as one of New Zealand's leading corporations.

Tau asks what economic conditions and set of ideologies enabled this massive transfer of wealth back to Māori to occur at a time when tribal groups were not well organized and did not pose a credible political threat to the government. He argues that the neo-liberal policies of the government, coupled with a judicial ruling by the Court of Appeal, paved the way for this action. Tau discusses some of the challenges and the tensions created as Ngāi Tahu converted itself from a tribe to a corporation, and argues that Ngāi Tahu in the twenty-first century reflects both its tribal heritage as well as the neo-liberal economic values of the 1980s.

Part III: Creating Ethical Leadership

The final part of the book deals with leadership of corporate organizations. In her chapter, 'Navigating the Tension between Global and Local: A Communication Perspective', Mills observes that over the last century, the world of business has moved from being comprised of largely loosely coupled local markets to a complex and highly integrated web of global markets. These markets are themselves increasingly the domain of large boundary-less corporations and conglomerates. At the same time, worldwide conflicts, advances in communication technology and more accessible international travel have encouraged people to reposition themselves, both psychologically and in many cases physically, as global citizens. This economic and social globalization means that on the one hand managers must operate in an environment where national and cultural boundaries are more permeable and open to the homogenizing effects of globalization, while on the other they are confronted with social diversity in their functional relationships on a scale that would have been unusual just a generation ago. Mills asks how can twenty-first-century managers define their practice and navigate this tension between the increasingly standardized management practices that accompany globalization and the subjectivities distinguishing the local and personal worlds of those they encounter in their management roles. Mills sees a communication perspective on management as offering the manager the necessary insights and tools to understand and resolve this tension. On the basis that management is essentially a communication function, this chapter explores the challenges of contemporary management from a communication management perspective and argues that core communication principles can provide the philosophical foundations from which ethical and sustainable management practices can be synthesized.

In 'Vocational Calling and the Search for a New Approach to Business Leadership', Cammock agrees with Mills that the complex demands of a post-modern global economy require more from business leaders. In particular, the global financial crisis has prompted calls for more ethical, sustainable and responsible practice. A leadership practice of this kind requires a particular work orientation on the part of the leader. There are indications that managers motivated primarily by a desire for short-term financial returns and rapid career advancement have led many of the organizations that have faced financial difficulties in recent years. Cammock argues for a return to the age-old virtues of vocation and calling as a foundation for leadership, and proposes this orientation as an antidote to the greed and self-interest that have been so prominent in recent corporate life. Vocation is defined as emerging from the place 'in which your deep gladness and the world's deep hunger meet' (Buechner 1993: 119). Cammock sees the emergence of leaders with such an orientation as one of the critical needs of our time, particularly in view of the call for more sustainable and socially responsible organizations. To describe the key elements of vocation, Cammock draws on recent leadership literature and the mytho-poetic tradition, as explored in Joseph Campbell's work and the Western poetic tradition of David Whyte. The chapter uses case studies to illustrate the ways in which leaders can identify and enact such an orientation in their own life and work. In particular, Cammock draws on his own engagement with leaders from Pacific communities to discuss the strengths and challenges of experiencing a strong sense of individual vocation in Pacific communities, which have a very different tradition of collective service and responsibility. He concludes that there are leadership benefits in both community and individual calling. However, there is also a need for younger people to forge new synthetic approaches to community and business leadership, which can require a movement against traditional cultural norms.

In Chapter 9, 'Cultivating Character: The Challenge of Business Ethics Education', takes up the theme of business leadership among the young. Drawing on his teaching experience in Indian business schools and industry, Alexander argues that inadequate attention to character formation in young adults is a major drawback of current business education which has widened the existing gap between the quality of managers that business schools and universities produce and what industry actually requires. Alexander develops a critique of the present dominant models of business education by examining justifications for a value-based business education and arguing that morally appropriate decisions for sustainable businesses are inextricably linked with the character and identity of decision-makers.

He emphasizes that both novice and experienced executives should be trained to assume the responsibility of creating positive organizational cultures that support and shape individual ethical behaviour. The chapter calls for a careful selection of pedagogical strategies and the practice of continuous mentorship for cultivating ongoing moral leadership in the workplace.

In the concluding chapter, 'New Directions in Corporate Social Responsibility', Buckingham and Nikalant return to the issue of the threefold characteristics needed for sustainable business: efficiency, justice and fairness. They argue that notions of economic justice need to be rethought in ways that will create a radical reconfiguration of management practice. A rethinking of justice genuinely expressed through management will enable business to function both efficiently and fairly, maintaining profit while also accommodating the broadest possible range of stakeholder interests. Buckingham and Nilakant draw on Sen's capability approach to economic measurement of individual well-being to consider how maximization of human capability can compete convincingly with self-interest maximization as a viable basis for sustainable approaches to business and management. The authors argue that genuine corporate social responsibility needs to address the most marginal of groups and to integrate management approaches that enable people to participate in the economy as employers, employees and consumers to the fullness of their capabilities.

*　　*　　*

As a whole, this book brings an interdisciplinary, globalized perspective to a field dominated by Anglo-American management ideologies. Its particular strength lies in the centralizing of non-Western perspectives on business and management practices and the explorations of tensions between dominant Western models and the multiple culture of the real-world global economy in which they play out. When so much of established management culture has proved itself both morally and economically bankrupt, integration of Pacific, Māori and Indian insights into not only Asia-Pacific but also Anglo-American and European management approaches are long overdue. After all, the economy is global.

References

Aras, G. and Crowther, D. 2009. *Global Perspectives on Corporate Governance and CSR*. Farnham: Gower.

Banerjee, S.B. 2007. *Corporate Social Responsibility: The Good, the Bad and the Ugly*. Cheltenham: Edward Elgar.

Beer, M. and Nohria, N. 2000. 'Cracking the code of change'. *Harvard Business Review*, 78(3), 133–41.

Boatright, J.R. 1996. 'Business ethics and the theory of the firm'. *American Business Law Journal*, 34(2), 217–38.

Booth, L. 1998. 'What Drives Shareholder Value?' Paper presented at the Federated Press 'Creating Shareholder Value' Conference, 28 October 1998, 1–33.

Buechner, F. 1993. *Wishful Thinking: A Seeker's ABC*. San Francisco, CA: Harper San Francisco.

Drucker, P.F. 2001. *The Essential Drucker*. New York: HarperCollins.

Friedman, M. and Friedman, R.D. 2002. *Capitalism and Freedom*. Chicago, IL: University of Chicago Press.

Ghoshal, S. 2005. 'Bad management theories are destroying good management practices'. *Academy of Management Learning & Education*, 4, 75–91.

Harvey, D. 2005. *A Brief History of Neoliberalism*. New York: Oxford University Press.

Hilimoniuk, R. 2011. *Institutional (Re)design for the Post-2007 Global Economic Order: Recalibrating the Multilateral-National Nexus*, http://www.cigionline.org/publications/2011/6/institutional-redesign-post-2007-global-economic-order-recalibrating-multilatera, accessed 26 March 2012.

Jensen, M. and Meckling, W. 1976. 'Theory of the firm: Managerial behavior, agency costs and ownership structure'. *Journal of Financial Economics*, 3, 305–60.

Joseph, A.V. 2009. 'Successful examples of corporate social responsibility'. *The Indian Journal of Industrial Relations*, 44(3), 402–9.

Manz, C.C. and Sims, H.P. 1993. *Business Without Bosses*. New York: John Wiley.

McCloskey, D.N. 2006. *The Bourgeois Virtues: Ethics for an Age of Commerce*. Chicago, IL: University of Chicago Press.

Nozick, R. 1974. *Anarchy, State, and Utopia*. New York: Basic Books.

Olson, E.E. and Eoyang, G.H. 2001. *Facilitating Organization Change: Lessons from Complexity Science*. San Francisco, CA: Jossey-Bass/Pfeiffer

Pfeffer, J. 1998. *The Human Equation*. Boston, MA: Harvard Business School.

Pfeffer, J. 2007. *What Were They Thinking? Unconventional Wisdom about Management*. Boston, MA: Harvard Business School.

Rappaport, A. 2005. 'The economics of short-term performance obsession'. *Financial Analysts Journal*, 61, 65–79.

Rawls, J. 1971. *A Theory of Justice*. Cambridge, MA: Harvard University Press.

Seddon, J. 2005. *Freedom from Command and Control: A Better Way to Make the Work Work*. 2nd edn, Buckingham: Vanguard.

Sen, A.K. 1987. *On Ethics and Economics*. Oxford: Blackwell.

Sen, A.K. 2009. *The Idea of Justice*. Boston, MA: Harvard University Press.

Stiglitz, J.E. 2004. 'Evaluating economic change'. *Daedalus*, 133(3), 18–25.

Sundaram, A.K. and Inkpen, A.C. 2004. 'The corporate objective revisited'. *Organization Science*, 15(3), 350–63.

Useem, M. 1993. *Executive Defence: Shareholder Power and Corporate Reorganization*. Cambridge, MA: Harvard University Press.

Useem, M. 1996. *Investor Capitalism: How Money Managers Are Changing the Face of Corporate America*. New York: Basic Books.

Woods, J.A. 1996. 'The six values of a quality culture', in *The Quality Yearbook*, ed. James W. Cortada and John A. Woods. New York: McGraw-Hill, http://my.execpc.com/~jwoods/6values.htm, accessed 26 March 2012.

Young, S.D. and O'Byrne, F. 2001. *EVA and Value-Based Management: A Practical Guide to Implementation*. New York: McGraw-Hill.

PART I
Making Managers Responsible

2

Selfish Managers: Can We Eliminate Perverse Incentives?

Amal Sanyal[1]

Introduction

The effects of managerial decisions on the economic system have come under renewed scrutiny following the latest spate of corporate scandals and failures. In this chapter, I will focus on a set of issues that arise from the interplay of managers' interests and the institutional arrangement in which they work. I assume that managers respond to their business environment as self-interested individuals. So the decisions they make tend to depend on their expectation of how such decisions would influence their rewards (or punishments). In developing this line of reasoning, I argue that corporate scandals and several types of large-scale management failure are directly related to the management's incentive structure, based on what resembles a principal–agent relation.

As is well known, this structure grew through the 1980s when shareholders wrested control from managers after a series of corporate debacles (Werner 1977, Kaufman, Zacharias and Karson 1995, Bratton 2001). Following these events,[2] managers in general tried to battle adverse public opinion by trying to satisfy the short-term expectations of shareholders and analysts. During this defensive phase, corporate governance arrangements seem to have changed radically as boards grew more and more active. These changes aligned managerial incentive with investor interests more closely than ever before (Useem 1996). By the late 1980s, the present arrangements were fully developed. I will argue that some

1   I am grateful to Ramzi Addison and Sagar Sanyal for comments that improved this chapter.

2   I would especially mention the bankruptcy of the Penn Central Transportation Company in 1970 and W.T. Grant stores in 1976. These were the two largest bankruptcies in US history at the time. They were among the events that stirred up shareholders against the discretion of management and their imperviousness to shareholder suggestions.

corporate problems arise directly from this institutional structure. Hence, to reduce their frequency, one possible route is to reform the institutions that define and fix managerial incentive. I will first try to establish this reasoning, and then investigate practical ways to introduce reforms.

Obviously, this chapter looks at only one aspect of a complex systemic problem. The literature shows its multidimensional nature as it probes into business ethics, corporate governance, managerial practice, and reform.[3] Foremost, there are the fundamental issues of personal and business ethics and the ethical limits of profit. Although profit-seeking precipitates the problems, it nevertheless continues as the driving force of our economies. This has led many authors to explore ethically acceptable ways of pursuing profit (Ulrich and Thielemann 1993, Quinn and Jones 1995, Carroll 2000, Machan 2007). Another part of the literature has focused on the trajectory of events in search of generalities and patterns (Conrad 2003, Marnet 2007, Rajagopalan and Zhang 2009). Some literature also tries to understand the trail in the aftermath of meltdowns (Duchin, Ozbas and Sensoy 2010, McCoy and Renuart 2008, Amromin and Paulson 2009, Demyanyk 2009, Poon 2009). Yet another group of studies examines corporate governance and its weak links, both in micro-level motivation factors and aggregate effects (Shleifer and Vishny 1997, Daily, Dan and Cannella 2003, Stansfield 2006, Isaksson and Kirkpatrick 2009). This chapter shares common ground with the last of the aforementioned literature, as I will also explore motives, incentives and the psychology of risk-taking.

My attention to corporate governance and agency relations does not indicate that I consider other dimensions less important. At the most fundamental level, the problems under discussion arise from self-interest. Self-interest used as motivation has the potential to break all ethical barriers. And the barriers are broken from time to time. Corporate governance, the focus of this chapter, induces socially harmful strategic behaviour because the interaction of managers and shareholders is primarily grounded in self-interest. If corporate owners and managers acted differently, for example, in the spirit of Gandhian trusteeship (Gandhi 1941), perhaps the situation would be quite different. Hence, a change of motivation is the surest way around the problem. But self-interest is so thoroughly woven into our social system and institutions that a

---

3   For a sample of the issues raised, see Kochan (2002), Huffington (2003), Bakan (2004), Jacoby (2004), Knee (2006), Shiller (2008), Salter (2008) and Foster and Magdoff (2009). Recent corporate scandals and problems have also had effects outside academic and business literature. For example, two powerful plays have been staged in London: *The Power of Yes* by Sir David Hare, in repertory at the National Theatre, and *Enron* by Lucy Prebble, at the Royal Court and the Noël Coward Theatre.

change of motivation is unlikely until there is a radical change in the social formation itself. Therefore, we need to explore solutions that would work in the indefinite interim. This is why I believe it is useful to explore mechanisms assuming that everyone continues to act with self-interest.

The rest of the chapter is organized as follows. The next section classifies corporate scandals and managerial failures of the recent past. It focuses on two types of problems that arose because of agency relations.

In the first problem, management covered up the poor financial health of a company while at the same time trying to set things right with covert measures. The process continued until the real state of finances and the covert operations came to light, but by then company finances were at breaking point. The company went down both because of poor finances and also because of mistrust in the managers.

In the second problem, management got into conflict with stakeholders other than the company's owners and precipitated certain large-scale social problems. Cases identified in the first problem raise the question why management chooses to misinform owners, while cases identified in the second one lead us to examine the nature of conflict between owners and other stakeholders.

I then turn to the issue of conflict between owners and other stakeholders. In this section I discuss why these conflicts do not generally get resolved in markets – contrary to the claim of some schools of economics – and how they drag managers into disastrous decisions. Following this, I explore why management chooses to hide bad news – a decision ending in ruin in most cases. I analyse the relationship between managerial decisions and the manager–owner relationship and show that it leads to: (1) managers' tendency to send false signals about the company's health; (2) more risk-taking by managers than warranted by financial news, and (3) ignoring the interests of other stakeholders if they are not commercially valuable to the company.

I then propose a structure in which management is responsible not only to owners, but also to other stakeholders. I provide real-life examples of such arrangements to explain how they handle incentive and efficiency.[4] In the final

---

4   It is often claimed that the prevailing agency relation leads management to maximize profit, and this in turn leads to efficient allocation of resources. Hence, other forms of owner–management relation may obstruct efficient resource use. Given this, it is important to check that other governance forms are not inefficient.

section I suggest practical means by which a multiple-stakeholder business can gain a foothold in the present system, then draw my conclusions.

Scandals and Failures: A Typology

We can identify three distinct types among the recent scandals and failures.

(1) The first are cases of large-scale but simple fraud, where managers use their position to generate private wealth at the cost of the company. Such cases lead to significant loss for shareholders and the public. For the company, the effect may range from loss of goodwill and credit rating to bankruptcy and collapse. A prime example from the last decade is the case of Bernard Madoff Investment Securities, where the chairman, Bernard Madoff, ran the firm as a Ponzi scheme. The loss to clients was almost US$65 billion (Chad and Ef 2009). In a more recent case, in 2009 the FBI charged the head of Stanford International Bank for misleading clients about their deposits and investing them in private equity and other risky assets. The firm raised an estimated US$8 billion from the public by promising much higher than market rates of return.[5] In the 1980s, the case of Barlow Clowes stands out. Its chairman Peter Clowes duped depositors and spent £110 million on items of personal consumption at their expense (Lever 1992). Similar frauds occur regularly, and I will refrain from citing further examples.

(2) In the second type of case, a sequence of events begins with managers providing reports of good health when the company is actually in a bad state. They use false accounting, set up special-purpose entities to dress up balance sheets, and use fabricated costs and profits. They expect to steer out of the difficulties through planned manoeuvres, and want to cover their losses until they can recover. Cases that come to light are obviously those where this strategy has failed. Once the fraud goes public, market value of stocks falls rapidly through panic selling. Shareholders' wealth is largely wiped out and jobs are lost. If the company has rewarded employees with its own stocks, then its employees lose significant amounts of savings. For a large company, the effect on the economy through backward and forward linkages is significant. The aftermath affects the company's bankers, financiers, suppliers and other companies in which the problem company had invested.

---

5   For details of the case, chronology of events and amounts involved, see 'Allen Stanford Arise and fall', *Economist*, 10 March 2012.

Recently, we have seen a surge of these cases, and they have brought down very large companies. Enron, for example, once the seventh largest US corporation, collapsed, wiping out jobs, wealth, savings and deposits. At Enron, dubious accounting, conducted with the complicity of its accounting firm Arthur Andersen, went on for several years till the fraud came to light in 2001. Many key executives were proven guilty and sent to jail. In the next few years, we saw a number of company failures precipitated by very similar managerial behaviour. From 1999 to mid-2002, WorldCom's Chief Financial Officer (CFO) and the Director of General Accounting used fraudulent accounting strategies to misrepresent the financial state of the corporation. Other large firms that have failed include Global Crossing, Tyco and Adelphia – and the pattern of events and management behaviour were similar in all these cases.

The reason for treating these cases as separate from the simple fraud described above is that the deceit in the second type of case is strategic. It is a calculated move, reasoned by analysing the response it would elicit from shareholders, suppliers, buyers and the market and deciding management counter-moves over a sizeable future time frame. Frauds in the first grouping are not strategic. A manager decides to cheat as a personal maximizing decision, having considered the gains, the probability of being caught and the expected penalty. The considerations are qualitatively similar to the decisions made by a shoplifter, and involve no strategic calculation of moves and counter-moves.

By contrast, strategic behaviour in the second grouping results from the management's incentive structure. Managers' reward and reputation depend on the performance of the company. For large companies, managers' remuneration is significantly – indeed, spectacularly – higher if the company reports a better financial picture. It is possible to claim a relation between the extraordinary rise of frontline managers' pay through the 1990s and the surge in stealth accounting at the turn of the century. Shareholders, too, believed there was a direct relation between the two. Following the collapse of Enron and a few others, shareholders of General Electric made the company charge its former boss, Jack Welch, for benefits that were already agreed to be given free. Similarly, fearing shareholders' opposition, GlaxoSmithKline's board gave up a plan to increase its CEO's pay.[6] Part of the shareholder reaction was, of course, simply vengeful, while some of it stemmed from the belief that higher remuneration packages contributed to the motive for deception.

---

6   For an account of shareholders' mood following Enron, see 'Humbled' (2003).

The role of remuneration and rewards was more evident in the failure of financial firms. After the sub-prime mortgage crisis and the spate of bank collapses in 2007–2008, senior executives' pay was identified as a major reason for the crisis. Shareholders were outraged by the size of the pension given to Fred Goodwin, a former chief executive of the Royal Bank of Scotland group, the executives' bonuses at American International Group, a company that had failed badly, and by the expensive tastes of John Thain, chairman and CEO of Merrill Lynch, as reported by media. To bring the executive pay issue into focus, a report in *The Economist* quoted a bank's chief executive as saying: 'It was better to be an employee than a shareholder' ('The revolution within' 2009). The general opinion was that colossal pay drives bankers to take foolish risks. Further, manoeuvres to ensure unsustainably high profit make the financial system itself vulnerable.

A section of applied game theory literature has analysed the strategic behaviour of managers given their incentive structure (Holmström 1999, Holmström and Ricart I Costa 1986). It produces useful insights into strategic dishonesty and false signalling. It is these kinds of false signals that we saw in the cases of Enron, WorldCom and so on. High remuneration packages increase the cost of failure for managers. Hence, reporting bad news has a very high personal cost, and managers tend to develop an unduly high personal stake in reporting good corporate health. A manager is likely to postpone bad news if there is any reasonable expectation of turnaround. Further, a higher remuneration package increases the amount of risk a manager is willing to take to hide failure.

(3) The third group comprises cases that are not scandals, but involve large-scale harm inflicted on stakeholders other than the owners of a company. As they act in the shareholders' interest, managers end up hurting the interest of others. A large part of the critique of corporate business derives from irresponsible behaviour towards workers, the environment and the ecosystem, human rights, Third World governments, less articulate buyers – for example, seniors and Third World consumers – and so on. Some of the damage done in the past has been so serious that it has prompted protest across the world and led to intervention by national governments and the United Nations, and even driven new legislation in some countries.

Examples are, indeed, abundant. As transnational corporations (TNCs) have spread in the last few decades, complaints have piled up about their human rights violations, manipulation of cross-country business and defence agreements, environmental damage, child labour, sweatshops, wage repression in host countries and so on. It is not only TNCs: large businesses in general have also been indicted. A recent report from the Council of Europe Parliamentary Assembly states:

> *The globalisation of the economy challenges the effectiveness of international human rights protection. Large multinational corporations have been criticised for violations of human rights, especially in developing countries. Child labour in the textile industry, environmental disasters caused by the oil industry or breaches of the right to privacy in telecommunication companies are examples of these concerns.*
>
> *(Council of Europe 2010)*

A number of corporations have been charged with bribing key personalities in other countries to sell arms and defence wares, producing unwarranted defence expenditure and escalation of political and territorial tension. This is evidenced by the mounting number of companies charged and convicted of violation of the Foreign Corrupt Practices Act in the US. A frequent allegation by Third World activists is that TNCs do not respect the environment of developing countries. Cases of violation range from minor infringement to major disasters. Some recent cases show the scale of these violations. For example, Shushufindi 61, a pit in the jungles of Ecuador, has been used as a dump for oil waste by Texaco, bought by Chevron in 2001. Apparently, Lago Agrio in the Ecuador jungle has been used by Texaco as a dumping ground since the 1960s ('Justice or extortion?' 2009). And in another event of stunning cynicism, the Sanlu Group of China was found to have been topping up the protein content of infant milk powder by adding melamine, a toxic chemical ('Formula for disaster' 2008, 'The poison spreads' 2008).

These examples illustrate the conflict between corporate management as representing owners, and the interest of other stakeholders. The point to note is that a corporate manager does not gain personally by actions that harm other stakeholders, by degrading the environment for example, except to the extent that it improves the corporation's financial performance. Adverse action towards other stakeholders results from the compulsions of contracts which require managers as agents to protect the interest of shareholders, who are their principals.

In this chapter, I will not discuss the cases of straight cheating and embezzlement – that is, those of group (1) above. The other two types, grouped as (2) and (3), have a common link. They are related to the incentive structure of management and I will pursue this link. For ease of reference, I will refer to managers' behaviour in group (2) as 'false signalling', and in group (3) as 'anti-social'.

Managers, Shareholders and Other Stakeholders

The work of a business relates to the interest of many others besides its owners, such as employees, input suppliers and consumers. With globalization and the growth of TNCs, stakeholders of a large business are now varied and spread out all over the world. They might include those who suffer the environmental effects of production, and the social and cultural effects of consumption.

Do Markets Take Care of Stakeholders' Interests?

As has been noted, damage – sometimes large-scale devastation – occurs because managers ignore the interests of others when chasing shareholders' profit. To see why this happens, I first need to dispel a point of view that denies such a transgression is at all possible. This claim is based on an influential strand of economics which argues that in market equilibrium, not only is business profit maximized, but so is the welfare of everyone else.

The underlying logic of this position is that other stakeholders – consumers, workers and suppliers – interact with business in competitive markets. Market interactions are intentions to sell and buy, as summarized in supply and demand in various markets. When businesses, their customers and suppliers freely interact in competitive markets, an economy-wide equilibrium is expected to emerge. In this equilibrium, prices of goods and inputs are expected to coincide with their opportunity costs. The opportunity cost of an item is what the society forgoes or misses out on when it produces the item. Hence, if prices equal opportunity cost and no more, that is surely the fairest possible outcome. If consumers, workers and suppliers do business with corporations at these prices, there is nothing to complain about.

This account is based on several simplifying assumptions, and is not expected to hold precisely. Its supporters believe that the real-world deviation from this prediction is not significant. They believe that just as the laws of mechanics hold closely enough to be useful in spite of frictions, so do the laws of market optimality in spite of real-world divergences.

The tendency to a fair equilibrium could not be denied if, indeed, all economic interactions occurred in competitive markets. However, most markets are not competitive – as is required by the logic of the above theory. Oligopolies, cartels, long-term business agreements, monopoly rights, patents, brand power, government regulation and trade unions make markets uncompetitive. Hence, many businesses have significant influence on their prices through non-market channels – something that should not happen in competitive markets.

Externalities

The market theory assumes that all economic interactions occur in and through markets, so prices fully reflect the balance of economic interest of all who have anything to do with a product. But the truth is that a large amount of economic interaction occurs without the mediation of markets. As an example, consider why a factory can pollute with impunity. The factory spews smoke and inflicts cost on neighbours but does not have to pay for it because there is no market to extract this cost. The factory pays for most other things – for example, it has to compensate workers for their time and labour. This happens because the factory interacts with workers in a market. By contrast, its interaction with neighbours is a non-market relationship. If neighbours could sell the right to pollute and factories were required to buy these rights, then factories would have paid the amount they cost their neighbours, and in effect, the amount of pollution would drop. These non-market effects called 'externality' naturally do not obey any market laws. The market mechanism fails to make businesses do the right thing with air, water and the ecosystem because relevant markets do not exist. It is therefore no wonder that some of the most spectacular managerial debacles have taken place precisely in these areas.

Public Goods

An important type of externality is embodied in public goods. These are goods with at least one of two rather peculiar features. For some public goods, it is not possible, or it is very costly, to stop anyone from consuming or using them once the goods have been produced. Examples are street lighting, clean air, law and order, defence services and so on. If the good is produced at all, it is there for everyone. Because no one can be deprived of the good, no one can be forced to pay either. Therefore, markets cannot work normally for such things. For another type of public good, once production has started, it costs hardly anything to produce an extra unit of it. Examples are radio and TV broadcasts, the Internet, maintenance of a road or bridge, and so on. Markets cannot work for these goods either, because there is no objective measure of the cost of an extra unit to charge to a buyer.

Public goods and other non-market economic interactions are widespread, and they are a major reason why markets do not automatically lead to optimal arrangements for all business stakeholders. Even when interaction takes place through markets, the markets may not be competitive. Hence, we do not expect the welfare of other stakeholders to be looked after as an automatic by-product of market activities.

Financial Firms

The market's performance is even more problematic in the case of financial firms. Financial markets trade in products with uncertain returns. Their managers have to distinguish themselves by generating a higher return than competitors. But if all information about financial assets and companies is publicly available, then there is no reason why one firm's manager would do any better than another's. Managers can, of course, do better if they have or can buy inside information – a course of action that can easily end up as criminal and sooner or later create a disaster for the firm. Alternatively, a manager can bet on specific assets or portfolios on the basis of hunches and take credit for foresight if this strategy succeeds. Note that this means the manager takes more risk on certain assets than market information would justify. The hunch may pay in the short run, but over a reasonable period, averages predicted by market information are more likely to prevail. If the hunch seems to be working, the manager's confidence grows and he or she puts more investment into these assets, which induces others to follow the example. But since the wager was not warranted by market information, sooner or later it would generally show itself as a poor bet.[7] When it does, it creates devastation, not only for the manager who championed the asset, but also for all the others who had joined the party.

---

7   Of course, the market may not always foresee coming economic tendencies. In that case, it may underestimate some assets and a smart manager may spot it. Such a manager would appear to be taking extra risk, but would do well.

If sufficiently large, it can generate an economy-wide crisis. This happened in the recent sub-prime mortgage episode, where the initial success of some firms with sub-prime mortgages quickly drew all financial firms into the same sort of asset portfolios (Chomsisengphet and Pennington-Cross 2006).

Given the reasons detailed above, management's effort to increase profit often hurts the interests of others related to the industry. This is what I term *anti-social decisions* – serious damage to environment and society by large corporate bodies. Further, when rewards for successful managers are significantly greater than the market average, their behaviour is even more seriously affected. This implies that bigger corporations, which pay their executives spectacularly, are also likely to be the more frequent offenders.

Agency and Strategic Misinformation

In the present corporate set-up, managers are appointed as owners' agents to increase the company's market value. This agency is inherently problematic because, in the short run, managers have most of the information about the corporation, and shareholders hardly any. The asymmetry of information diminishes with time, and in the long run, the market and shareholders get a fair idea from various channels about the state of the company. Managers can exploit the short-run information asymmetry to 'buy time' in order to protect their interests when necessary.

This is the basis of the strategic misinformation game many managers have played in the last few years. Because higher profits and a better financial state are rewarded handsomely, managers have a serious disincentive to disclose bad news. If there is a reasonable chance of recovery by implementing specific measures, then the rational response is to postpone the report of bad health and heal the company in the mean time. In the interim, managers continue to present positive news using false accounting and other methods to alter reports. Because these acts are culpable, managers in effect take a gamble that the manipulations will not be exposed. If possible, they buy the complicity of auditors, as happened in the Enron case. If the company's problem is soon sorted out, the accounts are retrospectively set back to order. If not, the managers have to be more and more inventive and deceitful, which increases the probability of being exposed. In the sad, but graphic, words of B. Ramalinga Raju, the former chairman of Satyam Computers: 'It was like riding a tiger, not knowing how to get off without being eaten' (quoted in 'India's Enron' 2009).

The mechanics can therefore be outlined as follows. The business system breeds a group of high-flying managers accustomed to spectacular rewards, adulation and media attention in the largest of corporations that have a system-wide footprint. The personal cost of losing their position is enormous. Apart from immediate monetary loss, there is considerable loss of the esteem of the market and media, which are related to future income. When the economy is in good shape, the managers maintain and enhance their reputation. When the going is not good, some of them are tempted to withhold the bad news in the short run and work for a turnaround. The cost of serving up bad news is so high that a significant amount of risk-taking to avoid it becomes a rational step. Measures to set things right either have to be camouflaged as normal business steps or have to stay secret. A fraction of these managers may attract the attention of corporate watchers and be exposed early. Others may succeed for a while until the difficulties pile up, and most of them are shown up in the end. We can speculate that, at least in some of the cases, managers succeed in getting everything right in the end. Such cases possibly provide the statistical basis[8] of their belief that reporting irregularities can eventually be amended.

The largest of companies are involved in these episodes because they have the highest-paid and most renowned managers. Because of their sheer size, their failure also leads to the failure of a number of other companies, with system-wide consequences. The sequence is more likely at the peak of a long-running boom. As business starts to weaken past the peak, managers of some of the largest companies are likely to decide to swap bad news with cooked-up good news, and thus start down the slippery path.

If Managers are Tasked to Manage Multiple Stakes

I have argued that most corporate crises result from managers' response to shareholder pressure, which works through managerial contracts. I would also claim that the frequency of these events would fall if management were made responsible to the wider group of stakeholders, not only the owners. But the idea of running an organization on behalf of a number of conflicting interests raises a few questions:

---

8   The Association of Certified Fraud Examiners (ACFE) tries to estimate the percentage of fraud that goes undetected using internal audit results, external audits and cases of detected fraud. It projected a loss of US organizations' revenue from undetected fraud at US$650 billion for 2006–2007. See ACFE (2006).

1.   Given that stakeholders have conflicting interests, how would managers decide anything at all?

2.   Who would appoint managers, who would pay them, and what would be the reward structure?

3.   If the focus on profit were removed, what would ensure that managers would maintain business efficiency?

Although these questions appear discouraging, organizations managed on behalf of several stakeholders are fairly common outside the corporate world. Some of them have remained viable through the centuries, and continue to function well in the present commercial milieu. These organizations have resolved the above questions in a variety of ways.

Broadly speaking, there are two types of arrangements that try to align management with the interest of non-owners. In the first, the interest of other stakeholders is introduced indirectly – for example, through regulation or pressure by government, international bodies, lending organizations and so on. In the second group, managers are directly contracted to work for other stakeholders – as in community-owned enterprises, family businesses, NGOs and not-for-profit businesses. Managers' contracts in these cases specify their responsibility to a number of extra-commercial objectives. I will briefly describe these arrangements and how they address the problem of multiple interests.

Regulation

Regulation as a societal response to the unwanted effects of private business is an ancient practice.[9] It constrains certain practices by prohibiting them outright or by imposing appropriate rates of taxation. Such taxes aim to increase the cost to a company by the amount of cost it creates for other stakeholders. Alternatively, regulation may prescribe rather than proscribe. For example, a business may be required to maintain safety norms for health and to protect from fire and other hazards on its premises. These regulations force it to spend the right amount on safety. They do not eliminate business profit, but reduce risk activities to a level agreeable to other stakeholders.

---

9   For examples of wide-ranging economic regulation in ancient times, see Rangarajan (1992).

Most countries have regulations about safety of products, the workplace, food and drugs, building consent, anti-trust, financial disclosure and so on. Note that these are generally areas where business creates externality or involves asymmetric information between buyers and sellers. As noted above, in the case of externalities some relevant markets do not exist. In the case of information asymmetry, although markets exist, interaction between buyers and sellers does not take place on a level playing field. Regulations restrain managers from passing on externality costs to other parts of society, or from taking advantage of asymmetry of information. This class of regulations reduces the occurrence of corporate decision-making I have termed 'anti-social'.

Business managers have worked for at least two centuries within the framework of a modern regulatory environment. This implies that it is possible to balance responsibility to owners with other requirements. In a sense, legal restrictions make it easy for managers to avoid harm to other stakeholders, because shareholders have to accept them. At the same time, profit continues to remain the objective, and hence general efficiency of operations and control of costs are not subverted.

In the past, serious episodes of business failure affecting the economy have been followed by new corporate regulations. Recent accounting frauds have also prompted a set of new regulations. They aim to increase the reliability of company reports. In the US, the Sarbanes-Oxley Act (SOX) came into force in 2002. Among other things, it established an accounting regulator, the Public Company Accounting Oversight Board, to oversee relations between accounting firms and their corporate clients. The Act specifies possible conflicts of interest in detail, sets rules to avoid them, and provides for tough penalties for violation. Some provisions of SOX have attracted criticism from a legal point of view, and some critics perceive SOX itself as harmful to business growth in the long run (Latham 2003). The point, however, is that properly framed regulation restrains the profit motive only at the boundary line where it starts violating other parts of society. It does leave enough room for business growth up to that point, and so enables the socially optimal amount of business growth.

However, legal restrictions tend to breed vested interest groups in the government, political establishments and the legal profession who profit from restrictions. As a result, governments may end up creating more regulations than warranted, and this may stifle enterprise.[10] Hence, regulation may not

---

10 Opinion on business regulation varies widely. Some scholars argue that regulations contravene
    individual freedom and restrict and pervert the development of society – recent statements of

be the ideal solution, and may be recommended as a last resort. It would be better if restraint could be introduced through voluntary arrangements or a mechanism of checks and balances.

Community Businesses

In a community business, managers enhance community profit while at the same time trying to advance some of that community's cherished values. They serve the community both as owners with a stake in the unit's profit and also as people with specific ethnic or cultural values. There are examples from all over the world of businesses adhering to a community value system and, at the same time, doing well commercially. For example, some of the community businesses owned by American Indians in the US or by Māori in New Zealand are among the better-run organizations in their niche areas.[11] An interesting example of community businesses solving the conflict between profit and social obligations is provided by the community-owned department stores in Wyoming, Montana and a few other north-eastern US states. In these states, mainstream supermarkets failed to resolve the conflict of profit and location, and progressively moved away from rural areas (Livingston 2007). This conflict between shareholders and consumers has been tackled by community stores. They do well commercially, and have resisted the urge to relocate to bigger centres as their profits grow. Community stores have also been able to increase stock from local suppliers – the stakeholders neglected by large discount retailers (Goetz and Swaminathan 2004). These examples show that community interests need not strangle profit and growth.

Family Businesses

Family businesses can be regarded as a special class of community business. The focus of a family business is family interest, defined more widely than in simple pecuniary terms. The profit and financial conditions of family businesses

this view are often traced back to Hayek (1960) and Friedman and Friedman (1962). At the other extreme, there is the argument that thorough regulation is necessary given the anarchic and exploitative nature of capitalism. The exploitative nature of capitalism was forcefully argued in Marx (1849), and a powerful case for government intervention was made in Keynes (1936). This chapter takes an intermediate position: regulation should curb anti-social business activities, but leave enough room for the development of business and ideas.

11 For a directory and information on American Indian community businesses, visit Nativeedge at http://www.nativeedge.org/. To see the profile of a very successful Maori business, Ngai Tahu Holdings, visit http://www.ngaitahuholdings.co.nz/.

have proven somewhat difficult to study, because the units split and acquire different owners after one or two generations. But there is enough information to make a few preliminary observations.

First, family businesses are no less efficient than other forms of business. They are also remarkably adaptable to the external environment. In India, for example, they have worked and succeeded in pre-British times, during British rule, during the forty years of licence Raj after independence, and now in a more liberal market environment.

Family businesses, of course, have their own characteristic tensions. Sociologically, there is a tension between the incumbent and successor generations. Unlike in ordinary businesses, where the basic values are invariant through time, the value system of different generations of a family business need not necessarily match, and room needs to be made for resolution of differences (Ramachandran 2005). This tension revolves around the relationship between owners and management, and is germane to our discussion. While a business is expected to bring in income, family management imposes some constraints on profit and wealth. Each generation has to agree to the constraints or modify them as they become owners.

In the Indian case, business families are generally joint families nested within a caste or sub-caste to which they are bound by implicit responsibility. Managers have to work with a given hierarchy of priorities, rather than prioritize business actions through profit calculation alone. A less profitable investment project may be chosen at times over a more profitable one because of family and community considerations.

Contrary to commonly held belief, family businesses are not on the way out. In India, they dominate several sizes and classes of business. About half of the 30 companies included in the Sensex (India's reference index for the stock market) are family businesses. Interestingly, family and community constraints help rather than hinder their competitiveness. A family business relies on other family-based business units for demand, supply, information and finance. Interactions occur repeatedly within a set of families and communities. The actions of the business units are keenly watched by others who have potential business relations with them – for example, people of the same caste or community. If a business breaks a contract or a promise, this becomes part of the business data for potential partners. It reduces the chances of the unit's long-term success. Hence, co-operation and behaviour according to established codes are the best strategy for family business units. This is probably how ties and trust develop among family business units over time. These ties cut down transaction and search costs, and increase the competitiveness of family businesses when compared with other forms of business.

The fact that family businesses continue to prosper implies that the conflict of other concerns with the profit and wealth motives can be resolved successfully even in the context of today's liberalized and globalized economies.

Not-for-profit and Non-governmental Organizations (NGOs)

A third group of examples are businesses run by not-for-profit organizations and NGOs. Not-for-profit units take up the interests of other stakeholders in their line of work. Likewise, an NGO business champions a mission and rallies a group of stakeholders around it. It advances the mission and stakeholders' interests by forming a business unit. The manager of an NGO business has to bear in mind the mission first, even though profit remains an important objective. NGOs are typically active in areas involving significant externality. These are the areas where profit-making firms would either hurt the interest of large segments of the society, or would fail to produce the appropriate amount.

A typical NGO business example will illustrate the NGO approach to the interests of social stakeholders. Consider an NGO providing immunization services against AIDS. The service is both a private and a public good. It is a private good because it directly benefits the immunized person, who is therefore expected to pay for it. At the same time, it is a public good because it produces benefits for others as well, through reducing contagion. Although others gain from the reduced risk of contagion, they may not be willing to pay for it. So the overall market demand – that is, demand backed by money – is significantly less than the optimal amount of immunization. Profit-making units catering to market demand would stop expanding immunization as soon as profit falls below other lines of business. After that point they would rather use their money elsewhere. However, an NGO would tend to produce the service until it reckons its provision is adequate.

Furthermore, in not-for-profit or NGO business units, profit is not ignored because it is required to increase operational capacity. These organizations remain quite aware of cost efficiency while advancing their social missions.

Managers' Incentives and Social Values

Large businesses are nearly always run by hired managers, whether they are a community or family business, or a not-for-profit or non-governmental organization (NGO). The success of community and family businesses, or NGOs, highlights the fact that managers need not be members of the community, family or NGO – nor personally believe or adopt the same values. The constitution of the business and the managerial contract can be used to propel the self-interested manager to work in a manner consistent with the values of the unit. A variety of formulas are used by NGOs to set managerial rewards, with differing emphasis on profit and other objectives. These induce alternative strategies for managers and different outcomes for the organization.

The rational strategy of a self-interested manager in these settings is to advance profit subject to fulfilling the value imperatives. This also minimizes the cost of operation subject to the value constraints. Therefore, managers employed to serve other values need not abandon business principles like economy or efficiency of resource use.

How To Go About It

Relationships between stockholders and managers have changed over the years. And after the recent spate of corporate disasters and the recession, regulators, shareholder groups and the legal profession have been actively thinking about how these relationships might – or should – change again. These efforts notwithstanding, it is worthwhile to propose a dilution of the influence of owners on management as a general principle. In this section, I will discuss possible ways to give this idea a practical shape.

CORPORATE GOVERNANCE LAWS

The foremost proposal should be about reform of legislation on corporate governance. We can insist on representation of other stakeholders on a company's board. Extended boards introduce the concerns of other parts of society. This can directly reduce the incidence of anti-social behaviour. Indirectly, the arrangement may reduce shareholders' pressure on management to push profits indefinitely, which in turn would also reduce cases of false signalling.

How would managers respond to opposing pressures from shareholders and other stakeholders? Would such arrangements lead to chaos in boardrooms and at shareholders' meetings? This fear is unfounded. In the last section, I gave examples of businesses and organizations where managers handle contradictory interests. As illustrated, these organizations do manage to work well, compete and grow. In the proposed structure, good corporate managers would be those who can prevail upon conflicting interests, set up dialogue among opposing groups, and imagine and arrange mutual accommodation. This, in fact, is the quality of good leadership in all walks of life – and my suggestion simply recognizes the social nature of modern business. It should be noted, however, that such proposed representation would easily be politicized, therefore the modus operandi has to be devised with care. It is beyond the scope of this chapter to develop the constitution of such boards.

GENERAL LEGISLATION

We can lobby for operational constraints for businesses that affect the environment, wildlife, health, children, minority groups and so on. There is a significant amount of regulation in most countries in these areas – but many of the regulations are ineffective and their enforcement is not transparent. Further, some arrangements create rent-seeking, and associations of those who are the targets of a regulation often capture the regulating bodies. We should ask for rationalization of existing regulations and regulating institutions. This is a challenging task, and requires the development of political and constitutional mechanisms with appropriate checks and balances.

COMPETITION

Community-owned businesses and NGOs should be encouraged to compete with mainstream businesses wherever possible. They should campaign by explaining the difference between their business and their competitors' – by highlighting their values and inviting consumer support. Experience shows that such organizations can expect significant support. There is substantial research and marketing evidence to suggest that a values system – and not just price – guides consumers' choice in many cases (Kahle 1996). Competition of this kind has been successful in areas where business has a reputation of being callous – for example, businesses with a focus on the environment, wildlife, organic food, forestry, child labour, women's empowerment, literacy and so on.

The purpose of this competition is to force mainstream businesses to adopt a similar values orientation to protect their market share. In the medium to long term, competition is expected to force mainstream businesses to introduce non-commercial values in their corporate missions and be seen to be working for them. They will be forced to care for other stakeholders' concerns even as they continue to look for profit.

Businesses will discover that a values orientation is a useful way to win consumers from their mainstream business rivals. In the last two decades we have seen examples of this new strategy and orientation. There are large corporations that have strategically adopted – for example – green values or a Third World orientation.[12] If some firms in an oligopoly pursue certain values that consumers appreciate, then the only possible equilibrium strategy for others would be to adopt them as well.

CREDIT RATING

Multiple-stakeholder businesses are less risky for lenders and investors, including shareholders, because management has less incentive to push for profits through excessive risk-taking or other dubious means. We can campaign for this to be incorporated into credit rating procedures. Rating agencies should be persuaded to rate multiple-stakeholder companies higher if other financial parameters are equal.

The result of differential rating can be substantial. Lower rating devalues business stock, therefore lenders charge higher interest for loans. Differential rating is expected to increase the cost of funding for mainstream businesses compared to multiple-stakeholder ones. I suggest that such competition might lead to the adoption of multi-stakeholder business units' values by mainstream units. Further, the cost differential may make multi-stakeholder business the preferred mode in the long term. When management is forced to adopt extra-profit missions to improve a company's credit rating, it will not face much opposition from shareholders, because the change would appear to deliver more, not less, profit.

---

12 For a discussion and some empirical facts on the issue, see Wang (2009). See also the cases of BP and General Electric discussed later in this chapter.

BUYING STOCKS

Stakeholders should try to buy stocks in anti-social corporations where possible. It is a financially wise proposition if a corporation regularly inflicts damage on a group of stakeholders. After acquiring shares, stakeholders can influence management to alter operations in order to reduce damage. It is worthwhile spending any amount less than the present value of the stream of future damages or costs to acquire shares in such a company. As an example, the combined present value of all future medical costs inflicted on people living near a large polluting factory is often enough to buy substantial shares in the factory – even 100 per cent in some cases – in densely populated countries.

There are, of course, reasons why polluting factories are not bought off by their victims in spite of this. Individually, each resident's future loss is probabilistic and small, and therefore does not induce them to take such a step. However, these actions can become feasible if the people affected are organized into a collective. They may be able to raise contributions from members or take out market loans. In developing countries, victim groups may not be able to raise loans because financial markets are imperfect and individuals often lack suitable collateral. NGOs can play a role here by organizing the victimized stakeholders, and raising contributions from the government and non-governmental sources.

GENERAL CAMPAIGNING

A general campaign to create awareness of the anti-social aspects of certain corporate activities has proven useful in the past. The medium for initiating such campaigns is frequently academia or NGOs. A critical amount of sustained campaign activity generally creates interest in the media to disseminate and participate in it, and eventually builds up political pressure.

Sustained campaigns by NGOs on the environment have led corporate organizations to be more careful. In 2005, General Electric started following a set of self-imposed restrictions on greenhouse gas emissions in response to widespread criticism of its large environmental footprint.[13] It now publishes an annual 'corporate citizenship report' describing its continuing efforts in the

---

13 For the self-imposed restrictions announced by General Electric in 2005 see 'A lean, clean electric machine' (2005). For a detailed list of criticisms levelled against the company, see the company profile of General Electric at Crocodyl, http://www.crocodyl.org/wiki/general_electric, accessed 26 March 2012 .

field of social responsibility. In some cases, corporations have re-branded their core values to emphasize business ethics. A prominent example is BP's new title: 'Beyond Petroleum'.

Attention to corporate social responsibility (CSR) is becoming common – as seen in the trend for large TNCs to establish special committees within the board to oversee CSR and sustainable practices. In some companies, executive remuneration has been tied to results in these areas. Corporations have come together to form groups to promote CSR. The European Alliance for CSR was created in 2006. It currently consists of 70 TNCs and 25 national partner organizations, and has become a resource for building capability in CSR.[14]

That those with wealth have extra social responsibility is an old idea. Religions propagate the idea, and norms of conduct have developed around it. This idea is very much alive in our materialistic society too, as is evident from charity funding of local public goods all over the world, and several huge altruistic funds at the global level.[15] However, this notion of personal responsibility has not transformed into a corresponding idea of corporate responsibility. CSR, which is often presented as an impersonal organizational responsibility, can be given more appeal and meaning by propagating it as the wealth owners' responsibility to society – a less abstract and more familiar idea.

INTERNATIONAL BODIES

We should persuade international bodies to establish wings to oversee global actions of TNCs. International bodies, like the UN or World Bank, can be quite effective in persuasion because they fund the clients of large TNCs. The UN has had some success in involving First World corporations in some of its Third World projects. Apart from the implicit threat that the UN or the World Bank may advise the loan/grant recipient countries to transact with a more complying rival, TNCs have other reasons to participate in these programmes. It enables them to project a responsible image in the developing world, where there is significant distrust of TNCs.

A number of global-level programmes have produced some success. The United Nations Global Compact, launched in 2000, has established a club

---

14 The history and the list of current members of the European Alliance for CSR are available at its homepage, http://www.csreurope.org, accessed 26 March 2012.

15 For example, the Bill and Melinda Gates Foundation (US), Stichting INGKA Foundation (the Netherlands), and Wellcome Trust (England) together have funds exceeding US$100 billion according to information published on their homepages.

of global companies committed to upholding human rights, labour rights, environmental stewardship and transparency. The initiative now has more than 7,000 corporate members and stakeholders from over 130 countries.[16] Some participants from developing economies belong to small and medium enterprises.[17] Another UN initiative – Principles for Responsible Investing (PRI) – began in 2005. It now includes over 170 institutions, representing US$15 trillion in assets. The member institutions take into account six key principles in the area of environmental, social and corporate governance when making investment decisions.

Corporations benefit by image-building through participation in these projects, which has significant cash value. Because their participation is, in this sense, opportunistic, it is sometimes suggested that it cannot really help. This argument is perhaps misleading. It is possible for a corporation to be ruthlessly commercial in some areas of its operation while at the same time participating in programmes like the United Nations Development Programme (UNDP) or the Global Sustainable Development Facility (GSDF), to enhance its image and disarm critics. But a corporation's participation in these so-called image-lifting activities does not cease creating the social benefits calculated by its sponsors (for example, UNDP or GSDF) because the company participates in irresponsible activity elsewhere. What is necessary for sponsoring agencies is to devise projects or activities that do produce significant benefits where they take place.

I should point out that all proposals in this section would not suit all industries and types of business. For example, an effective procedure in social service industries would be to engage the NGOs into competition with mainstream business. However, industries involving large initial investment, where NGOs are not expected to operate as business units, have to rely on other measures. It is necessary to examine the characteristics of each industry to plan for the kind of measure that would suit, and then work on the modalities. A discussion of these procedures is beyond the scope of this chapter, but they certainly merit thorough research and planning in order to apply the ideas proposed here.

---

16 For up-to-date information, visit http://www.unglobalcompact.org/, accessed 26 March 2012.
17 For example, the Indian chapter has 168 members, including TNCs, small and medium enterprises, and industry associations.

Conclusion

In this chapter, I have suggested that extending the responsibility of managers to a wider social group is both desirable and feasible. It is desirable because: (1) it tends to reduce the anti-social tendency of corporations, and (2) it frees management from the pressure of advancing profit by any, including unscrupulous, means. This freedom reduces the chance of false signalling that often leads to corporate failure.

I expect substantial change in the culture of managerial reward and remuneration if managers are made responsible to several stakeholders. Shareholders, of course, would continue to remain active in selecting managers, because they are the principal stakeholders. But they would realize that managers' abilities to deliver profits are circumscribed by other mechanisms. This will curb the excesses of salary and perks offered to managers in the expectation of sky-high profits. The more the reward structure loses the excesses, the less will be the manager's perceived personal cost from objective reporting of a bad financial state. Managers will feel more secure in their jobs, therefore cases of false signalling to maintain a company's reputation would decline.

I have given several examples of well-functioning arrangements where managers are responsible to several stakeholders. Most production activities involve some conflict of interest. Good management should involve resolving the conflict in the most suitable and expedient manner – something the present corporate governance arrangement does not even attempt. This cause can be advanced by moving towards multi-stakeholder organizations.

References

'A lean, clean electric machine: The greening of General Electric'. 2005. *The Economist*, 8 December, http://www.economist.com/node/5278338, accessed 26 March 2012.

'Allen Stanford Arise and fall', *Economist*, 10 March 2012.

ACFE (Association of Certified Fraud Examiners). 2006. *Report to the Nation on Occupational Fraud and Abuse*. Austin, TX: ACFE.

Amromin, G. and Paulson, A.L. 2009. 'Comparing patterns of default among prime and subprime mortgages'. *Economic Perspectives*, Federal Reserve Bank of Chicago, 33(2), 18–37.

Bakan, J. 2004. *The Corporation: The Pathological Pursuit of Profit and Power.* Toronto: Viking.

Bratton, W.W. 2001. 'Berle and Means reconsidered at the century's turn'. *Journal of Corporation Law*, 26, 737–70.

Carroll, A.B. 2000. 'Ethical challenges for business in the new millennium: Corporate social responsibility and models of management morality'. *Business Ethics Quarterly*, 10(1), 33–42.

Chad, B. and Ef, A. 2009. 'Bernard Madoff pleads guilty to massive fraud'. *The Wall Street Journal*, 13 March.

Chomsisengphet, S. and Pennington-Cross, A. 2006. 'The evolution of the subprime mortgage market'. *Federal Reserve Bank of St. Louis Review*, January/February, 88(1), 31–56.

Conrad, C. 2003. 'Setting the stage: Introduction to the special issue on the "Corporate Meltdown"'. *Management Communication Quarterly*, 17(1), 5–19.

Council of Europe. 2010. *Human rights and Business.* Parliamentary Assembly (Doc. 12361), http://assembly.coe.int/Main.asp?link=/Documents/WorkingDocs/Doc10/EDOC12361.htm, accessed 26 March 2012.

Daily, C.M., Dan, R.D. and Cannella Jr, Albert, A. 2003. 'Corporate governance: Decades of dialogue and data'. *Academy of Management Review*, 28(3), 371–82.

Demyanyk, Y.S. 2009. 'Quick exits of subprime mortgages'. *Federal Reserve Bank of St. Louis Review*, 91(2), 79–93.

Duchin, R., Ozbas, O. and Sensoy, B.A. 2010. 'Costly external finance, corporate investment, and the subprime mortgage credit crisis'. *Journal of Financial Economics*, 97(3), 418–35.

'Formula for disaster: The politics of an unconscionable delay'. *The Economist*, 18 September, http://www.economist.com/node/12262271, accessed 26 March 2012.

Foster, J.B. and Magdoff, F. 2009. *The Great Financial Crisis: Causes and Consequences.* New York: Monthly Review Press.

Friedman, M. and Friedman, R.D. 1962. *Capitalism and Freedom.* Chicago, IL: University of Chicago Press.

Gandhi, M.K. 1941. *Constructive Programme: Its Meaning and Place.* Ahmedabad: Navajivan Publishing House.

Goetz, S.J. and Swaminathan, H. 2004. *Wal-Mart and County-wide Poverty.* AERS Staff Paper no. 371, University Park, PA: Pennsylvania State University.

Hayek, F.A. 1960. *The Constitution of Liberty.* Chicago, IL: University of Chicago Press.

Holmström, B. 1999. 'Managerial incentive problems: A dynamic perspective'. *Review of Economic Studies*, 66(1), 169–82.

Holmström, B. and Ricart I Costa, J. 1986. 'Managerial incentives and capital management'. *Quarterly Journal of Economics*, 101(4), 835–60.

Huffington, A.S. 2003. *Pigs At The Trough: How Corporate Greed And Political Corruption Are Undermining America*. New York: Three Rivers Press.

'Humbled: Pity the poor, post-Enron company boss'. *The Economist*, 18 December, http://www.economist.com/node/2281938, accessed 26 March 2012.

'India's Enron: Scandal hits India's flagship industry'. 2009. *The Economist*, 8 January, http://www.economist.com/node/12898777, accessed 26 March 2012.

Isaksson, M. and Kirkpatrick, G. 2009. 'Corporate governance: Lessons from the financial crisis'. *OECD Observer*, 273.

Jacoby, S.M. 2004. *The Embedded Corporation: Corporate Governance and Employment Relations in Japan and the United States*. Princeton, NJ: Princeton University Press.

'Justice or extortion? Ecuador, Chevron and pollution'. 2009. *The Economist*, 21 May, http://www.economist.com/node/13707679, accessed 26 March 2012.

Kahle, L.R. 1996. 'Social values and consumer behaviour: Research from the list of values', in *The Psychology of Values*, ed. C. Seligman, J.M. Olson and M.P. Zanna. Hillsdale, NJ: Lawrence Erlbaum Associates.

Kaufman, A., Zacharias, L. and Karson, M. 1995. *Managers vs Owners: The Struggle for Corporate Control in American Democracy*. Oxford: Oxford University Press.

Keynes, J.M. 1936. *The General Theory of Employment, Interest and Money*. Cambridge: Macmillan and Cambridge University Press, for the Royal Economic Society.

Knee, J.A. 2006. *The Accidental Investment Banker: Inside the Decade that Transformed Wall Street*. New York: Oxford University Press.

Kochan, T.A. 2002. 'Addressing the crisis in confidence in corporations: Root causes, victims, and strategies for reform'. *The Academy of Management Executive*, 16(3), 139–41.

Latham, J.L. 2003. 'The legislative and judicial response to recent corporate governance failures: Will it be effective?' *Tennessee Journal of Business Law*, 5(1), 72–89.

Lever, L. 1992. *The Barlow Clowes Affair*. London: Macmillan.

Livingston, J. 2007. 'Outside the box: Community-owned department stores an alternative to big-box chain stores', http://findarticles.com/p/articles/mi_m0KFU/is_1_74/ai_n18630538/, accessed 26 March 2012.

Machan, T.R. 2007. *The Morality of Business: A Profession of Human Wealthcare*. New York: Springer Science and Business Media.

Marnet, O. 2007. 'History repeats itself: The failure of rational choice models in corporate governance'. *Critical Perspectives on Accounting*, 18(2), 191–210.

Marx, K. 1849. *Wage Labour and Capital*, http://www.marxists.org/archive/marx/works/1847/wage-labour/index.htm, accessed 26 March 2012.

McCoy P.A. and Renuart, E. 2008. *The Legal Infrastructure of Subprime and Nontraditional Home Mortgages*. Cambridge, MA: Joint Center for Housing Studies of Harvard University.

Poon, M. 2009. 'From new deal institutions to capital markets: Commercial consumer risk scores and the making of subprime mortgage finance'. *Accounting, Organizations and Society*, 34(5), 654–74.

Quinn, D.P. and Jones, T.M. 1995. 'An agent morality view of business policy'. *Academy of Management Review*, 20(1), 22–42.

Rajagopalan, N. and Zhang, Y. 2009. 'Recurring failures in corporate governance: A global disease?' *Business Horizons*, 52(6), 545–52.

Ramachandran, K. 2005. *Indian Family Businesses: Their Survival beyond Three Generations*, Working Paper Series, Indian School of Business, Hyderabad. Presented at the 35th EISB Conference, Barcelona, 12–14 September 2005.

Rangarajan, L.N. 1992. *Kautilya: The Arthashastra*. Mumbai: Penguin Classics.

Salter, M. 2008. *Innovation Corrupted: The Origins and Legacy of Enron's Collapse*. Cambridge, MA: Harvard University Press.

Shiller, R.J. 2008. *The Subprime Solution: How Today's Global Financial Crisis Happened, and What to Do about It*. Princeton, NJ: Princeton University Press.

Shleifer, A. and Vishny, R.W. 1997. 'A survey of corporate governance'. *Journal of Finance*, 52(2), 737–83.

Stansfield, G. 2006. 'Some thoughts on reputation and challenges for global financial institutions'. *The Geneva Papers*, 31(3), 470–79.

'The poison spreads: Food regulation in China'. *The Economist*, 25 September, http://www.economist.com/node/12304845, accessed 26 March 2012.

'The revolution within'. 2009. *The Economist*, 14 May, http://www.economist.com/node/13604627, accessed 26 March 2012.

Ulrich, P. and Thielemann, U. 1993. 'How do managers think about market economies and morality? Empirical enquiries into business-ethical thinking patterns'. *Journal of Business Ethics*, 12(11), 879–98.

Useem, M. 1996. *Investor Capitalism*. New York: Basic Books.

Wang, Y. 2009. 'Examination on philosophy-based management of contemporary Japanese corporations: Philosophy, value orientation and performance'. *Journal of Business Ethics*, 85(1), 1–12.

Werner, W. 1977. 'Management, stock market and corporate reform: Berle and Means reconsidered'. *Columbia Law Review*, 77(3), 388–417.

3

Corporate Environmental Responsibility: Whose Business, Whose Health?

Arindam Basu

Introduction

Increasingly, society expects that the best industries and business practices are not only socially responsible, but also committed to sustaining a healthy environment. In this sense, corporate environmental responsibility (CER) is embedded within the notion of corporate social responsibility (CSR) – a construct that represents the ethics of conducting business within the context of a healthy society and the expressed commitment of a business to uphold the principles that govern healthy society. CER refers to a commitment towards a sustainable local and global environment, with the assumption that a healthy environment is instrumental to sustaining a healthy society. In this chapter, I consider CER along with a discussion of the different approaches related to sustainable practices for the environment. However, as will be demonstrated, the process is not simple.

Businesses have traditionally been viewed in the light of profit-maximizing initiatives, where generation of wealth and using natural resources were considered to be their only roles (Friedman 1962). However, increasingly, for their own advantage, businesses have adopted 'greener' and 'leaner' technology, and there are mechanisms in place that both mandate and enable them to adopt practices that are geared towards environmental sustainability. Thus, protection of the natural environment and conducting business are not necessarily incompatible. The different stakeholders in the process – including individual consumers, civil society representatives, government officials, and business leaders themselves – have important roles to play in this harmonization process.

Even so, industrial accidents continue to happen, and the presence of industries and industrial activities continues to lead to environmental degradation in a number of ways. Thus, in the face of thriving businesses and increased productivity, environmental protection poses a challenge both for environmentally conscious businesses and the governments in countries where these industries are located. Local government and administration have a responsibility to ensure environmental protection for the safety of the population. Industrial accidents, continuous emission of pollutants into the environment and residual damage to the environment even after closure of factories pose important challenges to the society. Other challenges include finding the best ways to integrate the role of government and industry to prevent accidents, ensure a healthy and sustainable environment, and foster industrial productivity. This chapter explains and discusses these challenges. While the scope of this problem is global, I have chosen to focus on India and New Zealand and discuss some of the challenges these countries have faced, both in the past and at present, and how administration and business in these two countries have addressed these opportunities.

The chapter is divided into two sections. The first section outlines the challenges that face society, governance and businesses. The second section describes the two main approaches to fostering environmental responsibility for businesses. One of these approaches looks at how the law and governance frame policies and put regulations in place so that businesses comply with the established laws of the land and conform to environmental sustainability. The other looks at how businesses regulate themselves, or take other steps to achieve more than the minimum compliance with environmental regulations. In essence, this initiative comes from within the industries themselves, where they have organized and formulated policies that enable them to conduct their businesses while at the same time keeping ecology and the environment in perspective.

The Challenges

Business and industrial processes are important for society, yet they are often associated with disastrous environmental and public health consequences, and as a result, pose challenges for the regulatory systems and processes within any society. On the one hand, industries and businesses provide livelihoods for millions of people and sustain the economy – and yet, on the other hand, industrial activities influence individual and public health through their impact on the environment. The continued operation and maintenance of an industrial production plant typically results in emissions of toxicants into the air, discharge of chemical and bioactive products into the air, water and soil, and the release of other products as runoffs or emissions into the environment. In addition, industrial activities and factory operations have considerable impact on the people who work in them, specifically those who are occupationally exposed to toxins and chemicals. Even after a factory shuts down or a business ceases to operate, unless the site is properly secured, toxins and residues continue to impact on the lives of people who live in the vicinity and perhaps for generations they can suffer from adverse health impacts resulting from toxic exposure. Uncontrolled or unrestrained market and economic growth are ecologically unsustainable, and as DesJardins has pointed out, 'ethically deficient' (DesJardins 1998: 826). The profit motive of businesses, frequent industrial accidents, and the impact on the physical environment as a result of industrial and business activities bring into question whether industry and a healthy environment can coexist and whether industries or businesses can foster environmentally sustainable development at all.

The question of whether industries and businesses can overcome the notions of profit motive and contribute to a sustainable environment is addressed by considering issues surrounding corporate social and environmental responsibility. CSR is a complex construct. It has been described as the framing of policy and other approaches that define the social sensitivity and responsiveness of a corporate organization. A uniform definition of this concept has not been achieved, and CSR is open to interpretation by authors and businesses that refer to these and other practices.

CER is, in principle, conceptually related to CSR. CER is about industry and corporate commitment, role and effort to support a sustainable and healthy environment. It aims to mitigate the adverse effects on the environment and public health from industrial and other corporate activities. The path to instituting robust CER practices is never easy, and indeed, experience shows that industrial processes have often been associated with significant harm to the environment, and consequently to public health.

IMPACT OF BUSINESS AND INDUSTRY ON ENVIRONMENT AND HEALTH

Industrial accidents and disasters continue to plague societies across the world. Examples of notable industry-caused ecological disasters in New Zealand include the environmental effects from the closed Tui mine, the Brunner and Pike River coal mine disasters and the environmental and health effects from continuous runoff of contaminants from the dairy industry. In India, such examples include the Bhopal gas tragedy, the Roro Asbestos mine disaster, the Kodaikanal mercury poisoning and, more currently, the pollution of the River Ganges from tanneries spread along the banks of the river in and around Kanpur in north India. These examples serve as stark reminders of how industrial activities continue to contaminate the environment.

Conceptually, industrial activities impact on the environment in three ways. The most devastating and visible of these is when industrial accidents result in large-scale and massive build-up and release of toxicants that can lead to disastrous consequences. These industrial disasters or accidents result from the sudden release of massive amounts of toxicants or environmentally harmful agents into the environment such as oil spills, chemical spills, and mine explosions, usually resulting in accidents that lead to significant loss of life over very short periods. A hallmark of this type of disaster is its dramatic immediate impact, including loss of life. In India, the most important example of this type of devastating industrial disaster is the 1984 Bhopal gas tragedy which occurred at the Union Carbide India Ltd (UCIL) pesticide plant in Bhopal, India. Describing the event, Broughton cited the official accident summary: 'At around 1 a.m., December 3, loud rumbling reverberated around the plant as a safety valve gave way sending a plume of MIC gas into the early morning air' ('Accident Summary' 1984). Around 3,800 people died immediately as a consequence of massive sudden exposure to methyl isocyanate (MIC), and over the next two decades more than 20,000 premature deaths were attributed to this event. Eventually, UCIL was closed and its parent company Union Carbide Corporation (UCC) was taken over by Dow Jones Industrial Corporation (Broughton 2005: 1).

In New Zealand, a more recent example of this type of event was the Pike River coal mine blast on the west coast of the South Island. In November 2010, a series of massive explosions at the Pike River mine left 29 miners dead and trapped underground in the collapsed mine. Although there was no environmental release of toxic chemicals and this accident did not result in the deaths of people living in the surrounding areas, it is clearly another example of an industrial accident that not only claims lives, but also significantly impacts on the local community. Following the disaster, the mine was closed and the company, Pike River Coal, was turned over to receivers, leading to loss of livelihood and jobs for hundreds of workers and contractors in the area. Although the scale of these two disasters cannot be compared, they both illustrate the characteristics of this type of disaster. In each case, significant loss of life occurs over a relatively short period, the business is adversely affected, and the various aspects of the disaster are highly visible.

Another way industrial accidents happen and impact on the environment is through small-scale continuous emission of toxicants resulting from industrial activities that enter the surrounding environment and contaminate air, water or land, leading to exposure to toxins for people who live around the industrial areas. Examples include exposure to dairy runoffs in New Zealand and the contamination of the River Ganges from tanneries dotted along its banks in the Kanpur region of India (Gupta and Sinha 2006, Iyer, Mastorakis and Theologou 2006). New Zealand produces about 2.2 per cent of the world supply of milk through its NZ$11 billion dairy industry. However, this productive, profitable industry is associated with significant contamination of the environment, in particular, high faecal pollution of New Zealand's waterways, putting hundreds of individuals at risk of gastrointestinal tract illnesses (Winkworth 2010). In India, effluents from the tannery and agricultural industries are associated with significant contamination of the water supply, and as a result, thousands of Indian households are continuously exposed to chromium and other heavy metals. Such exposure is continuous, even while the industries thrive, and is potentially responsible for a significant proportion of disease attributed to toxicants in the community. However, because of the slow and continuous release of toxicants, significant cumulative effects take several decades to emerge in the community, and gauging the impact of such industries requires careful environmental monitoring and disease surveillance. Therefore, the detection and effects are less dramatic than those that result from major industrial accidents or disasters.

The third way industries pollute the environment is through contamination from residual contaminants. This happens when, after an industrial plant closes, people in the surrounding area are exposed to the waste products left behind as the industrial protection controlling release of such toxins is removed. The cases of the Roro asbestos mine and Kodaikanal mercury plant in India and the Tui metals mine in New Zealand are examples of such contamination by attrition. These disasters are all associated with incorrectly managed closure of industrial plants which resulted in prolonged, continual release of toxicants into the environment. As a consequence, people living in the vicinity of these operations have been exposed to high levels of industrial toxicants. For example, after the asbestos mine in the Roro Hills, Jharkhand, India, was abandoned in 1983, the company, Hyderabad Asbestos Cement Products Ltd, left hazardous waste out in the open in several tailing ponds, and people in the surrounding villages were exposed to it for years. Subsequently, many of them developed signs and symptoms of asbestos-related diseases (Dutta, Sreedhar and Basu 2002). The Anglo-Dutch company Unilever and its Indian subsidiary Hindustan Lever manufactured thermometers in an industrial plant in the hill resort town of Kodaikanal, in the state of Tamil Nadu, India. In 2001, the residents of Kodaikanal discovered that the plant was dumping mercury-laced waste from the factory onto a dump site. This led to the closure of the plant. Even nine years after closure, however, several thousand tons of mercury-contaminated waste and soil were still found lying inside and around the factory (Mukherjee et al. 2009, Rajgopal, Ravimohan and Mascarenhas 2006).

In New Zealand, the Tui mine, located on the western slopes of Mount Te Aroha, in Waikato, has long been associated with significant environmental contamination from abandoned tailing ponds. In the 1960s, the mine extracted copper, lead and zinc sulphides. It was abandoned in 1973 after the company, Norpac Mining Ltd, went into liquidation. However, rock ore dumps and tailings were left behind, and significant amounts of heavy metals have leached into the soil and nearby streams. The impact of the pollution is increased by the amount of water discharged from the site, including drainage from adits, contaminated under drainage from waste rock and tailings, and natural sources.

These examples illustrate that the inter-relationships between industry and business processes – governed, in turn, by industrial outputs and profitability – can have a significant impact on environmental and human health. Calculating the associated costs of such disasters on the industry and local economy is far from simple. Further, they highlight the need to institute appropriate management strategies and establish environmental control of aspects of industrial processes and practices. Bhopal and the experience of Unilever (Hindustan Lever) at Kodaikanal in India have also shown that businesses and industrial processes that are not sensitive to environmental needs and fail to respond to their local community eventually become unsustainable. There is also a strong case for industries and corporations to formulate strategies to minimize environmental harm and put checks and balances in place to protect not only the environment, but also the lives of people living in the surrounding areas after closure. As the examples of Roro in India and the Tui mine in New Zealand illustrate, inappropriate closure of the factories and improper maintenance of the tailings and disposal of hazardous waste can lead to major environmental and human health disasters. These, in turn, involve significant societal costs.

These situations pose a dilemma. On the one hand, if industrialization is allowed to continue without any restriction, then it is possible that there will be continuous environmental damage and the risk of other major industrial disasters claiming many lives. Industries will continue to pursue increased output goals without much regard to the impacts on the environment. This situation is summed up by DesJardins as 'ethical disaster' (DesJardins 1998: 826). On the other hand, if the societal controls are so tight that the focus is entirely on protection of the environment, without any consideration as to how CER operations can be funded and maintained from the industry's operational perspective, then it may be financially discouraging to some businesses, as they might see only the costs required to continue to operate. The result will be that they will move away from the area of production, and that, in turn, will lead to economic loss and unsustainable community. The loss of industrial activities and the absence of sustainable livelihoods will lead to lack of revenue, loss of employment and productivity, and following the closure, as described above, there may be residual pollution and damage to the environment.

The challenge, then, is to find a middle path, one that not only mitigates the potentially harmful effects of industrial activities on the environment, but at the same time seeks to identify ways to maintain economic sustainability and competitiveness, so that industrial activities continue to contribute to the local economy. This dilemma essentially relates to how industrial productivity and activities can be controlled – or industry and business be conducted – in ways that can be responsive and sensitive to the environmental sustainability issues around the business and industrial processes. This can be achieved both from a perspective of policy and regulation, as well as from the company's perspective of what is needed to maintain and sustain the environment, or a combination of both.

The Responses

These challenges can be addressed using two complementary approaches. One approach is to meet these challenges from a governance perspective, with a view to policy and regulation to control corporate and industrial activities and minimize environmental harm. The other approach emerges from a self-regulation perspective, a more 'ground-up' approach, at the level of the corporations, industries and businesses. The second approach is grounded not only in the ethical and moral principles of conducting business, but also on sound business principles, and with a view to long-term benefits. It builds positive images of corporate social and environmental responsibility and responsiveness. A possible third approach is to identify elements within each, and combine elements of both governance and industrial self-regulation so that companies and industries regulate their processes to be environmentally sensitive within a negotiated framework in consonance with governmental and societal environmental policies. An example of this is the Accord between Fonterra, the independent agency representative of New Zealand's dairy industry, and New Zealand's Ministry for the Environment (Fonterra Co-operative Group 2003).

THE POLICY AND REGULATORY APPROACH

Industries and businesses are currently viewed as profit-maximizing entities. Following the Second World War, the extent to which a firm was socially responsible was measured in terms of its business efficiency and profitability. Friedman famously stated: 'Few trends would so thoroughly undermine the very foundations of our free society other than to make as much money for their shareholders as they possibly can' (Friedman 1962: 133). Given the traditionally understood nature of businesses and industries and their relationship with the environment, society has entrusted governments, regulatory bodies and other relevant agencies with the responsibility of protecting national resources and environments. As guardians of the environment and protectors of public health, they play an important role in putting into place the policies and regulations that control environmental threats.

In India, the Environment (Protection) Act of 1986 resulted in the establishment of the Ministry of Environment and Forests, and is an example of a policy and regulatory approach. The framework and background work for this policy had been in existence since at least the 1970s. The push came following the massive disaster of the Bhopal gas tragedy and its aftermath (Broughton 2005).

In New Zealand, the Conservation Act of 1987 resulted in the establishment of the Department of Conservation (DOC), which takes a leading role in conservation work, environmental protection and sustainability. While the Resource Management Act of 1991, administered by the Ministry for the Environment, is New Zealand's main piece of legislation that sets out how the country manages its environment. In this case, the urge was to protect the environment, particularly in response to the ecological damage and toxin releases of the emerging and growing dairy industry, and keeping in mind the nature of agribusiness, to ensure that a plan was put together that integrated relevant existing, but fragmented, statutes and provided a comprehensive framework (Gunder and Mouat 2002, Jackson and Dixon 2007).

Policy and regulatory approaches can be effective, but they have also been criticized for being punitive. The real punishments in terms of costs are still more frequently borne by the ordinary staff of the companies concerned and by the general public, rarely by the top executives involved, so they have little deterrence value. Further, this strategy is dissociated from the participatory approach that would allow better co-operation and collaboration with industries and businesses in order to foster better integration and more effective control over environmental situations.

Kagan, Thornton and Gunningham reported the results of a mixed-methods cross-sectional study of 14 paper pulp mills spread across New Zealand, Australia, Canada and the United States. The study looked at and tested the effects of different approaches (strict regulatory approaches, as in the United States and Canada, versus a more participatory approach, as experienced in New Zealand) on the overall compliance of these industries. They found that over a period of three decades, tightening regulatory requirements and intensive political pressures did bring about large improvements in compliance with respect to environmental factors among these paper and pulp processing mills. Some even showed over-compliance, in that they went beyond what was expected of them in terms of compliance specified by the regulatory processes. On analysis of qualitative interview-based data, the authors found that pressure to maintain a healthy environment from the local community and environmental activists (relevant to the New Zealand context) – a process the authors termed 'social licence' – together with a corporate management style that was favourable to the environment encouraged some firms towards better compliance (Kagan, Thornton and Gunningham 2003). On the other hand, depending solely on regulation and policies may not work. There is an element of inherent resistance to the regulatory process if the industries perceive that compliance to regulations can add to their costs and adversely impact their business prospects. In India, for instance, Curmally has argued that an approach to control environmental contamination and pollution by enactment of laws and monitoring can result in failure, primarily because India has poor infrastructure and a relatively low institutional capacity for effective monitoring of compliance. As a result, in spite of strict and relatively high penalties and costs associated with non-compliance, the compliance rates in India are lower when compared to other countries, such as New Zealand, that allow a more participatory approach in dealing with this issue. Faced with relatively rigid options, most companies choose either to flout the norms or laws, or not to enforce the standards at all (Curmally 2002).

ECOLOGICAL MODERNIZATION

In general, irrespective of governmental and societal control, industrial processes have tended to move closer to being greener and leaner – that is more eco-friendly – and to using fewer resources than before. As Tilt argued in a content analysis of Australian corporate environmental policies, most industries prefer to be seen as environmentally friendly in their operations. For most modern corporations, a focus on environmental responsibility is deemed a part of the larger CSR. Corporate environmental policies are seen as 'stepping stones' for corporations embracing environmental concerns as an agenda (Tilt 2001).

Consider the example of UCIL in Bhopal, India, which produced Sevin, a pesticide. At the time of the Bhopal disaster, the company was about to be sold. The usual checks and balances that ensure that safety norms and procedures are followed were probably never strictly observed when compared to the procedures to be expected of a corporation of the stature of Union Carbide. This tragic event was largely a result of shoddy safety systems, poor maintenance and equipment failure – and the subsequent leak of a cocktail of noxious gases into the environment, against which no adequate protection was or could be offered. Thousands of people died overnight in Bhopal, and in the aftermath, the company was closed. Eventually, as a result of the crass negligence of environmental safety issues, events in a remote city in India, Bhopal, pushed a giant global corporation to the brink of bankruptcy. Union Carbide was eventually bought by the Dow Chemical Corporation. In 1989, the Supreme Court of India directed final settlement of all Bhopal litigation, and UCC, UCIL and the Government of India agreed to a settlement of US$470 million. Clearly, mere responsiveness to the immediate shareholders as stakeholders alone is not sufficient for sustainability, nor can it be a sectoral role for a corporation – environmental sensitivity and safety should be a major goal as well.

As the extraordinary example of Bhopal illustrates, the environment and business are linked in more complex patterns than can be measured in terms of profitability and productivity alone. The World Business Council for Sustainable Development has echoed this complexity of mutual association between business and environment. Moir has argued that CSR should be framed in the debates about enlightened self-interest of a company, and that a moral or ethical imperative can be linked to social expectations of businesses. The issues around environmental responsibility need to be considered from an ethical perspective (Moir 2001). This argument extends the concepts of stakeholders in a firm, and challenges Friedman's argument about satisfying the shareholders alone.

CSR therefore acknowledges the role of primary and secondary stakeholders in businesses. Primary stakeholders – such as company representatives or major investors – expect that a company should be responsive and responsible to their demands and expectations. However, there are also secondary stakeholders to consider. Their needs and demands may not match the profitability of business productivity of the firm. Nevertheless, there is a societal demand or urgency to meet their expectations. Among these different groups of stakeholders, the answer to the dilemma about whose interests come first is not easy to resolve. Stakeholder theory enables one to analyse the reasons why companies may conduct CSR exercises based on people and their social interactions. Theorists have built models of stakeholder identification on the basis of 'salience' characteristics: notably power, legitimacy and urgency. Power refers to the lobby and the pressure groups or financial importance of specific stakeholder groups; legitimacy refers to the notion that the actions are desirable and appropriate within socially constructed norms and values, and the environmental argument is the urgency component of the model. The impact on the environment and its effects need not only be analysed in terms of whom they impact upon, but also over what period and how responsive the company is in addressing those issues (Moir 2001).

THE GLOBAL COMPACT AND THE 'ACCORD' APPROACH

For environmental protection and best practices for businesses and industries in environmental sustainability, the two complementary approaches have been governmental or societal regulation, along with a push from the corporations themselves to enhance their image in order to be perceived as being environmentally friendly. When policy and regulatory approaches are tempered by corporate policies and promoted by the community, activists and lobbyists within society, this creates a framework that supports acceptance of environmental and ecological roles. Hopefully, the best results with respect to environmental sustainability will emerge from such a meeting of expectations and practice.

Over the last decade, an interesting middle ground, forged by regulatory bodies in collaboration with industries, has received the support and participation of the United Nations (UN). Known as the 'Global Compact', it is a programme based on industries' voluntary initiatives and a consultative approach by the UN and its constituent countries to foster CSR. The focus is not entirely on the environment. However, three of the ten principles on which the Global Compact is based are relevant to protection of the environment. These include that businesses should support a precautionary approach to environmental challenges, that businesses should undertake initiatives to promote greater environmental responsibility, and that businesses should encourage the development and diffusion of environmentally friendly technologies (Hall and Cruse 2010).

Another example of this harmonious process where governmental regulations meet the company initiatives and environmental sustainability is built around a negotiated agreement is the aforementioned Accord between dairy industry representatives Fonterra and the New Zealand Ministry for the Environment and Ministry of Agriculture and Forestry which aims to ensure ecological improvement and maintenance of soil and waterways (Fonterra Co-operative Group 2003). Despite the robustness of these approaches, the outcome in terms of fostering environmental protection is still uncertain.

Conclusion

In summary, big businesses and multinational corporations use environmental resources, and their massive production processes are associated with the release of toxins into the environment. In the process, people living near industrial production plants are exposed to harmful environmental agents. In general, three related but distinct patterns of environmental harm can be identified:

1.   The sudden release of massive environmental toxins and noxious agents, as happened at Bhopal in India, or the Pike River coal mine in New Zealand.

2.   A relatively slow but continuous process of leaching of harmful agents into the environment, leading to environmental degradation, as happens with effluents from the dairy industry

in New Zealand and tannery industries and factories around the River Ganges in India.

3.   Residual damage to the environment following closure of an industrial plant or mine, as happened at the Tui mine in New Zealand, or the Roro asbestos mine in India.

These phenomena suggest that while industrial developments and business processes are vital to the sustenance of the economy, there is also a need to control and regulate them, in order to minimize environmental harm and harmful effects on public health.

Societies, governments, businesses and industries have in general used three approaches, grounded in two complementary strategies, to address this challenge of environmental protection in the face of the risk of environmental degradation as a result of industrial activities. Societies have used what has been described as a 'top-down' approach, where policies and regulations have been drafted to control industrial emissions and processes that could potentially have harmful effects on the environment. Indian lawmakers and government have largely taken this approach, with the most prominent example being the Environment (Protection) Act of 1986, following the Bhopal gas tragedy. In a complementary approach, industrial bodies and business councils take self-regulatory steps, keeping in mind the 'greenness' of their business processes and ethical considerations from a business and moral perspective. Such an approach can be labelled 'ground-up'. Finally, in some countries, notably New Zealand, an approach based on a negotiated space between lawmakers and industry has shaped policies and taken steps to minimize environmental harm from industrial activities and businesses – the 'accord' approach.

In this chapter, I have discussed some of the key issues surrounding the relationship between business and the environment, specifically with respect to public and environmental health. In it, I have described the impact of a number of industrial disasters that have taken place in India and New Zealand, and explored some of the strategies used to mitigate such environmental health effects. It is reasonable to speculate that accord-based approaches – where lawmakers, government agents, and representatives of businesses and industries create a negotiated agreement on how best to meet and manage environmental needs – are better than either the isolated approaches of governmental control alone or industry self-regulation. I believe a dialogue between stakeholders, industry and the enforcers of environmental protection is the best process to shape CER accords. However, if the outcomes and expectations of all concerned are not laid out clearly, such approaches are also fraught with the possibilities of confusion and eventual failure. The point is to strike a balance between profitability from an industry perspective, environmental safety, and sustainability of businesses and society. The best paths are still open and continue to be built.

References

'Accident Summary, Union Carbide India Ltd., Bhopal, India: December 3, 1984', in Hazardous Installations Directorate, Health and Safety Executive. 2004, cited in E. Broughton. 2005. 'The Bhopal disaster and its aftermath: A review'. *Environmental Health*, 4(6), doi: 10.1186/1476-069X-4-6.

Curmally, A. 2002. 'Environment and rehabilitation'. *India Infrastructure Report 2002*, 96–137.

DesJardins, J. 1998. 'Corporate environmental responsibility'. *Journal of Business Ethics*, 17, 825–38.

Dutta, M., Sreedhar, R. and Basu, A. 2002. 'The blighted hills of Roro, Jharkhand, India: A tale of corporate greed and abandonment'. *International Journal of Occupational and Environmental Health*, 9(3), 254–9.

Fonterra Co-operative Group, Regional Councils, Ministry for the Environment and Ministry of Agriculture and Forestry. 2003. *Dairying and Clean Streams Accord*. Wellington: New Zealand Ministry for the Environment, http://www.mfe.govt.nz/issues/land/rural/dairying-accord-may03.pdf, accessed 26 March 2012.

Friedman, M. 1962. *Capitalism and Freedom*. Chicago, IL: University of Chicago Press.

Gunder, M. and Mouat, C. 2002. 'Symbolic violence and victimization in planning processes: A reconnoitre of the New Zealand Resource Management Act'. *Planning Theory*, 1(2), 124–45, doi: 10.1177/147309520200100203.

Gupta, A. and Sinha, S. 2006. 'Chromium levels in vegetables and grains grown on tannery effluent irrigated area of Jajmau, Kanpur, India: Influence on dietary intake'. *Bulletin of Environmental Contamination and Toxicology*, 77(5), 658–64, http://www.springerlink.com/index/K1728Q340613224M.pdf, accessed 26 March 2012.

Hall, C. and Cruse, S. 2010. *United Nations Global Compact Annual Review: Anniversary Edition June 2010*. New York: United Nations Global Compact Office.

Iyer, G.V., Mastorakis, N.E. and Theologou, A.I. 2006. 'Assessment of pollution load from unsafe chromium leather tanneries in India'. *WSEAS Transactions*

on Environment and Development, 2(3), 207–15, http://www.wseas.us/
e-library/conferences/2006evia/papers/516-512.pdf, accessed 26 March 2012.

Jackson, T. and Dixon, J. 2007. 'The New Zealand Resource Management Act:
An exercise in delivering sustainable development through an ecological
modernisation agenda'. *Environment and Planning B: Planning and Design*,
34(1), 107–20, doi: 10.1068/b32089.

Kagan, R.A., Thornton, D. and Gunningham, N. 2003. 'Explaining corporate
environmental performance: How does regulation matter?' *Society*, 37(1),
51–90.

Moir, L. 2001. 'What do we mean by corporate social responsibility?' *Corporate
Governance*, 1(2), 16–22.

Mukherjee, A.B., Bhattacharya, P., Sarkar, A. and Zevenhoven, R. 2009. 'Mercury
emissions from industrial sources in India and its effects in the environment'.
Mercury Fate and Transport in the Global Atmosphere, 81–112, http://www.
springerlink.com/index/W75216665775124V.pdf, accessed 26 March 2012.

Rajgopal, T., Ravimohan, H. and Mascarenhas, P. 2006. 'Epidemiological
surveillance of employees in a mercury thermometer plant: An occupational
health study'. *Indian Journal of Occupational and Environmental Medicine*, 10(1),
11–18, doi: 10.4103/0019-5278.22889.

Tilt, C.A. 2001. 'The content and disclosure of Australian corporate
environmental policies'. *Accounting, Auditing & Accountability Journal*, 14(2),
190–212, doi: 10.1108/09513570110389314.

Winkworth, C. 2010. 'Land-use change and emerging public health risks in New
Zealand: Assessing *Giardia* risks'. *New Zealand Medical Journal*, 123(1,322),
http://www.nzma.org.nz/journal/123-1322/4341/, accessed 26 March 2012.

PART II

Traditional Values and Ethical Management

4

The Duty of Corporate Management: From the Perspective of Dharma

Venkataraman Nilakant and Marjolein Lips-Wiersma

Introduction

In this chapter, we examine the role of corporate management through the lens of *dharma* – a Hindu concept that refers to both appropriate conduct and one's duty. First, we discuss the notion of dharma, and examine the evolution of the role of corporate management. Contemporary business practices are strongly influenced by a particular stream of economic theory, which we refer to as the contractarian perspective (Boatright 1996, Jensen and Meckling 1976). We identify the notion of dharma within the contractarian perspective, which is to enhance shareholder value, and discuss its dysfunctional consequences – and then propose an alternative notion of the dharma of corporate management, to mitigate the negative consequences of the contemporary business practice of exclusively focusing on the interests of shareholders.

The dharma of managers cannot give exclusive attention to shareholder value enhancement. Instead, we believe four tensions need to be balanced in corporate organizations – and the duty of managers is to balance the interests of the various stakeholders. This requires balancing self-interest with concern for others. Any alternative conception of managerial work must acknowledge the tension or contradiction between pursuing self-interest and concern for others. It may not always be possible for managers to easily reconcile these and arrive at 'win–win' situations. Shareholder interests may have to be sacrificed in certain circumstances, if they are inconsistent with a higher moral and ethical purpose that will inevitably involve putting others' interests above managerial or shareholder interests.

The Concept of Dharma

A complete exposition of dharma is beyond the scope of this chapter. However, the concept of dharma is central to Hindu philosophy and practice (Kane 1968, Creel 1972, O'Flaherty and Derrett 1978). As Creel (1972: 155) points out: 'There is no precise Western equivalent' for the concept of dharma. Usually, dharma is loosely translated as one's duty. For our purposes, we consider dharma to be a multi-dimensional concept that, among other things, 'refers to what one should do and why one should do it' (Creel 1972: 155). What one should do, or what one does, also reflects the innate characteristic, or nature, of the person or the role – and another interpretation of dharma is that it also refers to the innate characteristic or essence of things. Thus, the dharma of water is to flow and the dharma of fire is to burn. If water does not flow, it ceases to be water. Similarly, if fire does not burn, it is no longer fire (Brown 1953, Karve 1961). In other words, dharma refers to a characteristic of a role. The role ceases to be if the characteristic is absent. Therefore, the characteristic is an essential feature of the role. If one applies this conception of dharma to managerial work, what would be the dharma of a manager? To answer this question, we need to examine how the role of corporate management has evolved over the years.

Evolution of Corporate Management

The organization of work in large American corporations in the post-war era, until the 1980s, was characterized by the dominance of professional managers. Referred to as 'the managerial revolution', corporate control of business shifted from owners to non-owning professional managers in the early twentieth century (Powell 2001). During this period, management models of structuring work and establishing authority diffused to other parts of the world, providing ideas for management practices (Guillen 1994b). These management models also incorporated social aspects of corporate organizations (Guillen 1994a). Around the mid-1980s, however, the dominance of professional managers began to be challenged (Useem 1993). Prior to the 1980s, shareholding in individual businesses was widely dispersed among a large number of small shareholders. An unwritten 'Wall

Street rule', which advised unhappy shareholders to divest their holdings rather than challenge the professional managers, became the norm (Useem 1993, Useem 1996), and during the same period, shareholding by institutional investors steadily increased (Brown 1998).

In 1950, pension funds, mutual funds, educational endowments and charitable foundations owned less than 15 per cent of the common stock outstanding in the United States. This increased to 40 per cent by 1980, and to more than 50 per cent by the end of the 1980s (Bernstein 1992). By 2005, institutional investors held about 68 per cent of the equity of the thousand largest US corporations (Conference Board 2007). These institutions also accounted for about 80 per cent of all trading activity in the stock market. For example, by the end of the 1980s, institutional investors held 52 per cent of General Electric, 59 per cent of Johnson & Johnson, 71 per cent of Digital Equipment and 83 per cent of Intel (Useem 1993). Changes in the pattern of ownership rendered the 'Wall Street rule' obsolete as it became unviable for large investors to divest their holdings. These large investors began to challenge the dominance of professional managers through individual and collective action – and although professional managers resisted the attempts of shareholders to wrest control, it gradually began to shift from them back to owners. The shifting of locus of control to owners or shareholders was accompanied by two other phenomena. An ideology of neo-liberalism emerged during the mid-1980s (Chomsky 1998), which viewed individual freedom as both the mark and aim of human progress. The rise of neo-liberalism and shift in control of corporations also coincided with other larger changes, such as deregulation, technological change and globalization.

One aspect of the rise of neo-liberalism was the emergence of economic theories that came to dominate the conduct of business. One particular stream of economic theory, which we refer to as the contractarian perspective, became the dominant model for corporate management. The contractarian perspective, characterized by theories such as the agency theory and transaction cost economics, views an organization not as a social institution, but as a nexus of contracts (Baiman 1982, Bradach and Eccles 1989, Donaldson 1990, Donaldson 1995, Eisenhardt 1989, Fama and Jensen 1983, Jensen and Meckling 1976, Lafontaine 1992, Levinthal 1988, Pfeffer 1997). Thus, a business is an arrangement that is the outcome of bargaining among various constituents, such as employees, suppliers, customers, shareholders, government and community groups. It is implicitly assumed that each constituent acts exclusively to promote its self-interest (the self-interest maximization principle). As these constituents seek to maximize their self-interest, the actual structure of an organization reflects an arrangement that permits them to do so while co-operating with each other.

The contractarian perspective, in itself, does not consider shareholder interests to be paramount. In principle, any constituent or stakeholder can lay claim to the control of the firm (Boatright 2002). However, in the agency theory variant of the contractarian perspective, shareholders are viewed as 'principals', and managers as 'agents'. Agency theory claims that shareholders, as principals, bear the most risk as they are vulnerable to 'moral hazard' by agents – that is, the managers. In other words, self-interest maximizing behaviour by managers can erode the welfare of shareholders, as managers may make decisions that benefit themselves to the detriment of shareholders. Therefore, shareholders have a claim on the fiduciary duty of managers. In the United States, this fiduciary duty is assigned to managers by corporate law. Agency theory claims that, as bearers of residual risk, shareholders are best suited to lay claims on managers' fiduciary duty, which is to enhance the wealth of shareholders (Boatright 1996, Jensen and Meckling 1976). It is argued that maximization of shareholder wealth 'promotes the welfare of society as a whole' (Boatright 1996: 223). In other words, the dharma of corporate management within the contractarian perspective has become the promotion of shareholder interests. The power of agency theory is evident in the fact that the economic reforms initiated in New Zealand in 1984 were based on agency theory ideas (Scott, Ball and Dale 1997).

As a consequence of this view of managerial fiduciary duty, the contractarian perspective opposes social initiatives by business corporations on three grounds (Margolis and Walsh 2003). First, engagement in social initiatives is tantamount to stealing, as shareholders – who are seen as the rightful claimants of corporate resources – may neither benefit from nor sanction such initiatives. Second, engagement in social initiatives reduces efficiency, since organizational resources are best suited to wealth creation rather than alleviating social ills. Third, it violates due process, since the rightful claimants of organizational resources are not fully consulted.

These arguments against social initiatives are based on the underlying philosophy of the contractarian perspective, which is a modified form of utilitarianism (Bentham 1789/2001, Mill 1861/1972). In the modified form, normative economic theory draws on two of the components of utilitarianism – consequentialism and welfarism – to argue that all choices must be evaluated by their outcomes, and outcomes must enhance individual utilities or personal well-being (Sen 1999). Coupled with the primacy given to property rights, this translates into evaluating corporate actions and managerial choices on the basis of their consequences for shareholder wealth, which it is assumed constitutes the personal well-being of an investor. Within such a narrowly defined ethical philosophy, an action not explicitly oriented to enhancing shareholder wealth in the short term is ethically wrong or bad. The dominance of the economic perspective is reflected in the view that corporate law in the United States requires managers not only to maximize shareholder wealth, but also to ignore other considerations (Bainbridge 2003). Lee (2005, 2006), however, challenges this view and argues that corporate law in the United States neither endorses exclusive attention to shareholder wealth creation, nor does it require managers to consider ethical factors in terms of profits alone.

The emergence of shareholder value as the almost exclusive metric and measure of organizational performance in recent years reflects the dominance of the contractarian perspective (Kennedy 2000, Koslowski 2000, Stiglitz 2003, Stiglitz 2004, Useem 1993, Useem 1996). Shareholder value is operationalized in terms of future cash flows. Chief executives are expected to maximize future profits, measured as dividends and the increase in the value of the firm in the stock market (Koslowski 2000).

Consequences of the Shareholder Value Principle

Research documents three significant consequences of the shift towards shareholder value enhancement (Khurana 2002, Useem 1993, Useem 1996).

First, organizations have been restructured to 'align' themselves with this goal of enhancing shareholder value. Organizational structures changed to decentralize authority, distribute information more widely and hold middle-level managers accountable to measures of shareholder value. A study by Barsky, Hussein and Jablonsky (1999) of downsizing in United Technologies demonstrates that financial reporting practices under such an organizational context privilege shareholder and management interests over other stakeholders, such as employees or the community. These practices may also favour actions that are detrimental to other stakeholders and to society at large. In other words, the shareholder value principle facilitates decisions that seem to ignore the social consequences of managerial actions (Cassidy 2003). In addition to internal financial practices, external corporate law also favours shareholder value maximization. An experimental study – with experienced corporate directors as subjects – found that while directors were aware of the ethical and social implications of their decisions, they nevertheless made decisions that favoured shareholders because these were legally defensible, while ignoring issues of personal ethics and social responsibility (Rose 2007).

Second, selection procedures in corporations changed to ensure the 'right' people were selected for managerial positions (Khurana 2002). Remuneration for these managers was tightly linked to indicators of shareholder wealth. In addition shareholders have given preference to external chief executive officer (CEO) appointments. A major impact of the shifts in corporate control has been in the area of executive compensation. Both the nature and amount of compensation for top executives, particularly CEOs, have changed significantly. In the 1980s, in response to public outcry about excessive compensation, the United States Congress enacted legislation to limit non-performance-based compensation for top executives. This led to a restructuring of executive compensation so that a major portion of it became contingent on performance, which was defined as shareholder value. Thus, compensation for CEOs was restructured toward stock options (Heron, Lie and Perry 2007). The rationale behind restructuring executive compensation in favour of stock options was based on a principal–agent model, in which CEOs were seen as agents working for principals: the investors (Jensen and Meckling 1976). It was argued that stock options would align the agents' efforts towards maximizing the principals' welfare. Between 1994 and 2005, the median value of the salary component of CEO compensation actually increased by 57 per cent, while the median value of the stock option component increased by 179 per cent (Heron, Lie and Perry 2007).

Third, under the new metric, employees are seen as costs, which leads organizations to downsize and restructure in order to enhance shareholder value. In the last two decades, the most visible of these changes has been in the area of employment. Corporations have shed hundreds of thousands of both blue-collar and white-collar jobs, exerting a significant toll on employees and communities (Powell 2001). The era of the lifelong job with clear career prospects has given way to contingent employment (Pink 2001). As a result of such shifting patterns of employment, Sennett (1998) argues that employees' ability to place themselves in a narrative and see continuity in their lives has been eroded. This loss of coherence, he claims, leads to loss of character, breakdown in ethical behaviour, loss of community involvement and loss of a sense of personal development. This change also relates to increasing inequality within business organizations ('The new titans' 2006). For example, while 'corporate America has increased its share of national income from 7% in mid-2001 to 13% this year ... the real weekly wage of a typical American worker in the middle of the income distribution has fallen by 4% since the start of the recovery in 2001' ('The new titans' 2006: 6).

The shareholder value principle that has become the dominant organizing logic is not confined to the United States alone. Thanks to globalization, this management model has also diffused to other parts of the world (Chen 2002). A direct observation study of eight CEOs of large corporations in Sweden found that shareholder value was used both as a goal and a control mechanism, resulting in senior managers working themselves to exhaustion (Tengblad 2004). The strong orientation toward alignment with shareholder value in these corporations resulted in the absence of critical and constructive discussion within each organization. Tengblad (2004: 599–600) characterizes the climate in these organizations as 'impatience':

> This impatience is present on every level. The shareholders expect superior returns on their investments, otherwise they would never have made the investment, and if they believe that the company will no longer provide superior returns they will probably sell their shares. The analysts and merchant banks are evaluated by investors on the quality of their investment suggestions and are thus under continuous pressure to perform themselves. The CEOs in their turn are evaluated on the basis of how well the share performs. The CEOs regarded their environment quite often as unfriendly and highly competitive and this was reflected in their work; there was not much room for 'considerate leadership' or discussions about alternative perspectives on governance.

In summary, the shareholder value principle – which embodies a particular strain of economic theory of organization – has become the dominant management model in recent years. Economists justify lack of attention to social issues by arguing that social welfare is maximized when organizations exclusively pursue profits (Friedman 1970). A corollary to this argument is that corporations need to focus on a single objective function, which is shareholder wealth creation (Jensen 2002, Sundaram and Inkpen 2004).

The contractarian perspective would argue that the dharma of the manager is to enhance shareholder value. Can this view be sustained through critical reasoning? The concept of dharma not only implies a natural order of things, it also entails a moral order (Creel 1972). Any departure from the natural order might result in some form of injury or injustice; one who doesn't follow the dharma prescribed by one's role can cause social chaos or disorder that might injure others. Exclusive attention to shareholders' interests can potentially disadvantage other stakeholders and create ethical issues for which there are no remedies within the contractarian perspective. Thus, the contractarian notion of dharma cannot be sustained, if it is subjected to critical scrutiny.

Ethical Problems and their Resolution within the Contractarian Perspective

If the long-term goals of a corporation were defined as wealth-creation for shareholders, there would be little to disagree with in the contractarian perspective. In practice, however, what makes this utilitarian philosophy particularly worrying is the insistence on immediate rather than long-term returns. Rappaport (2005) notes that investment analysts and corporate managers have a mutually reinforcing obsession with short-term performance. Even those organizations that profess to have a long-term orientation struggle to match their practice with rhetoric in times of economic downturn.

In reality, there is ubiquitous tension between the economic imperative of immediate shareholder value enhancement and the social obligations of the firm to its other stakeholders. Economic theory does away with this tension by banishing social obligations beyond the purview of corporate management. The insidious effect of this is that moral dilemmas, ethical tensions and value-based choices are no longer part of the legitimate discourse in business organizations. As Bird and Waters (1989) found, managers show a reluctance to describe their actions in moral terms, even when they are acting for moral reasons: 'They talk as if their actions were guided exclusively by organizational interests, practicality, and economic good sense even when in practice they honour morally defined standards, codified in law, professional convictions, and social mores' (Bird and Waters 1989: 73). The avoidance of moral talk creates and reinforces a caricature of management as: an amoral, neutral activity; stonewalling extensive discussions in situations where no illegal or blatantly deviant actions are involved; individual managers absorbing stress as a result of denying the relevance or importance of particular normative expectations, and the neglect of moral abuses and a decreased authority of moral standards. They conclude that it 'is impossible to foster greater moral responsibility by business people and organizations without also facilitating more open and direct conversations about these issues by managers' (Bird and Waters 1989: 83).

The suppression of ethical and moral discourse is an inevitable outcome of the separation of economic and social-ethical aspects of organizing and managing. The separation of economics from ethics, although relatively recent, arises from an emphasis on rationality that is narrowly defined as self-interest maximization. In other words, rational behaviour is viewed as self-interest maximization, and any behaviour other than self-maximization is seen as non-rational, and hence beyond the purview of economics (Sen 1987). This traditional microeconomic paradigm has had a dominant influence on political science, sociology and organization theory. The notion that individuals pursuing their self-interest necessarily advance the interests of society is now an almost taken-for-granted assumption in neo-liberal economic theory (Stiglitz 2004). Under conditions of perfect markets, perfect competition and perfect information, self-interested profit-maximization can indeed lead to economic efficiency that is also Pareto-optimal – that is, no one can be made better off without making someone else worse off. However, when there are information asymmetries, markets not only lead to economically inefficient outcomes, but can also lead to socially unfair effects (Stiglitz 2004).

Supporters of the contractarian perspective argue that it does not ignore ethical issues that might arise in a firm; they are just treated differently. The ethical issue within the contractarian perspective is the treatment of non-shareholders, such as employees, customers, suppliers and others. Specifically, the issue is whether it permits non-shareholders to advance their interests. In the contractarian perspective, non-shareholder interests are protected by four means: (1) legally enforceable explicit contracts; (2) adjudication by courts in instances where explicit contracts may be incomplete; (3) implicit contracts whose violation may results in adverse economic consequences, and (4) government regulation (Boatright 1996). However, there are three types of ethical problems that may arise out of contractual relationships for which there are no explicit remedies within contractarian theory. First, a firm's actions in pursuit of shareholder wealth can create negative externalities, such as pollution, customer injury, rising unemployment and so on. Second, there may be misallocation of resources, allowing shareholders to benefit at the expense of other groups, such as employees. Third, there may be misappropriations, where shareholders enrich themselves by violating settled agreements (Boatright 1996). For each of these problems, remedies within the framework of contractarian theory may include intervention by courts, extending legal responsibility of managers to safeguard community interests, and finally, political action (Boatright 1996).

There are, however, other ethical problems that lie outside the purview of the contractarian theory. Safeguarding shareholder interests by making it a fiduciary duty of managers can: (a) reinforce existing power relations; (b) lead to hidden social costs such as long-term environmental damage; (c) understate the institutional role of corporations in addressing social problems such as poverty and inequality; (d) unleash economic forces that can lead to redistribution of resources in favour of the wealthy, and (e) elevate economic efficiency above other values such as human dignity and meaningful work (Boatright 1996).

In an eloquent critique of the contractarian perspective, Ghoshal (2005) argues these economic theories are pretences for knowledge, ideologies masquerading as science and devoid of any morality or ethics. More importantly, as Ghoshal observes, adopting these false ideas dehumanizes managerial practice. Despite a number of organization theorists voicing concerns (Donaldson 1990, Ferraro, Pfeffer and Sutton 2005, Ghoshal 2005), the contractarian perspective has persisted not only in research and practice in management (Margolis and Walsh 2003), but in other fields as well (Hansmann and Kraakman 2000).

There are problems with confining rational choice solely to self-interest maximization. If we extend the notion of rational choice to include choices we can sustain if we subject them to critical reasoning (Sen 2009), we could perhaps mitigate some of the ethical issues associated with the contractarian perspective. Modern economics justifies its narrow ethical foundation of prudence by referencing the work of Adam Smith (Sen 1986, Smith 1776/1976, Smith 1790/1975, Stigler 1981). However, in his book *The Theory of Moral Sentiments*, Smith distinguishes between two types of behaviour in terms of concern for others (Smith 1790/1975, Sen, 2009). When our self-interest is served by concern for others, we are acting with 'sympathy', or enlightened self-interest. However, when we decide to ignore our self-interest in order to help others, we are acting with 'commitment' (Sen 1999). The notion of commitment is distinct from enlightened self-interest because it involves making sacrifices in order to pursue values such as social justice or protecting the environment.

This notion of commitment is beyond the purview of contractarian economic theory.

Until about the eighteenth century, the seven cardinal virtues of hope, faith, charity, justice, courage, temperance and prudence, were an integral part of Western philosophy and religious tradition (Aquinas 1270/1984, McCloskey 2006). As McCloskey argues so persuasively in her book *The Bourgeois Virtues*, these seven virtues were not only fundamental to the development and flourishing of free-market capitalism in the West, but could also be found in Eastern wisdom traditions (McCloskey 2006). While Adam Smith believed prudence – broadly defined as self-interest, although more appropriately characterized as enlightened self-interest or sympathy – was most beneficial to the individual, he also said that 'humanity, generosity and public spirit are the qualities most useful to others' (Smith 1790/1975: 139, Sen 2009). In terms of theory development, it would be foolish to deny the importance of self-interest in economic exchanges. However, it is rather limiting to consider it as the sole purpose of human behaviour. It is probably more useful to consider self-interest, or prudence, as one of the many virtues that contributes to human flourishing – to consider self-interest as one of the virtues individuals possess as they pursue a meaningful life. Since the middle of the eighteenth century, Western philosophy and social sciences have elevated prudence as the dominant virtue, while neglecting or relegating other virtues to the background (McCloskey 2006). Yet all the virtues need to be considered as a whole; they constitute an ethical system of which prudence is a constituent part.

In the following sections, we will discuss the implications of adopting a more nuanced and complex view of rational choice. In particular, we will invoke the notion of dharma to critically examine the duty of managers in corporate organizations.

Re-conceptualizing the Dharma of Corporate Management

What alternative notions of the dharma of managerial work could be sustained? The chief characteristic of corporate managerial work is that a manager is someone who achieves goals and gets work done through the actions of others. Managers also mediate the relationship of the organization with different constituents or stakeholders. Therefore, the appropriate dharma for managers is to balance various stakeholder interests without privileging any specific constituent. This would not only be ethically and morally sustainable, but would also ensure long-term growth of the organization. However, balancing various stakeholder interests is a complex task.

Corporate social responsibility (CSR) is an area of management that has gained prominence in recent years. Advocates of CSR argue that organizations have social obligations that extend beyond maximizing profits or shareholder value (Bowen 1953, Godfrey and Hatch 2007, Windsor 2006). CSR has become a significant movement (Godfrey and Hatch 2007), and has generated an impressive body of research, writing and action (Vogel 2005). Stakeholder theory is one strand of both CSR and strategic management that emerged in the 1990s. The stakeholder model of CSR has had a significant impact on theory and practice of CSR under the shareholder value maximization principle. While acknowledging that CSR is more than just the stakeholder perspective, we nevertheless focus on this strand of CSR, since it occupies a position of prominence within the literature (Clarkson 1995, Lee 2008).

Stakeholder theory was proposed by Freeman (1984) and also developed by others (Donaldson and Preston 1995, Friedman and Miles 2002, Jones, Felps and Bigley 2007, Mitchell, Agle and Wood 1997). Stakeholders are defined as 'any group or individual who can affect or is affected by the achievement of the organization's objective' (Freeman 1984: 46). Donaldson and Preston (1995) propose three types of stakeholder theory: normative, descriptive and instrumental. Normative stakeholder theory is seen as being rooted in the idea that all stakeholders' interests have intrinsic value, and therefore stakeholders ought to be treated as 'ends' (Jones and Wicks 1999). This deontological view is firmly rejected by Freeman (1999), who views stakeholder theory as being rooted in utilitarianism and being managerial and instrumental in nature. According to Freeman (1999), the instrumental thesis of stakeholder theory is that paying attention to key stakeholder relationships will increase shareholder value over an uncertain time frame (Freeman 1999, Freeman, Wicks and Parmar 2004). Some researchers have focused on explicitly identifying key stakeholders and their salience (Mitchell, Agle and Wood 1997). Others have claimed that the instrumental approach underlying stakeholder theory is also moral, by arguing that morality and prudence can co-exist (Gibson 2000). Despite such conciliatory efforts to accommodate shareholder interests, stakeholder theory has been criticized for ignoring agency problems between managers and shareholders, not paying enough attention to the interests of shareholders, and ignoring the normative basis of the shareholder value approach (Heath and Norman 2004, Jensen 2000, Velamuri and Venkataraman 2005).

Despite the recent prominence of the corporate goal of shareholder wealth maximization, corporations and managers face both external and internal limits in pursuit of this goal. The relationship between basic economic conditions and corporate behaviour is mediated by several institutional conditions, such as: private and public regulation; the presence of other organizations that monitor corporate behaviour; institutionalized norms regarding appropriate corporate conduct; associative behaviour among corporations, and organized dialogue between corporations and their stakeholders (Campbell 2007). Organizations are also driven to engage in social initiatives by many different actors, each driven by a variety of motives (Aguilera et al. 2007). In reality, corporate managers face both convergent and divergent goals of economic performance and appropriate social behaviour. This tension needs to be acknowledged in both theory and practice.

In practice, achieving the balance – particularly in corporate business organizations – is not easy, since it requires managers to first acknowledge and then address the tensions between prudence and other virtues. These tensions are natural and inevitable, constituting the reality of corporate life. The tensions may not always be perfectly resolvable, and at times managers may have to abandon prudence in favour of justice or charity. In other instances, they may have to act prudently. Inevitably, they have to make choices – and these choices arise in specific local and historical circumstances that may not be amenable to universal guidelines or the categorical imperative. Contrary to the business ethics approach, it is not realistic to provide checklists and guidelines to help managers address their unique tensions. Managers must engage with local conditions and make choices under conditions of uncertainty and ambiguity. The choices they make will shape not only their character, but also the character of their corporate organization.

In order to make choices, managers need to address the tensions. This requires them to engage in a dialogue that focuses on the ethical tensions between prudence and other virtues, and constitutes the ethical discourse of the organization. It is only through a process of engagement, dialogue and learning that managers can make ethical choices. The dominant economic model and responses to it have attempted to resolve the tensions by simply ignoring them. Ignoring the tensions reduces a corporate organization to a wealth-creating instrument that privileges shareholders. If the organization is to be more than this – if it is to be an arena where human capability can develop and flourish in productive ways – then the tensions need to be acknowledged and addressed.

Managers rarely have the choice of being exclusively self-interested. In practice, most managers seek to pursue enlightened self-interest, or what is referred to as a 'win–win' situation in popular managerial jargon. This of course refers to sympathy, in Adam Smith's terminology. The challenge for an alternative theory of the firm is to explore the tensions between sympathy (enlightened self-interest) and what Smith (Sen 2009) referred to as 'commitment' – that is, virtues that embody humanity, generosity and public spirit. An alternative theory of the firm must acknowledge the possibility of this tension, and build theory and practice on how it may be resolved without privileging any exclusive group of stakeholders. Resolving contradictions and confusion between diverging values requires dialogue. Such equivocality as is present in ethical dilemmas can create opportunities for integration of ethics in organizational life, by prompting discussion on higher ethical principles (Jovanovic and Wood 2007).

In the following sections, we discuss four possible tensions corporate managers may face as they attempt to move beyond an exclusive attention to sympathy, or enlightened self-interest. These tensions are meant to be illustrative rather than exhaustive. They could also constitute a building block for an alternative theory of the firm.

Tension between Empowerment and Autonomy

Employee empowerment is touted as one of the strategies to ensure both employee growth and commitment, and organizational performance. In reality, under the economic framework, empowerment is constrained freedom – that is, autonomy granted to employees to act in prescribed ways to enhance shareholder value. Thus, empowerment represents prudence, or enlightened self-interest. True autonomy, however, focuses on the capabilities of people to do and be what they value (Sen 1999). While it might seem that with increased focus on employee empowerment, individual employees have gained more freedom, others argue that 'however well-meaning the intentions of empowerment programs, they will always be constrained by managerial/ executive prerogatives and notions of inclusivity – who is, and who is not, to "be" empowered and in what form' (Fineman 2006: 277).

The tension between human development and controlled freedom is recognized within ethics literature. According to Maclagan (2007), 'there is a fundamental tension in business ethics between the apparent need to ensure ethical conduct through hierarchical control and the encouragement of individual potential for autonomous moral judgment' (Maclagan 2007: 48). He argues that genuine, non-manipulative participation by employees (and others) is the only way forward for the ethical management of business, whereas Weaver and Trevino (1999) make a distinction between compliance-based approaches (the detection and discipline of rule violations) versus values-based approaches (the development of shared principles regarding ethical behaviour), and argue that ethics programmes should combine accountability for violations of agreed-upon norms with a strong values focus. Stansbury and Barry (2007) identify the tension between ethics and the neo-liberal business environment:

> *Although a values orientation is necessary for enabling control, it is not sufficient: if the firm outlines its values without prioritizing them or otherwise providing guidance for acting on them, then managers may be expected to favor those goods for which they are rewarded, such as contribution margin or return on assets.*
>
> *(Stansbury and Barry 2007: 247)*

However, in their suggestions for practical or theoretical ways forward, they ignore such a tension by suggesting that it is important to distinguish between *coercive control* and *enabling control* (where employees are provided with an understanding of the process and purposes of control).

Given the competitive environment in which businesses operate, there will always be a tension between coercive control and enabling control. In employee empowerment programmes, human capital is revitalized through management styles that foster cohesiveness, complicity, initiative, creativity, collaboration and morality, to achieve the goal of improved performance. However, it is the performance drive itself – with the associated increase in managerial control, hyper-competition and short-term orientation – that inhibits cohesiveness, moral conduct and human creativity. This essential tension cannot be easily resolved. It forces managers to make choices either to favour true autonomy or to choose control, even if such control is framed as an empowerment programme. The choice will depend upon the extent to which managers are able to foster true autonomy and build capability in the organization without threatening the organization's viability and existence. Awareness and acknowledgement of the tension can itself lead to meaningful dialogue that promotes true autonomy.

Tension between Organizational Image and its Character

An organization's image is its reputation – that is, how others perceive it. It is driven by two assumptions: (1) that the organization has a set of values to enhance corporate image (Pruzan 2001), and (2) that such a set of values is to be manipulated to increase employee productivity and customer perception, also referred to as 'reputational capital' (Fombrun, Gardberg and Barnett 2000). Organizations strive to create a positive image as it facilitates resource mobilization. Therefore, organizational image is associated with enlightened self-interest. However, the character of an organization is the combined set of virtues that, at any given time, provides the basis for ethical judgements and actions. Such virtues are viewed as good habits acquired through experience. The extent to which virtues are practised demonstrates the character of the organization. Character is not static and is not 'contained' within the organization, but rather is formed through interactions between 'insiders' and 'outsiders' (Coupland and Brown 2004). Character has been described as the extent to which the organization understands 'what is' and lives up to 'what should be' rather than what 'appears to be' (Pruzan 2001).

In the late 1990s, the websites of over 80 per cent of the Fortune 500 companies claimed to engage in corporate social responsibility (Esrock and Leichty 1999). Some research claims that CSR is an excellent way to enhance the legitimacy of a firm among its stakeholders and develop a positive image of social responsibility (Handelman and Arnold 1999), and it can also be an innovative and effective form of advertising (Drumwright 1996). These studies assume that character and image are not in tension with each other, and in fact, no distinction has been made between the image and the character of the company. Concurrently, a growing body of literature questions the integrity of the 'image-driven' CSR agenda – and its accompanying issues of greenwashing – and the ethics of cause-related marketing, as well as claims made with regard to environmentally sensitive and ethically considerate products (Laufer 2003, Smith and Higgins 2000). This suggests that there are indeed tensions between 'character' and 'image'. Such tension is not easily resolvable – and managers may have to make choices as to what they are willing to support to enhance corporate reputation, and whether such reputation is consistent with the virtues they hold dear. Awareness and acknowledgement of tension between image and character can lead to dialogue that inspires managers and employees to reflect on higher ethical values, such as truth and obligation to stakeholders.

Tension between Stakeholder Management and Stakeholder Inclusion

Berman et al. (1999) distinguish between *stakeholder management* and *stakeholder commitment*. The ultimate objective of stakeholder management is marketplace success. Relationships that produce the best prospective outcomes for the firm are pursued, but not to advance the morally legitimate claims of stakeholders, other than shareholders. Intrinsic stakeholder commitment is where managerial relationships with stakeholders are based on normative moral commitments, rather than on the desire to use those stakeholders solely to maximize profits. We refer to this as *stakeholder inclusion*.

Many mining companies have long had a questionable reputation for social responsibility, especially in developing countries. There appear to be two types of motivation for their involvement in social initiatives (Kapelus 2002). They do so either because it is prudent to do so – that is, to minimize costs or protect a licence to operate – or because they have a strong ethical and moral commitment to improving the lives of those affected by their business. The difference in actions based on economic versus moral intent is manifested quite clearly in the decision-making processes regarding, for example, the involvement of local communities. When a company follows a prudent course of action, it is primarily concerned with minimizing disruption to its activities. It will want to keep the number of stakeholders as small as possible. Preferably, it would like to deal with only one person who has uncontested, legitimate authority. This results in consulting with the local elite only, and ignoring the distribution of benefits deriving from its activities among other stakeholders. To the extent that the company is interested in reducing costs, it will also want to limit the number of stakeholders, as this will limit the claims that might eventually be made upon it. The more restricted their notion of community, the more restricted their vision of their 'ecological footprint' (Kapelus 2002). Companies that go beyond prudence, or enlightened self-interest, make a conscious effort to include the local community, even to the detriment of profits. The choice between stakeholder management and inclusion is not easily reconcilable. Managers will have to make their choice taking into consideration local conditions, the character of the corporation, and what is feasible in a specific set of circumstances. If the tension is brought to the attention of the stakeholders, it can lead to meaningful interaction as they search for ways in which both the organization and its stakeholders can exercise their mutual responsibilities.

Tension between Advancing Business Interests and Leaving a Legacy

Corporations can engage in social initiatives out of enlightened self-interest with a view to advancing the business interests of the corporation – which, under the contractarian perspective, is shareholder value enhancement. They could also engage in social initiatives in areas such as education, climate change or public health, with a view to leaving a legacy for future generations. As discussed earlier, much corporate social responsibility literature views these as being consistent with each other. In other words, a business corporation can advance its interests while leaving a legacy. While this might be possible in certain situations, the two goals are not always congruent. Leaving a legacy will require the organization and its managers to marshal all their ethical resources by actively engaging in a dialogue about: (a) what they consider important; (b) how they view their obligations to society, and (c) what they can offer the society beyond their obligations, so that future generations can flourish both in economic and social terms. As McCloskey (2006) argues, not all business corporations pursue predatory profits. The so-called 'robber barons' – Andrew Carnegie, J.P. Morgan and Rockefeller – were also generous philanthropists. They left considerable fortunes for public causes. However, in the present context, with a dominant economic model that extols self-interest, it is not always easy to reconcile prudence with charity and justice. Going beyond prudence requires managers to view business as a calling and draw upon their spiritual and ethical resources (Moore 2003, Novak 1996).

Shell is one of the most extensively documented cases in the corporate social responsibility literature. Its public communications ignore the tension between advancing business interests and leaving a legacy: 'We hope, through this report and by our future actions, to show that the basic interests of business and society are entirely compatible – that there does not have to be a choice between profits and principles' (Shell, cited in Kok and Vanderwiele 2001). However, a detailed examination of Shell case studies shows it has experienced consistent tensions between advancing business interests and leaving a legacy (Taylor 2006, Livesey and Kearins 2002, Coupland and Brown 2004, Schwartz, 1997, Wheeler, Fabig and Boele 2002). In omitting the normative questions raised by these tensions, we ignore questions that may hold great promise for developing new theory and addressing practical management challenges (Margolis and Walsh 2003). We suggest that it would be particularly interesting to understand the processes through which corporations, such as Shell, become aware of such tensions – and the decision-making factors that, in the case of such tensions, lead a corporation to prioritize legacy over business interests, or vice versa.

Conclusion

We contend that the contractarian perspective has strongly influenced both theory and practice in corporate management. Its main consequence has been the elevation of shareholder value – narrowly defined as future cash flow and profits – over the interests of others, such as employees, the community and customers. We believe that this narrow orientation is now firmly entrenched in a philosophical perspective that equates rational behaviour with maximization of self-interest. The contractarian perspective argues that managers have a fiduciary duty to protect shareholders' self-interest, since shareholders bear the residual risk. Translated into practice, the contractarian perspective has stifled all ethical concerns, conversations and dialogue that seek to put others' interests above shareholder interests.

Invoking the Hindu notion of dharma, we suggest that the dharma of managers cannot be to pay exclusive attention to shareholder value enhancement. Instead, we propose that the appropriate duty of managers in corporate organizations is to balance the interests of various stakeholders. This requires balancing self-interest with concern for others. Any alternative conception of managerial work must acknowledge the tension, or contradiction, between pursuing self-interest and concern for others. It may not be possible for managers to easily reconcile these positions and arrive at a 'win–win' situation. Shareholder interests may have to be sacrificed in certain circumstances, if they are inconsistent with a higher moral and ethical purpose that will inevitably involve putting others' interests above managerial or shareholder interests. At other times, managers may need to consciously ignore others' interests and pursue shareholder interests. This makes organizational life and managerial decision-making inherently more complex than has been described in recent economics or ethics literature. Research programmes employing qualitative methodologies, such as ethnography, case studies, grounded theory and action research, can help uncover the tensions and the nature of choices that managers face as they try to balance prudence with other virtues. It would, however, mean abandoning the current paradigm that views rationality exclusively as maximization of self-interest.

As a first step toward an alternative theory, we suggest four tensions that could be meaningfully explored in corporations: empowerment and autonomy; organizational image and its character; stakeholder management and stakeholder inclusion, and advancing business interests and leaving a legacy. These might be illustrative rather than exhaustive, but they reflect an underlying tension between enlightened self-interest, or prudence, and a higher purpose, such as freedom, justice, charity or legacy. We hope this will lead to further debate and help develop an alternative theory of the firm based on more realistic and reasonable premises.

References

Aguilera, R.V., Rupp, D.E., Williams, C.A. and Ganapathi, J. 2007. 'Putting the S back in corporate social responsibility: A multilevel theory of social change in organizations'. *Academy of Management Review*, 32(3), 836–63.

Aquinas, St Thomas. 1270/1984. *Treatise on the Virtues*, trans. J.A. Oesterle. Notre Dame, IN: University of Notre Dame Press, 49–67.

Baiman, S. 1982. 'Agency research in managerial accounting: A survey'. *Journal of Accounting Literature*, 1, 154–213.

Bainbridge, S. 2003. 'Director primacy: The means and ends of corporate governance'. *Northwestern University Law Review*, 97, 547–606.

Barsky, N.P., Hussein, M.E. and Jablonsky, S.F. 1999. 'Shareholder and stakeholder value in corporate downsizing: The case of United Technologies Corporation'. *Accounting, Auditing & Accountability Journal*, 12(5), 583–604.

Bentham, J. 1789/2001. 'An introduction to the principles of morals and legislation', in *Selected Writings on Utilitarianism*. Ware: Wordsworth Classics of World Literature.

Berman, S.L., Wicks, A.C., Kotha, S. and Jones, T.M. 1999. 'Does stakeholder orientation matter? The relationship between stakeholder management models and firm financial performance'. *Academy of Management Journal*, 42(3), 488–506.

Bernstein, P.L. 1992. *Capital Ideas: The Improbable Origins of Modern Wall Street*. Hoboken, NJ: John Wiley & Sons.

Bird, F.B. and Waters, J.A. 1989. 'The moral muteness of managers'. *California Management Review*, 32(1), 73–88.

Boatright, J.R. 1996. 'Business ethics and the theory of the firm'. *American Business Law Journal*, 34(2), 217–38.

Boatright, J.R. 2002. 'Contractors as stakeholders: Reconciling stakeholder theory with the nexus-of-contracts firm'. *Journal of Banking and Finance*, 26, 1,837–52.

Bowen, H.R. 1953. *Social Responsibilities of the Businessman*. New York: Harper & Row.

Bradach, J.L. and Eccles, R. 1989. 'Price, authority, and trust'. *Annual Review of Sociology*, 15, 97–118.

Brown, C. 1998. 'Rise of the institutional equity funds: Implications for managerialism'. *Journal of Economic Issues*, 32(3), 803–21.

Brown, D.M. 1953. *The White Umbrella: Indian Political Thought from Manu to Gandhi*. Berkeley, CA: University of California Press.

Campbell, J.L. 2007. 'Why would corporations behave in socially responsible ways? An institutional theory of corporate social responsibility'. *Academy of Management Review*, 32(3), 946–67.

Cassidy, D. 2003. 'Maximizing shareholder value: The risks to employees, customers and the community'. *Corporate Governance*, 3(2), 32–7.

Chen, M. 2002. 'Post-crisis trends in Asian management'. *Asian Business & Management*, 1, 39–58.

Chomsky, N. 1998. *Profit Over People: Neoliberalism and Global Order*. New York: Seven Stories Press.

Clarkson, M.B.E. 1995. 'A stakeholder framework for analyzing and evaluating corporate social performance'. *Academy of Management Review*, 20(1), 92–116.

Conference Board. 2007. *US Institutional Investors Continue to Boost Ownership of US Corporations*, http://www.thefreelibrary.com/U.S.+Institutional+Investors+Continue+to+Boost+Ownership+of+U.S..-a0158105262, accessed 26 March 2012.

Coupland, C. and Brown, A.D. 2004. 'Constructing organizational identities on the Web: A case study of Royal Dutch/Shell'. *Journal of Management Studies*, 41(8), 1,325–47.

Creel, A.B. 1972. 'Dharma as an ethical category relating to freedom and responsibility'. *Philosophy East and West*, 22(2), 155–68.

DiMaggio, P. 2001. 'Introduction: Making sense of the contemporary firm and prefiguring its future', in *The Twenty-first Century Firm: Changing Economic Organization in International Perspective*, ed. P. DiMaggio. Princeton, NJ: Princeton University Press, 3–30.

Donaldson, L. 1990. 'The ethereal hand: Organizational economics and management theory'. *Academy of Management Review*, 15(3), 369–81.

Donaldson, L. 1995. *American Anti-management Theories of Organization: A Critique of Paradigm Proliferation*. Cambridge: Cambridge University Press.

Donaldson, T. and Preston, L.E. 1995. 'The stakeholder theory of the corporation: Concepts, evidence, and implications'. *Academy of Management Review*, 20(1), 65–91.

Drumwright, M.E. 1996. 'Company advertising with a social dimension: The role of noneconomic criteria'. *Journal of Marketing*, 60(4), 71–87.

Eisenhardt, K.M. 1989. 'Agency theory: An assessment and review'. *Academy of Management Review*, 14(1), 57–74.

Esrock, S.L. and Leichty, G.B. 1999. 'Corporate World Wide Web pages: Serving the news media and other publics'. *Journalism and Mass Communication Quarterly*, 76(3), 456–67.

Fama, E.F. and Jensen, M.C. 1983. 'Agency problems and residual claims'. *Journal of Law and Economics*, 26, 327–49.

Ferraro, F., Pfeffer, J. and Sutton, R. 2005. 'Economic language and assumptions: How theories can become self-fulfilling'. *Academy of Management Review*, 30(1), 8–24.

Fineman, S. 2006. 'On being positive: Concerns and counterpoints'. *Academy of Management Review*, 31(2), 270–91.

Fombrun, C.J., Gardberg, N.A. and Barnett, M.L. 2000. 'Opportunity platforms and safety nets: Corporate citizenship and reputational risk'. *Business and Society Review*, 105(1), 85–107.

Freeman, R.E. 1984. *Strategic Management: A Stakeholder Approach*. Boston, MA: Pitman/Ballinger.

Freeman, R.E. 1999. 'Divergent stakeholder theory'. *Academy of Management Review*, 24(2), 233–6.

Freeman, R.E., Wicks, A.C. and Parmar, B. 2004. 'Stakeholder theory and "the corporate objective revisited"'. *Organization Science*, 15(3), 364–9.

Friedman, A.L. and Miles, S. 2002. 'Developing stakeholder theory'. *Journal of Management Studies*, 39(1), 1–21.

Friedman, M. 1970. 'The social responsibility of business is to increase its profits'. *New York Times Magazine*, 13 September, 32–3, 122–6.

Ghoshal, S. 2005. 'Bad management theories are destroying good management practices'. *Academy of Management Learning and Education*, 2005(1), 75–91.

Gibson, K. 2000. 'The moral basis of stakeholder theory'. *Journal of Business Ethics*, 26(3), 245–57.

Godfrey, P.C. and Hatch, N.W. 2007. 'Researching corporate social responsibility: An agenda for the 21st century'. *Journal of Business Ethics*, 70, 87–98.

Guillen, M.F. 1994a. *Models of Management: Work, Authority, and Organization in a Comparative Perspective*. Chicago, IL: Chicago University Press.

Guillen, M.F. 1994b. 'The age of eclecticism: Current organizational trends and the evolution of managerial models'. *Sloan Management Review*, 36(1), 75–86.

Handelman, J.M. and Arnold, S.J. 1999. 'The role of marketing actions with a social dimension: Appeals to the institutional environment'. *Journal of Marketing*, 63(3), 33–48.

Hansmann, H. and Kraakman, R.H. 2000. *The End of History for Corporate Law*. Yale Law School Working Paper no. 235; NYU Working Paper no. 013; Harvard Law School Discussion Paper no. 280, doi: 10.2139/ssrn.204528.

Heath, J. and Norman, W. 2004. 'Stakeholder theory, corporate governance and public management: What can the history of state-run enterprises teach us in the post-Enron era?' *Journal of Business Ethics*, 53, 247–65.

Heron, R.A., Lie, E. and Perry, T. 2007. 'On the use (and abuse) of stock option grants'. *Financial Analysts Journal*, 63, 17–27.

Jensen, M. 2000. 'Value maximization, stakeholder theory, and the corporate objective function', in *Breaking the Code of Change*, ed. M. Beer and N. Nohria. Boston, MA: Harvard Business School Press, 37–58.

Jensen, M. 2002. 'Value maximization, stake-holder theory, and the corporate objective function'. *Business Ethics Quarterly*, 12, 235–56.

Jensen, M. and Meckling, W. 1976. 'Theory of the firm: Managerial behavior, agency costs and ownership structure'. *Journal of Financial Economics*, 3, 305–60.

Jones, T.M., Felps, W. and Bigley, G.A. 2007. 'Ethical theory and stakeholder-related decisions: The role of stakeholder culture'. *Academy of Management Review*, 32(1), 137–55.

Jones, T.M. and Wicks, A.C. 1999. 'Convergent stakeholder theory'. *Academy of Management Review*, 24(2), 206–21.

Jovanovic, S. and Wood, R.V. 2007. 'Dialectical interactions: Decoupling and integrating ethics in ethics initiatives'. *Business Ethics Quarterly*, 17(2), 217–38.

Kane, P.V. 1968. *History of Dharmashastra*. Poona: Bhandarkar Oriental Research Institute.

Kapelus, P. 2002. 'Mining, corporate social responsibility and the community: The case of Rio Tinto, Richards Bay Minerals and the Mbonambi'. *Journal of Business Ethics*, 39(3), 275–96.

Karve, I. 1961. *Hindu Society: An Interpretation*. Poona: Deccan College.

Kennedy, A.A. 2000. *The End of Shareholder Value: Corporations at the Crossroads*. Cambridge: Perseus.

Khurana, R. 2002. *Searching for a Corporate Savior: The Irrational Quest for Charismatic CEOs*. Princeton, NJ: Princeton University Press.

Kok, P. and Vanderwiele, T. 2001. 'A corporate social responsibility audit within a quality management framework'. *Journal of Business Ethics*, 4(31), 285–97.

Koslowski, P. 2000. 'The limits of shareholder value'. *Journal of Business Ethics*, 27(1/2), 137–48.

Lafontaine, F. 1992. 'Agency theory and franchising: Some empirical results'. *RAND Journal of Economics*, 23(2): 263–83.

Laufer, W.S. 2003. 'Social accountability and corporate greenwashing'. *Journal of Business Ethics*, 43(3), 253–61.

Lee, I.B. 2005. 'Corporate law, profit maximization, and the "responsible" shareholder'. *Stanford Journal of Law, Business & Finance*, 10(2), 31–72.

Lee, I.B. 2006. 'Efficiency and ethics in the debate about shareholder primacy'. *Delaware Journal of Corporate Law*, 31, 533–87.

Lee, M.D.P. 2008. 'A review of the theories of corporate social responsibility: Its evolutionary path and the road ahead'. *International Journal of Management Reviews*, 10(1), 53–74.

Levinthal, D. 1988. 'A survey of agency models of organizations'. *Journal of Economic Behaviour and Organization*, 9, 153–85.

Livesey, S.M. and Kearins, K. 2002. 'Transparent and caring corporations: A study of sustainability reports by The Body Shop and Royal Dutch Shell'. *Organization and Environment*, 15(3), 233–58.

Maclagan, P. 2007. 'Hierarchical control or individuals' moral autonomy? Addressing a fundamental tension in the management of business ethics'. *Business Ethics: A European Review*, 16(1), 48–61.

Margolis, J.D. and Walsh, J.P. 2003. 'Misery loves companies: Rethinking social initiatives by business'. *Administrative Science Quarterly*, 48(2), 268–305.

McCloskey, D.N. 2006. *The Bourgeois Virtues: Ethics for an Age of Commerce.* Chicago, IL: University of Chicago Press.

Mill, J.S. 1861/1972. 'Bentham', in *Utilitarianism*, ed. M. Warnock. Glasgow: William Collins. Mitchell, R.K., Agle, B.R. and Wood, D.J. 1997. 'Toward a theory of stakeholder identification and salience: Defining the principle of who and what really counts'. *Academy of Management Review*, 22(4), 853–86.

Moore, G. 2003. *Faithful Finances 101.* West Conshohocken, PA: Templeton Foundation Press.

Novak, M. 1996. *Business as a Calling: Work and the Examined Life.* New York: Free Press.

O'Flaherty, W.D. and Derrett, D.J. 1978. 'Introduction', in *The Concept of Duty in South Asia*, ed. W.D. O'Flaherty and D.J. Derrett. New Delhi: Vikas, xiii–xix.

Pfeffer, J. 1997. *New Directions for Organization Theory: Problems and Prospects.* New York: Oxford University Press.

Pink, D.H. 2001. *Free Agent Nation: The Future of Working for Yourself.* New York: Warner Business Books.

Powell, W.W. 2001. 'The capitalist firm in the twenty-first century: Emerging patterns in Western enterprise', in *The Twenty-first Century Firm: Changing Economic Organization in International Perspective*, ed. P. DiMaggio. Princeton, NJ: Princeton University Press, 33–68.

Pruzan, P. 2001. 'Corporate reputation: Image and identity'. *Corporate Reputation Review*, 4(1), 50–64.

Rappaport, A. 2005. 'The economics of short-term performance obsession'. *Financial Analysts Journal*, 61(3), 65–79.

Rose, J. 2007. 'Corporate directors and social responsibility: Ethics versus shareholder value'. *Journal of Business Ethics*, 73, 319–31.

Schwartz, B. 1997. 'Psychology, idea technology, and ideology'. *Psychological Science*, 8, 21–7.

Scott, G., Ball, I. and Dale, T. 1997. 'New Zealand's public sector management reform: Implications for the United States'. *Journal of Policy Analysis and Management*, 16(3), 357–81.

Sen, A.K. 1986. 'Adam Smith's prudence', in *Theory and Reality in Development*, ed. S. Lall and F. Stewart. London: Macmillan.

Sen, A.K. 1987. *On Ethics and Economics*. Oxford: Blackwell.

Sen, A.K. 1999. *Development as Freedom*. New York: Alfred A. Knopf.

Sen, A.K. 2009. *The Idea of Justice*. Boston, MA: Harvard University Press.

Sennett, R. 1998. *The Corrosion of Character: The Personal Consequences of Work in the New Capitalism*. New York: W.W. Norton.

Smith, A. 1776/1976. *An Inquiry into the Nature and Causes of the Wealth of Nations*, ed. R.H. Campbell, A.S. Skinner and W.B. Todd. Oxford: Clarendon Press.

Smith, A. 1790/1975. *The Theory of Moral Sentiments*, ed. D.D. Raphael and A.L. Macfie. Oxford: Clarendon Press.

Smith, W. and Higgins, M. 2000. 'Cause-related marketing: Ethics and the ecstatic'. *Business and Society*, 39(3), 304–22.

Stansbury, J.M. and Barry, B. 2007. 'Ethics programs and the paradox of control'. *Business Ethics Quarterly*, 17(2), 239–61.

Stigler, G.J. 1981. 'Economics and Ethics?', in *Tanner Lectures on Human Values*, ed. S.M. McMurrin. Cambridge: Cambridge University Press.

Stiglitz, J.E. 2003. *The Roaring Nineties: A New History of the World's Most Prosperous Decade*. New York: W.W. Norton.

Stiglitz, J.E. 2004. 'Evaluating economic change'. *Daedalus*, 133(3), 18–25.

Sundaram, A.K. and Inkpen, A.C. 2004. 'The corporate objective revisited'. *Organization Science*, 15(3), 350–63.

Taylor, B. 2006. 'Shell shock: Why do good companies do bad things?' *Corporate Governance* 14(3), 181–92.

Tengblad, S. 2004. 'Expectations of alignment: Examining the link between financial markets and managerial work'. *Organization Studies*, 25(4), 583–606.

'The new titans: A survey of the world economy'. 2006. *The Economist*, 16 September.

Useem, M. 1993. *Executive Defence: Shareholder Power and Corporate Reorganization*. Cambridge, MA: Harvard University Press.

Useem, M. 1996. *Investor Capitalism: How Money Managers are Changing the Face of Corporate America*. New York: Basic Books.

Velamuri, S.R. and Venkataraman, S. 2005. 'Why stakeholder and stockholder theories are not necessarily contradictory: A Knightian insight'. *Journal of Business Ethics*, 61, 249–62.

Vogel, D. 2005. *The Market for Virtue: The Potential and Limits of Corporate Social Responsibility*. Washington, DC: Brookings Institution Press.

Weaver, G. and Trevino, L. 1999. 'Compliance and values oriented ethics programs: Influences on employees' attitudes and behavior'. *Business Ethics Quarterly*, 9(2), 315–35.

Wheeler, D., Fabig, H. and Boele, R. 2002. 'Paradoxes and dilemmas for stakeholder responsive firms in the extractive sector: Lessons from the case of Shell and the Ogoni'. *Journal of Business Ethics*, 39(3), 297–318.

Windsor, D. 2001. 'The future of corporate social responsibility'. *International Journal of Organizational Analysis*, 9(3), 225–56.

Windsor, D. 2006. 'Corporate social responsibility: Three key approaches'. *Journal of Management Studies*, 43(1), 93–114.

Zald, M.N. 2002. 'Spinning disciplines: Critical management studies in the context of the transformation of management education'. *Organization*, 9(3), 365–85.

5

Guilds and Governance in Ancient India: Historical Practices of Corporate Social Responsibility

Jane Buckingham

Introduction

Contemporary debate about ethical corporate practice is crystallizing around a set of attitudes and practices loosely termed corporate social responsibility (CSR). The notion of a 'triple bottom line' of economy, environment and society as a measure of company performance is gaining credence as a viable means of increasing company sustainability. However, the details of the concept remain fluid, and contemporary companies struggle to find coherent methods of implementing links between government, business and community which will support broader CSR values while increasing profit. Typically, ideas of ethical business practice and ethical leadership are historically and geographically grounded. In an increasingly globalized and internationalized corporate environment, India's historical contribution to ideas of ethical practice are as relevant to North American and European development of business models as they are to doing business in the sub-continent.

This chapter offers historical insight into CSR as expressed through the character and function of guilds in ancient India. It suggests that exploration of historical examples of corporate business activity which demonstrate some CSR values can support the development of culturally appropriate models for contemporary ethical business practices. The chapter focuses on the links between business and community, and the importance of broader value systems in maintaining ethical practice from local to state levels. First, the chapter outlines the understanding in ancient India that economic activity is essential to the working of both state and community, and is an intrinsic element in the ethical framework of both. Then it explores the tradition of government involvement in regulation of business and co-operation with guilds in enforcement of ethical standards. Second, the chapter discusses the strong ancient tradition of internal guild regulation and accountability between guild members and the local community in both economic and social regulation. Third, it examines ancient ideas and methods of corporate donation to highlight the interaction between guilds and broader socio-religious culture. In ancient India, economic and cultural values are clearly deeply integrated and mutually influential.

By investigating the relationship between social and economic values in a historical context, the chapter emphasizes that any discussion of CSR and business ethics must recognize that business does not, and cannot, exist separately from its ideological and cultural context. The political, social and ideological culture in which business functions will not only support the development of particular corporate values, but also be influenced and even transformed by them. The increasingly globalized nature of corporate business makes such investigation of traditional business practice in India a useful resource for understanding the complex interaction between business practice, values and culture. This chapter contributes to the growing awareness of CSR as necessarily culturally variable, and asserts the need for corporate ethics to be discussed outside the dominant framework of Anglo-American models (Rossouw 2009, Young 2009, Reddy 2009, Koslowski 2009). Current research into CSR does little to bridge the gap between the ideology and practice of ethical business (Lindgreen and Swaen 2010: 1). However, an exploration of ethical practice by India's ancient guild formations suggests ways that companies can be committed for the common good both to profit and to constructive functioning in relationship with government and community (Alexander and Buckingham 2011).

Economic Classes and Early Guilds

The notion that economics was essentially a valuable element in the ideological fabric of ancient Indian society is clear from the earliest religious traditions. The idea that economic classes were necessary to the functioning of society can be identified in the Vedas, the first records of ancient Indian ritual and social tradition. The *Brihad-Aranyak-Upanishad* mentions the supreme deity Brahma's decision to create classes among the gods to parallel those among humans – that is, Brahmin, Kshatriya, Vaishya and Sudra.[1] The class of Vaishya (merchant) was created among the gods because the first two levels, Brahmin (priest) and Kshatriya (warrior), could not create wealth. The Vaishya class was given the title *ganasah* in recognition of the idea that the creation of wealth could not be by individual effort alone, but required co-operation. Some scholars have interpreted the term *pani* in *Rg Veda* texts as referring to merchant traders, and inferred that this earliest Vedic literature notes the existence of merchant communities working together for mutual protection in often dangerous trading environments. The terms *sreshthi* and *gana* in Vedic literature also suggest the existence of artisan communities. Although there is insufficient evidence to argue that economically based corporate communities existed in Vedic society, it is likely that such formations had already occurred where the benefits of mutual co-operation in the creation and protection of wealth were present (Majumdar 1922/2009: 1,216).

As a Brahmanic textual culture – expressed through the literature of the *dharmasastra* – developed from earlier Vedic foundations, the ethical dimensions of business activity in ancient India became increasingly formalized within the concept of *dharma* (duty/essence). Merchant guilds (*sreni*) are recorded in the *dharmasastra* literature as functioning according to a specific *sreni-dharma* (the duty of the merchant). Their economic activity formed part of the tradition of *Artha* (the art of economic welfare and material gain), which was particularly the responsibility of the king and state (Thapar 1993: 76, Rangarajan 1992b: 74–5). Ancient Indian society saw an essential link between economics and ethics. Economic activity was a core aspect of the broader ethical tradition that regulated society, from the level of the king and state to the ordinary village or town. The tendency in modern business and management to see ethics as separate from economic activity was absent from the ancient Indian model (Sen 1993).

---

1   The Varna system, comprising the four categories, Brahmin, Kshatriya, Vaishya and Sudra, is a hierarchical hereditary system of social stratification found in India. The Brahmin is considered the highest and most pure of the Varna categories, and the Sudra the lowest and least pure. Varna tends to describe an idealized broad social categorization, and is recognized throughout India. Varna is homologous with the caste system, with caste being a more fluid local expression of hierarchy, which accommodates the lower-caste communities not recognized in the Varna system (Dumont 1980, Sheth 1999, Smith 1994).

By the fifth century BC, guilds were not only of economic value in terms of contributing to economic growth, but were also recognized by the state as having a critical role in the ethics of wealth creation. An essential element in the traditions of state management expressed in the Brahmanic literature of the *Arthasastra* – manuals of statecraft and economic management for kings (Trautmann 1979) – was that the king was responsible for the overall welfare of his people, and that wealth was essential to the stability and well-being of the state (Rangarajan 1992b: 21–5, 33–41, Kautilya 1992: 149 {1.19.34}[2]). The creation of wealth was understood to be an essential element of the king's *rajadharma* (the duty of kings). As such, it functioned within the broader ethical paradigm of *dharma* (Rangarajan 1992d: 90). The literature on *Artha* was itself an element in the *dharmasastra* (literature relating to the duties of society) (Mackenzie Brown 1953). However, the king was not expected to regulate the economy without substantial state bureaucracy and community support provided through guild structures. Merchant guilds worked collaboratively with the state within the broader values framework of *Artha* (Majumdar 1922/2009: 25–8, Thapar 1993: 76). The merchant guilds helped king and state to ensure mechanisms for wealth creation and labour regulation were conducted according to the specific ethics linked to their *sreni-dharma*.

By the time of the earliest Buddhist *Jataka* stories of the seventh and sixth centuries BC, robust guild organization was a prominent feature of ancient Indian economic life. The notion of the guild already included both informal and formal notions of association. At the early stage of merchant and manufacture guild formation, individuals could be members of a variety of guilds and could come from any caste. This open membership strengthened networking opportunities for the trade and manufacturing communities. References to guilds in both Brahmanic and Buddhist texts as well as in inscriptions indicated that they were not exclusive to one ideological tradition. The *Jataka* literature of the period states the conventional number of guilds as eighteen. Although guild formation appears to include every branch of mercantile and artisanal activity – from money-lending to garland makers and metal workers – the establishment of a conventional number emphasizes that the guild had already become institutionalized as a component of the conceptual apparatus of the state (Majumdar 1922/2009: 17–20, 23–4).

---

2   References to the text of the *Arthasastra* will be identified by Kautilya, the author/compiler of the version translated by Rangarajan (Kautilya 1992) and cited throughout this chapter. The verse numbers in double brackets {} refer to the verse numbers in Kangle's earlier translation of the *Kautiliya Arthasastra* (Kangle 1969). Kangle's text is the master for Rangarajan's translation. The page number refers to the location of the verses in double brackets in Rangarajan's translation (Kautiliya 1992, author's note).

Guilds developed in north India from their early Vedic traces as the economic and political strength of the Mauryan Empire consolidated in the Magadha region. By about the fifth century BC, corporations of traders, manufacturers and other economic participants had become critical elements in the economic functioning of the state and were recognized by the king as having the right to develop laws for themselves and to have a voice in the royal court (Lingat 1973: 19–20). Majumdar cites the *Gautama Dharma-Sutra*, dated third century BC, as giving authority to 'cultivators, traders, herdsmen, money-lenders and artisans' to set rules for their classes. Further, it stipulated that the king would only give legal judgment after consulting with 'those who in each class have the right to speak' (Majumdar 1922/2009: 24). The state's granting of internal authority to the guilds and willingness to consult them in legal matters involving guild members reflected its recognition of the value of guilds in practical economic and social regulation, beyond the rules laid down in the *Arthasastra* tradition.

The capacity of guilds to regulate economic activity was linked to the guilds' ability to exercise ethical authority among their members. Guild structure had ancient roots, continuing elements of early government structures associated with tribal republics which had preceded the development of monarchic and imperial political formations in north India. They were essentially merchant and artisan co-operatives with governance structures including a general assembly, guild head and supporting executive, which both represented their members' interests and had the authority to implement executive and judicial decisions over their members. Guild formations were not limited to north India. From the twelfth century AD, multiple inscriptions in the modern south Indian states of Karnataka, Tamil Nadu, and offshore in Sumatra and Sri Lanka, reflect the complex activities linked into guild structures. A Tamil merchant guild comprising five hundred people and based in the town of Barus in Sumatra stipulated the fees which were to be given by guild members to the guild's local agents. The close but hierarchical relationships within the guild were expressed in the description of the guild agent as 'our son'. Those contributing membership fees included a ship owner, ship's captain and boatmen (Karashima 2009a: 181). The range of similar inscriptions throughout the Indonesian archipelago and Sri Lanka are testament to the richness of the Chola period in south India, which at its height, from the tenth to the thirteenth centuries AD, supported the development of international trade and economic associations in much the same way as the Mauryan, Kushan and Gupta periods had done in the north.

Ancient Indian guilds reflect the lack of a division more typical of modern economies between the ethics of the home or community and of the workplace. Guild membership required commitment and allegiance. All income was shared equally between members, and leaving before work was completed or neglecting to do the allocated share of work was punished with fines and even expulsion by guild authorities. Guild duties included not only business, but also internal community regulation, and it was part of the responsibility of the state to understand and respect the nature of the guild's interaction with the local community. The state's Superintendent of Accounts was required to keep up-to-date records of the traditions and professions connected with each guild, in addition to recording the guild's transactions. The internal authority of the guilds, and the recognition of the authority of their *sreni-dharma*, was such that even the king was expected to accept it. The state had only limited rights to intervene in guild affairs, and the strictness of guild discipline was internally enforced. Not only economic practice, but also relationships between guild members were overseen by the guild. By the Mauryan period (321–185 BC), internal guild authority was so substantial that the guild even had the power to intervene in certain disputes between a guild man and his wife (Majumdar 1922/2009: 25–7, Thapar 1993: 76, Kautilya 1992: 89 {4.1.2–3}, 340 {2.22.8, 15}).

Guild authority continued to grow. By around AD 400, as the *Narada Smirti* indicates, guilds could make their own laws with regard to both economic matters and social and customary practice. The economic and social authority of the guild within the urban context is reflected in their minting of coins and the status of the guild seal (Majumdar 1922/2009: 25, Thapar 1993: 76). By the tenth century AD, guild authority in south India included the capacity to mediate justice in criminal cases. A south Indian inscription, dated AD 900, records guild involvement in expiating criminal acts by guild members. A member of a major merchant guild who had killed a man deposited gold with two merchant guilds to pay for the burning of a perpetual lamp in atonement for his crime. Non-guild members were also within the ethical authority of the guild when their actions harmed a member. In AD 1055, a south Indian merchant guild ordered a revenue officer found guilty of hounding a merchant woman to suicide to burn a lamp in expiation for his actions. The funds were deposited with an oil merchant guild which then supplied the oil (Karashima 2009a: 175, 181). In ancient India, most dispute resolution, and even violent crime, was dealt with at the village or urban level without recourse to any higher judicial authority. The authority wielded by the guilds in criminal matters, together with their capacity to mint coins, gave them a status which rivalled, in some senses, even that of a king.

Buddhism and the Rise of Guilds: Culture and Business Ethics

The linkage of guilds to the well-being of both the state and local communities was supported in ancient India by transitions in the socio-religious culture. Buddhism, Jainism and other non-Brahman 'sects' developed from the sixth century BC in the economically rich Gangetic region of Magadha (contemporary Bihar), which later became the cradle of the Mauryan Empire. In north India, the rapid urban growth of the fifth and fourth centuries BC was supported by the rise of Buddhist philosophies. Buddhist philosophy emerged as a more socially egalitarian alternative to the ritual hierarchies and practice of Brahmanic Hinduism and appealed to the merchant and artisanal communities who were gaining social status and wealth in the flourishing urban centres. The idealized hierarchical Varna system – based on degrees of ritual purity and pollution and associated with Brahmanic culture – did not allow merchant and artisanal communities a high ritual status, no matter how wealthy or influential they had become in the urban context. The stability and infrastructure provided by the Mauryan state increased trade and artisanal wealth and contributed to a commensurate increase in expectations of social value, which were frustrated by the existing Brahmanic hierarchies (Darian 1977, Thapar 1978: 133).

In Mauryan India, Buddhist philosophies provided a religio-cultural framework, which complemented the economic and social aspirations of merchant and artisan communities who were prospering in the stable economic environment. The development of a strong and socially engaged merchant guild formation in the Mauryan period was linked to both the clustering of merchant communities in towns and the opportunities provided by the development of the institutional culture of the *sangha* (Buddhist community) for the expression of patronage by merchant guilds. Such links between ideological opportunity and economic prosperity also emerge in the European tradition in terms of a relationship between Protestantism and the rise of capitalism, famously articulated in 1930 by Max Weber in *The Protestant Ethic and the Spirit of Capitalism* (Weber 1930/1958). In the Mauryan period, Buddhist philosophy endorsed economic practices which supported the expansion of merchant culture and guild formation (Darian 1977: 231–2). Furthermore, the emerging Mauryan Empire, while maintaining respect for Brahmanic tradition saw advantages in aligning itself with the ideologies which appealed to the rising urban economic classes. Ashoka, the third Mauryan emperor, who like his father and grandfather had been influenced by both traditional Brahmanic ideas of statecraft and the Jain and Buddhist heterodoxies of the time, gave strong public support to the rise of Buddhism in his empire. Consistent with the Brahmanic *Arthasastra* tradition of statecraft in which he was trained, Ashoka saw an essential relationship between his position as emperor and the well-being of his people. In a heterodox economic climate, there were advantages in developing a synthetic approach to imperial leadership which allowed opportunities for the economic energies of the merchant and artisan communities to develop within the emerging Buddhist communities (Darian 1977: 230–31, Alexander and Buckingham 2011).

The Buddhist emphasis on merit as attainable by all, without any particular need for ritual or specialized practices, supported the consolidation of guilds by freeing up capital and satisfying merchant and artisans' social and philosophical aspirations. The Buddhist proscription against animal sacrifice and spending large sums on ritual and ritual specialists allowed the merchant or artisan to enjoy the ideological benefits of association with Buddhist philosophy in terms of giving opportunities for merit and enlightenment while avoiding the costs. Merchants were left free to invest resources such as livestock and capital in business ventures, rather than spending them on ritual mediation. While the Brahmanic Varna system rated mercantile activity as ritually less pure than that of the priest or warrior, Buddhist philosophy rejected pollution and purity as a form of ranking and saw the opportunity for gaining merit as applying equally to any member of the social hierarchy (Darian 1977: 231–5). The *Arthasastra* attributed to Kautilya[3] assumes that merchant, manufacturing and artisan communities are bound by dharma to pursue the creation of wealth through their specializations. As a manual of statecraft for rulers, Kautilya's *Arthasastra* stipulates legal means to force artisans and others to practise their trade and crafts honestly as benefited the state (Rangarajan 1992c: 423, Kautilya 1992: 428 {3.12.3637}). Surviving Buddhist texts do not have the same emphasis on state forms of control, but do encourage the ethical pursuit of wealth as an aspect of meritorious character. The *Digha Nikaya*, believed to embody early Buddhist teachings, particularly supported ethical mercantile activity: 'The wise and virtuous shine like a blazing fire. He who acquires his wealth in harmless ways like to a bee that honey gathers, riches mount up for him like [an] ant hill's rapid growth' (Davids 1899/2007: 1, *Digha Nikaya*, cited in Darian 1977: 235).

---

3   Kautilya's identity as a member of the court of Chandragupta Maurya, Emperor Ashoka's grandfather, his role as author or compiler and interpreter of the *Artha* tradition and the date of this text remain a matter of historical debate. The consensus is that he, or representatives of his school, compiled the existing version of the *Arthasastra* during the Mauryan period or possibly as late as the second century AD, and that this text represents the accumulation of centuries of thinking on *Artha* and the role of the king in managing the state (Rangarajan 1992b: 16–21, Trautmann 1979).

Merchants, frustrated by the relatively low ritual value placed on their caste communities, found in Buddhist institutions new opportunities for social and ritual acceptance outside the existing Brahmanic frameworks. Merchants and other guilds could invest their growing wealth in Buddhist *sangha* (communities) and monasteries, certain that their social standing and merit would be significantly enhanced by such economic engagement. The importance of the Buddhist *sangha* to the guild culture of the Mauryan period and the degree to which the guild held authority over its members is reflected in the inclusion among areas of guild regulation of decisions to allow wives to join the *sangha* as nuns. The permission of the guild was required before a wife could take such a step (Majumdar 1922/2009: 25). Such requirements gave the guild the kind of executive and judicial authority, even over areas of domestic life, usually associated with the state. That guilds considered such personal affiliation to the *sangha* as a legitimate area of regulation suggests that linkages to Buddhist institutions were becoming normalized.

Guilds were not static entities, and even those affiliated with unorthodox traditions remained affected as much by the ideas of dharma and social and ritual hierarchy which permeated Brahmanic Hindu society as by economic change. From about the eighth century AD, the Indian economy slowed, the fluidity and mobility of merchant and artisan communities lessened, and guild organizations declined. Guilds continued to regulate the cultural practices of their members, which became increasingly localized. Inter-caste communities of potters, for example, became specialized in the sense that they became increasingly fixed to a particular master, his family and his home. Immobilized by these loyalties and increasingly following dietary habits, forms of dress and ritual practice linked to a particular local deity, philosophy or *guru* (teacher), the inter-caste guild associations themselves became new caste groupings, marrying internally and becoming hereditary (Sharma 2003: 35, 208–10). As Sharma notes: 'It is an irony of history that the religious sects that sprang up to remove caste disparities and privileges based on birth were themselves swallowed up by the caste system' (Sharma 2003: 210). As guild membership became caste-based, guilds of higher caste status such as merchant guilds were able to exert authority over guilds of lower caste status, particularly those of the artisan castes. As centralized government power waned, the guilds themselves became local authorities. Like land owners, temples and religious institutions, guilds became able to control their own wealth and membership, and also to control sections of labour. Just as artisans could be transferred with a parcel of land or with management of a temple, an artisan community could be transferred into the control of a local merchant guild (Sharma 2003: 188).

Like modern corporate bodies, ancient guilds flourished when cultural and economic conditions allowed. The concept of ethical practice and appropriate guild behaviour was ultimately affected by what the broader religio-social environment endorsed. While egalitarianism spurred the growth of urban mercantile and artisanal guilds, the persistence of hierarchical caste values ultimately encouraged a return to more orthodox guild practices. This shift illustrates the real challenge of developing new cultures of corporate values in the twenty-first century, when 'self-interest'-based corporate models are entrenched. The ancient Indian example emphasizes that broader social and cultural expectations of change are necessary for deep structural alterations in economic practice. In the twenty-first century, a highly connected global community can, however, help to force change. As Seidman recently argued, 'fortress capitalism' is now breached by the speed and reach of communication. While in the past corporations could 'manage reputation the old-fashioned way, by hiding behind lawyers and crisis-management consultants', now they must earn a good reputation by living and doing business ethically. When it takes only a few seconds to broadcast misdemeanours through cell phones, weblogs and video, it is in a company's interests to behave more ethically than its competitors (McGill Murphy 2010). However, as in ancient India, the notion of what is ethical remains very much culturally determined.

Regulation of Economic Practice: State and Guild Co-operation

Kautilya's *Arthasastra* details the network of government ministries which regulated primary production and manufacture in the ideal ancient Indian state. The text also refers to the existence of guilds, and the relationship between these local regulatory bodies and the ethical regulation of the state's economic apparatus. Kautilya's *Arthasastra* had no illusions about the need for government intervention to enforce ethical regulation in business practice and the creation of wealth. The king's *rajadharma* included using fines and corporal punishment as deterrents to the exploitation of the consumer by business and service providers. In the ideal state, as described in Kautilya's *Arthasastra*, branches of government needed educating in the techniques of deception in order to ensure consumer protection from the full range of people participating in the economy. Kautilya's *Arthasastra* declares: 'Merchants, artisans, craftsmen, nomadic mendicants, entertainers and similar persons are all thieves, in effect, if not in name; they shall be prevented from harassing the people' (Kautilya 1992: 242 {4.1.65}). The *Arthasastra* provided instruction to government officers in the many opportunities taken to defraud the customer in manufacture and production. Goldsmiths, for example, could tamper with scales in weighing metal, substitute other metals for gold when doing repairs or plating, and steal gold purchased by the customer. A trained state representative could detect such attempts at fraud by, for example, boiling the suspect article to reveal the goldsmith's use of salt and sand in making gold leaf (Kautilya 1992: 243 {2.14.1842}). Service provision was also closely watched for breaches of consumer rights. The *Arthasastra* stipulates that: 'Washermen and Tailors shall not wear, sell, hire out, mortgage, lose or change a customer's garment' and 'shall return the garments within the time prescribed' (Kautilya 1992: 245 {4.1.16, 25}).

In the ideal state as described in Kautilya, branches of government had oversight of all areas of production associated with primary resources such as mining and forestry, and with manufacture, including metals and textiles (Rangarajan, 1992a: 305–8). The Chief Textile Commissioner, for example, had responsibility for all aspects of the manufacture and trade in yarn and finished textile work such as clothing, straps, ropes and bed sheets (Kautilya 1992: 332 {3.23.1,9,19}). He regulated the workforce to ensure that preference in employment was given to women who were dependent on spinning for a living, including those who were particularly marginalized such as widows, unmarried women, women who were disabled in some way, and those women who were paying off fines or were mothers of prostitutes. However, weaving of the spun thread was the responsibility of men (Kautilya 1992: 333 {2.23.2,7,10–12, 17–18}). The principal regulatory functions of the Chief Controller, meanwhile, related to quality control of the goods produced, negotiating wages and ensuring that propriety was observed between men and women. The Chief Controller had equal power to punish unethical work practices and breaches of social morality between his workers. He could permanently incapacitate a worker by ordering the amputation of the thumb and finger of a woman who stole materials or did not deliver the work she had been paid for (Kautilya 1992: 333–4 {2.23. 38; 1214,16}).

The severity of punishments for theft and labour misdemeanours mark their importance as deterrents to unethical work practice. The state used punishment under the law to enforce standards of work practice at its discretion. At the same time, state regulation of economic activity included recognition of the economic needs of weaker members of society. Women without other means of support and people with disabilities are included in the framework of ethical business activity. This mandated inclusiveness is in marked contrast to modern Euro-American models of economy which see disability as an impediment to profitable production and thus tend to exclude people with disabilities (Ville 2010, O'Brien 2001). The inclusiveness of state economic models suggests recognition of social responsibility as a key element in ancient Indian state understanding of how economy should function. Economy remained a priority in the structure of the ideal state, and there was a clear understanding that profit was essential to the state's power and the security of the king (Kautilya 1992: 304 {2.12.37}). Trade was to be directed towards markets which were 'profitable; losses must be avoided' (Kautilya 1992: 304 {2.16.25}). Even so, there was a place for the poor and weaker members of society in the economy, and a stipulation that heavy-handedness by officials would not be tolerated in the exercise of their duties: 'Any official who incurs the displeasure of the people shall either be removed from his post or transferred to a dangerous region' (Kautilya 1992: 304 {13.5.21}).

In addition to the regulatory mechanisms provided by government, merchant and artisan guilds played a major role in establishing and maintaining forms of ethical business practice, both within their corporations and in relationship with the state. In terms of concern for ethical economic practice, the internal governance of guilds complemented state priorities. The state came to rely heavily on the guilds to manage the integration of economy and ethical wealth creation at the local community level. Although guilds frequently functioned within large-scale inter-continental trade networks, they were deeply embedded in their local communities and were major players in the urban context (Thapar 1993: 76, Karashima 2009b: 200–201). Merchant guilds, in particular, even employed troops to protect traders and goods from pillage (Karashima 2009b: 213–16). Typically, guild membership rarely exceeded one thousand, and although members could belong to more than one guild and guild communities could be mobile and move between town and village, each guild held a local monopoly in its area of trade. Guilds which were not representative of the local village or town were prevented from activity by the local guild bodies. Consequently, there was a strong connection between the local trade, manufacturing and labour interests of the guild and the terms of its self-regulation. The dharma (duty and activity) of the guild, which regulated the ethical practice of the guild, was linked to the local customs, religious allegiances and social and cultural aspirations of its local membership (Majumdar 1922/2009: 26, Thaplyal 2001).

By the fifth century BC, the state expected guild organization to provide an extra-governmental system of regulation on which government could rely for local management of artisans and craftsmen. The guilds were registered with government and were required to use their executive structures to regulate manufacture, production quality, prices and movement of goods in co-operation with the state. With regard to artisans and craftsmen, Kautilya's *Arthasastra* notes:

> *All goods entrusted to repairers of articles, employers of [groups of] artisans, middlemen to undertake to get work done as well as self-employed artisans and craftsmen shall be covered by a guarantee from the appropriate guild. The guild shall be responsible for compensating [the owner] in case death of the person to whom the article was entrusted.*
> *(Kautilya 1992: 245 {4.1.2–3})*

The importance of guilds to economic regulation remained even as the political culture of north India changed. The Charter of Visnusena (*Maitraka Visnubhata*), dated AD 592, instructs merchant guild leaders in Indor, Gujurat to regulate weights, measures and prices in their local markets and to comply with state requirements for ethical practice. The charter stipulated that guild leaders were required to present to state authorities weights and measures for checking twice a year; financial transactions based on undeclared or smuggled goods were to incur fines; guild leaders were to post lists of fixed prices in shopping areas every five days and would be fined for non-compliance, and loss of the authorized stock list and failing to appear before the state's registrar were to be punished by fines and restriction on movement (Kosambi 1959: 285, 287).

In return for the work undertaken by guilds in managing and controlling substantial interconnecting areas of trade, the state was expected to recognize and provide benefits and concessions to guild members at every level of the guild hierarchy. Kautilya shows the depths of state support for the guild structures, in that the state provided guilds with extra provisions and concessions such as an additional seven days for delivery of contractual obligations for labourers who were also guild members (Majumdar 1922/2009: 27). The state's continued respect for the guilds is also recorded in the Charter of Visnusena (*Maiitraka Visnubhata*), which exempts all guilds from 'single-market-tax'. Further, it stipulates that guilds are exempt from the usual requirements of providing lodging and cooked food to the king's representatives – a duty which could be a substantial financial and material burden (Kosambi 1959: 281, 286).

The co-operation between guild and state reflected a strong mutual dependence: Certainly, the guild benefited the state, but the strength of guild organization was linked to the vigour and stability of the economy in which it functioned. While guild formations dated from the earlier Vedic period, the flourishing of merchant and artisan guilds under the Mauryan emperors was a consequence of the stability of the empire and the development of a strong economy, based on agricultural surplus and supportive of trade and mercantile initiative. The Mauryans, as the first major imperial dynasty in India's history, brought more land under cultivation than any rulers before them. A sophisticated bureaucracy regulated the collection and distribution of revenue from agriculture and also contributed to the collection of wealth from the mercantile economy through taxation and the gathering of tolls. The third Mauryan emperor Ashoka, in particular, supported opportunities for trade. He improved roads, and provided shelter, shade and other infrastructure supports for merchants, carriers and other travellers. In his Pillar Edict VII, Emperor Ashoka informed his people of the infrastructure improvements he had made:

> On the roads ... I have had banyan-trees planted to give shade to man and beast; groves ... of mango trees I have had planted; at every half-kos I have had wells dug; rest houses, too, have been erected; and numerous watering-places have been provided by me here and there for the enjoyment of man and beast.
>
> (Pillar Edict VII, in Smith 1920/2002: 209)[4]

Provision of infrastructure to support economic development benefited the state as much as it did the merchant and producer guilds. Guilds supported the state by paying taxes, tolls and duties and stimulating the flow of capital. Further, they developed their own financial surpluses which could be accessed by the government, and directly invested gold and coin into government funds. The king could even borrow money from guilds, though guilds were somewhat limited in their ability to enforce repayment (Majumdar 1922/2009: 26–7).

As guilds developed in ancient India, they engaged with the formal bureaucratic and legal systems by which government regulated the economy. While functioning as extra-governmental structures, the guilds supplemented and supported the ethical requirements of the state, and in particular the king's *raja dharma*. As such, merchant, producer and manufacturing guilds contributed to the implementation and maintenance of ethical business practice at the state level, both by participating in administration of ethical business practice and

---

4   Emperor Ashoka communicated with his subjects through his edicts, which were engraved in the local vernaculars on prominent naturally occurring rocks and on specially made pillars. The edicts functioned as bulletin boards, and were located in marketplaces and along roadsides where they could be read and disseminated along trade routes. References to the Edicts of Ashoka will be to the Pillar Edicts and Rock Edicts as they appear in Smith (1920/2002).

by internally regulating sections of society engaged in wealth production. The major company scandals which have affected India as much as other globalized economies in the last few years indicate that although implementation and regulation of values within companies is an uneasy process, ethical business practice is essential for the creation of sustainable and non-exploitative profitability.

The guild structures of ancient India offer models of the potential for government and business to work co-operatively. The deep linkages of the guilds to their local communities meant that their participation in the development of wealth had immediate impacts on those connected to their membership. Consequently, guilds had a strong investment in embedding ethical approaches in business practice and in expecting the same from the state. The details of ancient Indian state methods of enforcing regulation are not culturally appropriate in modern economies. However, the notion of shared guild/state commitment to economic regulation provides an approach to ensuring ethical wealth creation consistent with aspects of contemporary notions of CSR. The relationship between the state and guild meant that economic activity was managed both at the state and local community level at all times. In addition to business involvement in philanthropic and charitable activities undertaken to benefit people outside the business, contemporary CSR tends to take the form of promoting social goods through their business, which can also be construed as 'enlightened self-interest'. Promotion of fire safety campaigns by insurance companies to reduce claims is one such example (Banerjee 2007: 19). In the case of ancient Indian guilds, the relationship between guild and local community was so close that there was not the sense of separation between community and guild values. What was good for the guild was good for the community, and vice versa. Methods of wealth creation consistent with community values and the state's dependence on local economic regulation through guilds meant that local values also acted as a check on state interventions. CSR was not separated from the ordinary activity of guilds because guild activities were embedded in the well-being of the local community of which they were a part.

Guilds as Corporate Donors

As they changed in terms of social and ritual formation, guilds remained embedded in traditions of gift-giving, particularly to institutions which provided ritual, educational and charitable services to the community. Some guilds were deeply imbedded in elements of Brahmanic tradition. Others were linked with 'unorthodox' philosophies such as Buddhism and Jainism, tending to provide economic services in co-operation with the temples and *sanghas* linked to their communities. Gift-giving was recognized in Kautilya's *Arthasastra* as an element of economy fraught with risk. There are clear stipulations that gifts should be freely given, not be given to a wicked or evil persons, and not to someone unworthy (Kautilya 1992: 443–4 {3.16.1–4, 6–8}). These principles encouraged larger-scale corporate gift-giving to institutions publicly endorsed as meritorious. Consequently, temples – which provided not only ritual services, but also education and charitable support to the surrounding community – were legitimate targets of gift-giving. As Buddhism developed its own institutional organization, donations were made to maintain the Buddhist community and for the building of stupas, the architectural focus of Buddhist ideology (Mitra 2007: 18). Guilds, local landlords and kings practised conspicuous gift-giving, their donations of goods, services and currency recorded in inscriptions on the walls of temples and stupa. Like the royal families, which rose and fell more rapidly than the guilds, guilds sought status and legitimization through their contact with institutions which mediated influence between this and the next world (Thapar 1994: 28–36).

The development of the stupas of Sanchi, Bharhut and Amaravati, from small reliquaries for objects of worship to large complexes, was attained through donations of goods and services. In addition to land owners, powerful families and Buddhist monks and nuns, corporate donors recorded on stupa inscriptions include guilds of artisans and craftsmen such as potters, perfumers, bead makers, garland makers, weavers and cloak makers. Corporate donation gave artisan guilds opportunities for patronage which confirmed the legitimacy of their social status and enabled them to elevate it further. Guilds dealing in building materials, blacksmiths, masons and builders, together with corn and timber merchant guilds, all contributed funds, materials and other services to the development of the stupas. The ivory carvers' guild from Vidisha donated its labour and skills to carving the stupa gates at Sanchi, using the opportunity to include scenes promoting the aspirations and values of its community and to gain renown for its craftsmanship (Thapar 1994: 28–29). In some instances, guilds moved between occupations depending on available work. A Tiruvidaimarudur inscription records the construction of part of a temple by a military group which later became an established weaver guild. As soldiers, this group was linked to the large merchant guild association of the region, working with other soldier guilds to protect the merchants and their goods along the various trade routes (Karashima 2009a: 175, Karashima 2009b: 215–16).

There were additional advantages to guilds in forming relationships of mutual trust and benefit with socio-ritual institutions. Temples and, as they developed, monasteries were not only sources of meritorious not-for-profit activity; they were powerful land owners and employers, and provided resources of tax, wealth and local authority necessary to the well-being of the state. As well as a source of ongoing revenue and economic stability which the state could draw on, in emergencies these institutions also provided a treasury which a ruler could pillage (Rangarajan 1992d: 53–4, Liu 1988: 106–7). From the first to sixth centuries AD, as Buddhism moved away from its aniconic and atheistic philosophical roots and became more ritualized, monasteries gained wealth rivalling that of the Hindu temples. Buddhist monasteries which were less land-rich than temples engaged in trade in their own right. Worship and donation became as important in Buddhism as it was in Hindu culture. This change in religious culture encouraged trade in precious items such as pearls, lapis lazuli, coral, rubies, gold, silver and silks. Such valuable materials were given to monasteries, literally by the cartload, enriching the donor with merit and the monasteries with the merit of acting as a broker for such offerings (Liu 1998: 2, 88–95, 106–9). In addition to supporting trade in items linked to worship, monasteries tended to be built along trade routes and gave material support to merchants. Their status as religious institutions assisted in transactions between local traders and foreigners coming to India to do business, and it is likely that the monasteries provided merchants with deposit and banking services as well as lodgings (Liu 1998: 120–21). Temples with substantial revenue bases had sufficient credit to act as bankers, lending money for local rural development and also to help finance trading guilds (Thapar 1994: 34–5). As places of pilgrimage, often built along trade routes, temples, monasteries and stupas typically became places of intersection between meritorious activity and business. The reputation of the guild as meritorious and associated with a particular centre of learning or religious sect became part of its corporate identity. The constant movement of merchants, artisans and pilgrims through temples and other auspicious places meant the reputation of the guild and its networks of association also travelled, connecting local markets with international trade and religious networks.

Even when trading internationally, guilds never lost sight of their local character, and they used the available religious and cultural contexts to constantly affirm their connection to the local community and its values. Tamil merchant guilds in south India are recorded as donating part of their trade profits for the maintenance of the temple and to support the temple festival in their local centre. Internationally based south Indian merchant guilds, enriched by the stability and strength of the late Chola dynasty, also showed their support for local infrastructure by building and financing water tanks in the Malay peninsula and deploying military strength to protect these tanks from attack and theft (Karashima 2009b: 201–4). Such activities were consistent with the specific dharma of each guild and with the value placed on social and religious transactions within guilds (Karashima 2009b: 210–11). Compared with contemporary profit-driven notions of commerce, economies in the ancient world were characterized in part by a strong emphasis on social and ritual values as valid motivations for material transactions. Consequently, ancient Indian business and commercial systems typically included a more complex range of transactions than exist in modern supply- and demand-based market systems (Liu 1988: 2).

In addition to conspicuous donation, guilds often brokered gift-giving and other not-for-profit transactions for non-guild members wishing to give to temples and other places of worship and learning. In Indor, for example, Jivanta, leader of the oilmen's guild, received money from a Brahmin, Deva-visnu, in AD 465, to provide for the supply of oil for a temple lamp. In effect, the oilmen's guild acted as broker for the donation of oil to the local temple. The funds were to be held by the guild in perpetuity, even if the guild itself moved location (Kosambi, 1959: 283). Such practices became widespread as guild culture developed throughout India. The guild's brokerage services supported a broader framework of charitable religious donation than simple direct donation from guilds as corporate bodies or guild members. Further, they helped cement the reputation of the guild as trustworthy in managing wealth, property and other transactions for a third party. In the tenth and eleventh centuries AD, members of the south Indian oil merchant guilds provided a channel for donations from royalty to other guilds. By acting as brokers in these non-profit activities, the oil merchant guilds gained additional benefits in terms of strengthening their ties to powerful local royal families and raising their own status by showing support for the local temple. By this time, in the south, the term for an individual oil merchant and for the guild of oil merchants was the same – *sankarapadi* – suggesting that individual merchants were deeply identified with their guilds. Guild donations recorded in inscriptions tend to be those of guildsmen, whether as corporate donors or individual merchants or artisans (Karashima 2009a: 171–4).

Donations brokered by guilds also cut across gender lines. In first- and second-century AD north India, while the growth of institutional Buddhist structures flourished under the Kushan Empire, women who were members of artisan and small-scale land owning families, were also recorded as donors, particularly to Buddhist and Jain institutions. In the north, royal families tended to divide their patronage on gender lines, with wives and queens giving to unorthodox sects, and kings to the Brahmanic institutions (Thapar 1994: 31). It was similar in the south. A south India Tillasthanam inscription of AD 950, for example, records that a major oil merchant/guild had received a portion of gold from a Pandyan queen and allotted one third to each of three oil merchants/guilds in a village to keep the temple lamps burning (Karashima 2009a: 174). The involvement of guilds in not-for-profit activity, both as corporate donors and as brokers for individual acts of charity, brought substantial benefits in terms of developing local and international networks, a reputation for excellence in their specialization, and for reliability in executing wealth transactions. Building strong links with local socio-religious organizations through donation and brokering philanthropic activities was seen as sound business practice in ancient India. Guilds saw economic advantage in clearly demonstrating how membership worked not only for profit, but also for the broader social good.

The contemporary CSR mantra that 'doing good is good for business' (Gillis and Spring 2001) reflects an increasing awareness that there is no need to sacrifice public good for profit. By 2004, research into the advantages of CSR had already shown that not only consumer choices, but also investor and employee attraction and commitment to the company were substantially influenced by awareness of company involvement in CSR practices. Andrew Grant, Ernst & Young Environment and Sustainability Services Principal, emphasized in the 2004 Asian-Oceanian Computing Industry Organization (ASOCIO) policy paper on CSR that seeing ethical practice as separate and potentially detrimental to business practice was no longer a viable business position: 'Corporate Social Responsibility is now a determining factor in consumer and client choice which companies cannot afford to ignore. Companies who fail to maximise their adoption of a CSR strategy will be left behind' (ASOCIO 2004: 1.3). Not just the appearance of ethical activity, but genuine practice of CSR is now necessary not only to boost market share, but also to protect the existing business footprint. Companies are now subjected to such high levels of informal and formal global scrutiny that attending to CSR issues protects the company from risk of legal prosecution or government regulation. Further, active CSR engagement protects it from public outrage over unethical practices and the resultant loss of customers (Levine 2008).

The degree to which contemporary companies pursue such activities out of genuine human interest rather than simply as aspects of 'customer-friendly' marketing exercises will vary dramatically. However, the example of philanthropic activity in ancient India demonstrates there can be very concrete advantages to gaining a reputation for quality, trustworthiness and ethical commitment. The Indian experience shows that business is not disadvantaged by participating in activities which are of local benefit. Indeed, in acting as brokers of charitable donations, the reputation of the guilds was enhanced by demonstrating trustworthiness in handling money and showing respect for community values. The separation of social and religious values from business and economic interest prevalent in current 'self-interest maximization' models of business activity was absent from some of the most robust corporate business activity in ancient India.

Conclusion

This chapter does not intend to suggest that close moral involvement in the personal life of employees is ideal corporate practice, nor that business activity should be limited to the local community. Rather, it emphasizes that there is business advantage to developing practices which do not harm communities and do not exploit either the labour force or the consumer. This chapter argues that ethics and business are not mutually exclusive. Business can flourish in an environment in which guardianship and contribution to ethical practice are both understood to be essential and are the responsibility of state and community. Business can flourish in contexts where the local needs of manufacturers and contributors to economic development are nurtured through business organizations, like the guilds in ancient India, and state ethical regulation is managed in co-operation with these same business organizations.

It would be naive to infer from the historical examples discussed above that business practice in India is always ethical. Indeed, the existence of rigorous punishment at both state and guild level indicates the persistent risk of breaches of ethical practice in ancient India. Contemporary India's reputation for systemic government corruption and the recent spectacular corporate scandals similarly prevent such an illusion (Noorani 2011, 'Dynamic but dirty' 2010). However, India's guild tradition suggests there is a link between ethics and business which lies deep in Indian culture. M.K. Gandhi's comment that 'True Economics … stands for social justice … promotes the good of all equally, including the weakest, and is indispensable for decent life' (cited in Biswas 1998: 1,064) resonates with the insistence of Kautilya's *Arthasastra* that good economics – and indeed good management – must include regard for the welfare of the people (Kautilya 1992: 10 {1.19.34}, 177 {1.19.35–6}).

Guild practice supports the soundness of a broader approach to economic value by insisting on strong engagement by guild members not only in profitable activity, but also in the cultural and ethical life of the local community and, more broadly, of the town and region to which they belong. In ancient India, profit remained a guild priority and the state relied on guilds to help in regulating the economy and maintaining its prosperity at both local and international levels. However, profit was not an alternative to ethical practice. The dharma-based terms of the state's political engagement with guilds included the expectation that activities of cultural and social benefit were part of economic activity. In ancient India, charitable brokerage and donor activity were not seen as costly diversions of management focus and resources, posing risks to business profitability. Rather, both state and guild membership understood such actions to be an integral part of the responsibility of corporate bodies functioning within an ethical approach to wealth creation. Economic activity was conceptualized as more than a profit-driven activity. An ethically orientated approach to business, based in a strong sense of corporate social responsibility, was seen as intrinsic to the welfare of the people and the security and stability of the state in which they lived.

References

Alexander, J. and Buckingham, J. 2011. 'Common good leadership in business management: An ethical model from the Indian tradition'. *Business Ethics: A European Review*, 20(4), 317–27.

ASOCIO (Asian-Oceanian Computing Industry Organization). 2004. *Corporate Social Responsibility*. ASOCIO Policy Paper, June.

Banerjee, S.B. 2007. *Corporate Social Responsibility: The Good the Bad and the Ugly*. Cheltenham: Edward Elgar.

Biswas, N.B. 1998. 'Economics and ethics in an Indian society: A reflective analysis'. *International Journal of Social Economics*, 25(6/7/8), 1,064–72.

Darian, J.C. 1977. 'Social and economic factors in the rise of Buddhism'. *Sociology of Religion*, 38(3), 226–38.

Davids, T.W.R. 1899/2007. *Dialogues of the Buddha: The Digha-Nikaya*. Charleston, SC: Forgotten Books.

Dumont, L. 1980. *Homo Hierarchicus: The Caste System and its Implications*. Chicago, IL: University of Chicago Press.

'Dynamic but dirty'. 2010. *The Economist*, 2 December, http://www.economist. com/node/17627577 accessed 26 March 2012.

Gillis, T. and Spring, N. 2001. 'Doing good is good for business'. *Communication World*, October–November, http://findarticles.com/p/articles/mi_m4422/is_6_18/ ai_80227334/ accessed 26 March 2012.

Kangle, R.P. (trans.) 1969. *The Kautiliya Arthasastra. Part 1 (Text) and Part II (Translation)*. 2nd edn, Bombay: University of Bombay.

Karashima, N. 2009a. 'Nagaram: Commerce and towns AD 850–1350', in *South Indian Society in Transition: Ancient to Medieval*, ed. N. Karashima, New Delhi: Oxford University Press, 165–95.

Karashima, N. 2009b. 'South Indian merchant guilds in the Indian Ocean and Southeast Asia', in *South Indian Society in Transition: Ancient to Medieval*, ed. N. Karashima, New Delhi: Oxford University Press, 199–223.

Kautilya. 1992. *The Arthasastra*, trans. and ed. L.N. Rangarajan. New Delhi: Penguin.

Kosambi, D.D. 1959. 'Indian feudal trade charters'. *Journal of the Economic and Social History of the Orient*, 2(3), 281–93.

Koslowski, P. 2009. 'The ethics of corporate governance: A Continental European perspective'. *International Journal of Law and Management*, 51(1), 27–34.

Levine, M.A. 2008. 'The benefits of corporate social responsibility'. *New York Law Journal*, 13 August, http://www.law.com/jsp/cc/PubArticleCC. jsp?id=1202423730339, accessed 26 March 2012.

Lindgreen, A. and Swaen, V. 2010. 'Corporate social responsibility'. *International Journal of Management Reviews*, 12(1), 1–7.

Lingat, R. 1973. *The Classical Law of India*, trans. J. Duncan and M. Derrett. Berkeley, CA: University of California Press.

Liu, X. 1988. *Ancient India and Ancient China: Trade and Religious Exchanges AD 1–600*. New Delhi: Oxford University Press.

Mackenzie Brown, D. 1953. 'The premises of Indian political thought'. *Western Political Quarterly*, 6(2), 243–9.

Majumdar, R.C. 1922/2009. *Corporate Life in Ancient India*. Poona: The Oriental Book Agency, reprint Charleston, SC: BiblioLife.

McGill Murphy, R. 2010. 'Why doing good is good for business'. *Fortune*, 2 February, http://money.cnn.com/2010/02/01/news/companies/dov_seidman_ lrn.fortune/index.htm, accessed 26 March 2012.

Mitra, M. 2007. *It's Only Business! India's Corporate Responsiveness in a Globalized World*. New Delhi: Oxford University Press.

Noorani, A.G. 2011. 'Make ministers pay'. *Frontline: India's National Magazine*, 28(3), http://www.frontlineonnet.com/fl2803/stories/20110211280309900.htm, accessed: 26 March 2012.

O'Brien, R. 2001. *Crippled Justice: The History of Modern Disability Policy in the Workplace*. Chicago, IL: University of Chicago Press.

Rangarajan, L.N. 1992a. 'Heads of departments', in Kautilya, *The Arthasastra*, trans. and ed. L.N. Rangarajan. New Delhi: Penguin, 305–8.

Rangarajan, L.N. 1992b. 'Introduction', in Kautilya, *The Arthasastra*, trans. and ed. L.N. Rangarajan. New Delhi: Penguin, 13–41.

Rangarajan, L.N. 1992c. 'Loans, deposits, pledges, mortgages etc.', in Kautilya, *The Arthasastra*, trans. and ed. L.N. Rangarajan. New Delhi: Penguin, 422–30.

Rangarajan, L.N. 1992d. 'The Kautilyan state and society', in Kautilya, *The Arthasastra*, trans. and ed. L.N. Rangarajan. New Delhi: Penguin, 42–98.

Reddy, Y.R.K. 2009. 'The ethics of corporate governance: An Asian perspective'. *International Journal of Law and Management*, 51(1), 17–26.

Rossouw, G.J. 2009. 'The ethics of corporate governance: Crucial distinctions for global comparisons'. *International Journal of Law and Management*, 51(1), 5–9.

Sen, A. 1993. 'Does business ethics make economic sense?' *Business Ethics Quarterly*, 3(1), 45–54.

Sharma, R.S. 2003. *Early Medieval Indian Society: A Study in Feudalisation*. Kolkata: Orient Longman.

Sheth, D.L. 1999. 'Secularisation of caste and making of new middle class'. *Economic and Political Weekly*, 34(34/35), 2,502–10.

Smith, B.K. 1994. *Classifying the Universe: The Ancient Indian Varna System and the Origins of Caste*. Oxford: Oxford University Press.

Smith, V.A. 1920/2002. *Asoka: The Buddhist Emperor of India*. 3rd edn, Oxford: Clarendon Press. [New Delhi: Asian Educational Services].

Thapar, R. 1978. *Ancient Indian Social History: Some Interpretations*. New Delhi: Orient Longman.

Thapar, R. 1993. 'Imagined religious communities? Ancient history and the modern search for a Hindu identity', in *Interpreting Early India*, ed. R. Thapar. New Delhi: Oxford University Press, 60–88.

Thapar, R. 1994. 'Patronage', in *Cultural Transaction and Early India*, ed. R. Thapar. New Delhi: Oxford University Press, 25–40.

Thaplyal, K.K. 2001. 'Guilds in ancient India (antiquity and various stages in the development of guilds up to AD 300)', in *Life Thoughts and Culture in India*, ed. G.C. Pande. Delhi: Munshiram Manoharlal, 995–1,006.

Trautmann, R. 1979. 'Traditions of statecraft in ancient India', in *Tradition and Politics in South Asia*, ed. R.J. Moore. New Delhi: Vikas, 86–102.

Ville, I. 2010. 'From inaptitude for work to trial of the self: The vicissitudes of meanings of disability/De l'ineptitude au travail à l'épreuve de soi.

Les vicissitudes des significations du handicap'. *ALTER: European Journal of Disability Research*, 4(1), 59–71.

Weber, M. 1930/1958. *The Protestant Ethic and the Spirit of Capitalism*. New York: Charles Scribner's Sons.

Young S.B. 2009. 'The ethics of corporate governance: The North American perspective'. *International Journal of Law and Management*, 51(1), 35–42.

6

Tribal Economies?

Te Maire Tau

Introduction

What is a tribal corporation, what does it look like, and how does it benefit tribal members? I remember asking this question in the mid-1990s, when it was clear that Ngāi Tahu, the largest tribal group in the South Island of New Zealand, was about to settle with the Crown one of the largest land claims in the South Island. The actual cash settlement was NZ$170 million. That, plus the transfer of capital assets, ensured that Ngāi Tahu received a major capital and cash settlement that made it the largest private land owner in the South Island, as well as one of New Zealand's leading corporations. The challenge before the tribe, which consisted of small rural village communities that in many instances managed themselves informally, without even a bank account let alone a legal identity, was how to successfully manage this new wealth without mimicking Western corporate behaviour. Embedded into this was the acknowledgement that tribal values needed to be retained.

The background to these events reaches back to the nineteenth century, to 1840, when Ngāi Tahu leaders, along with other tribal groups, signed the Treaty of Waitangi, a pact between local *iwi* (tribe) and *hapu* (sub-tribe) and the British Empire. 'The Treaty', as it became known in New Zealand, was never legislated in the United Kingdom, although it was seen as a formal agreement among Māori. Under the Treaty, Māori recognized the Crown as possessing sovereignty, and in return for this concession, the tribes (*iwi* and *hapu*) were guaranteed their *tino-rangatiratanga* (chieftainship/ownership) over the fisheries, estates, properties and all other *taonga* (prized possessions). Included in these conditions was the principle that if land were to be sold by Māori to the new settlers, the Crown would have the right of 'pre-emption', whereby it was the sole purchaser (Kawharu 1989).

In the South Island, huge tracts of land were purchased by contract. The land purchases started with the Otakou purchase in 1844, where the Crown bought 400,000 acres from Ngāi Tahu for £2,400. The last purchase, in 1863, was when Rakiura (Stewart Island) was bought for £6,000 (Evison 1988). Of these, the largest (in 1848) was for 20 million acres of land, from Canterbury down to Otakou, for £2,000. As most readers of British imperial history would know, the contracts of purchase were not honoured, and by the end of the century, the native inhabitants had been reduced to a landless people, living in extreme poverty (Evison 1988). Moreover, thirty-seven years after the signing of the Treaty of Waitangi, the judicial system had formally reached the conclusion that the Treaty was a 'simple nullity' in New Zealand, leaving Māori with no case to argue before the courts. Consequently, the nineteenth century was for Māori a century where the British Empire oversaw the settlement of New Zealand, with a white migrant population bent upon removing from Māori all their capital assets and property rights. Later, for much of the twentieth century, Māori lived and worked as a brown proletariat, bereft of capital assets and overseen by a government intent on assimilating them into a derivative of the British Empire. By the 1980s, not only had tribal groups been stripped of their assets, but the Crown had also spent an entire century removing the basic pillars of the way in which they managed themselves socially by undermining the foundations of tribal structures (Banner 2000).

Today, Māori talk casually about their tribal affiliations and how their *iwi* manage their tribal assets. Yet this was not the case before the 1990s, because then Māori could not answer a basic question fundamental to all groups wishing to collectively share a common vision and future: 'Who am I?' While tribal members and Māori could answer this question in a customary manner, the legal fact was that tribal bodies did not and were not allowed to exist in any legal sense. As Hernando de Soto has argued so well, legal identity is critical to asset ownership (de Soto 2000).

Before its settlement with the Crown in 1998, Ngāi Tahu was the first tribal corporation in New Zealand, as acknowledged under the Te Runanga o Ngāi Tahu Act of 1996. This Act was the first in the nation's history that actually recognized *iwi*, or tribal groups, as legitimate political bodies. Before this Act, tribal bodies were not recognized in New Zealand law. The Act allowed Ngāi Tahu to become a corporation, and as I have suggested, the movement towards the negotiation of a settlement meant that Ngāi Tahu would be a corporation with serious financial leverage in its community.

Yet for most members of the tribe at that time, the idea of a corporation and its meaning and effect upon us was barely imaginable. At the time, most tribal members were uneducated and poor – and many still are. The majority of our leaders who now sit as directors of the Ngāi Tahu Trust Board would have left high school with no qualifications, and few were financially secure. In fact, most had worked as labourers or small farmers, and had faced rounds of redundancy and upskilling in the era of New Zealand liberal economic reform of the 1980s and early 1990s, popularly known as Rogernomics and Ruthanasia, after former Ministers of Finance Roger Douglas and Ruth Richardson, (Kelsey 1990, Hill 2009). None had any past experience as directors upon a board of any note.

During the period in which tribal leaders were negotiating the Ngāi Tahu Claim, a number of my generation, generally known now as Generation X (post-1964–86) adopted supportive roles in managing the negotiations or by acting as specialist advisers, which naturally meant that wide-ranging discussions were held on the nature of the settlement we were to advance. The basis for the Ngāi Tahu negotiations centred on the findings of the Waitangi Tribunal, a body established by the Crown to investigate grievances by Māori who believed the Crown had ignored the promises made in the Treaty of Waitangi (Sorrenson 1989: 158–79). Besides finding that Ngāi Tahu had, in fact, been wrongfully dispossessed of their land and resources, the Tribunal also made a number of findings on the social and cultural status of the tribe. The Tribunal essentially supported the Ngāi Tahu grievance that the Crown had promised schools and hospitals upon Ngāi Tahu reserves. That is, as Ngāi Tahu was to cede the bulk of the land to the Crown, tribal members would be relocated to reservations, which would be resourced with schools and hospitals. The Tribunal's findings read:

> It remains for us to state our conclusions on Ngāi Tahu's grievance that the Crown failed adequately to fulfill Mantell's promises as to schools and hospitals. We have found that these promises were made by Mantell to induce Ngāi Tahu to part with their land in the Kemp and Murihiku purchases. We have further found that, given the grave dissatisfaction of Ngāi Tahu chiefs both with the price and the totally inadequate extent of the reserves proposed or insisted on by Mantell, that the prospect of the provision of schools, hospitals and other government assistance constituted material inducements to Ngāi Tahu to sell their lands, many millions of acres in extent.
>
> (Waitangi Tribunal 1991: 19.5.1)

The Walter Mantell referred to in the Tribunal's findings was a Crown agent who, in 1848, took on the office of Commissioner for Extinguishing Native Titles. As the name suggests, Mantell's duty was to extinguish all 'native title' and to allocate to tribal members lands that were identified as 'Crown Grants'. What this meant was that the land purchased was presumed to have had all 'customary rights' removed, allowing it to then be reallocated to tribal members as land granted to them from the Crown, free of previous customary traditions. As his duty was to allocate land, Mantell was required to negotiate and minimize the contractual and oral promises made to Ngāi Tahu by the Crown agents at the time of the purchases. These negotiations were to be anything but reasonable, as Mantell recorded in Greek the instructions from his superior, Lieutenant-Governor Eyre, who told him that if there were any disagreements with Ngāi Tahu, then he should: 'Let them leave it. I must kari maters with a hi hand [sic]' (Evison 1997: 217). Mantell was given free rein to negotiate as he pleased, and as Ngāi Tahu claimed and the Tribunal found, he had promised tribal communities schools and hospitals on their reserves without any intention of delivering upon the plan. Schools were certainly set aside within villages, but only after Māori provided land and, in most cases, contributed the majority of the financial aid for the school buildings. Medical facilities, such as hospitals or clinics, were simply not provided.

The question for our negotiation team was to ask how the Waitangi Tribunal's findings were to be articulated in a meaningful way for the present generation. How could these findings have any meaning for tribal elders who were likely to die at an age well below the national average, or for families who were struggling to meet health costs for young children when the government had removed medical subsidies for infants? It is timely to remember that, except for New Zealand, in the mid-1990s the developed world was enjoying a financial boom (Goldfinch and Malpass 2007).

And what about education? Māori university graduates were few, and this was the least of our problems. Young Māori frequently left school with no qualifications, just as their elders had done before them. On top of the failure of the Crown to meet its obligations to educate our people, the mono-cultural education system actively undermined the cultural beliefs, knowledge systems and language of Māori. Consequently, by the time Māori left the education system in early adulthood, they were unable to function in either the Western-dominated world or in any traditional Māori world of their ancestors (Waitangi Tribunal 1999). The outcome for tribal leadership was that, in the main, our tribal leaders were unable to advance their people's grievances in any effective manner simply because most were illiterate, which left the few literate members with a university education a larger load to carry.

The issue facing the Ngāi Tahu tribe and its negotiators was simple: How could the Waitangi Tribunal's findings on schools and hospitals be resolved in a meaningful way, by the then and successive governments, when the economy had been in decline since the 1970s? I had asked these questions of our tribal leaders, who were participating in the Ngāi Tahu negotiations. At this stage, Ngāi Tahu's tribal leaders were Tipene O'Regan and Henare Rakihia Tau (Stokes 1980: 69, Ngāi Tahu Māori Trust Board 1993).[1] Both had attended university, with Tipene O'Regan always maintaining an interest in the academic community. Tau had trained as an accountant, although he left university before graduating. Both had eventually become *Upoko* (head leaders) in their communities. In the 1980s, these two leaders focused on much of the hard grind of articulating on paper formal tribal policy before the Crown and local communities, within the South Island and in Wellington.

In response to these and similar questions, a series of initial solutions were proposed. The Crown could subsidize Ngāi Tahu health care and education (Ngāi Tahu Māori Trust Board 1993).[2] The Crown could provide, for example, a number of medical centres within villages, and tribal colleges could be established in Christchurch and Dunedin. However, for a range of reasons, these ideas were set aside. The Crown could not be seen to be privileging one ethnic group over and above another, and tribal members no longer lived in their ancestral villages as new Crown land policies had prohibited it.

As these ideas were debated, the initial response – and one that was to become the orthodox response – was that with the settlement, Ngāi Tahu could purchase its own hospitals and care for its own elderly. The argument placed before tribal members was that with the expected settlement of NZ$170 million and the transfer of capital assets, the tribal corporation would generate enough profit to manage the issues of health and education among tribal members (Te Runanga o Ngāi Tahu 1997). This argument was essentially a classic neo-liberal economic response best captured as the 'trickle-down' theory, where social and cultural problems were dependent upon the capacity of the state to

---

1   At the time, Tipene O'Regan was Chair of the Ngāi Tahu Māori Trust Board and Henare Rakihia Tau was Deputy Chair, as well as being claimant before the Waitangi Tribunal for the Ngāi Tahu claim. For a commentary on issues of leadership, see Ngāi Tahu Māori Trust Board (1993) and Stokes (1980).
2   The emergence of these issues as topics of debate among Ngāi Tahu were flagged in the Board's 1993 *Annual Report* (Ngāi Tahu Māori Trust Board 1993).

generate enough wealth to resolve social concerns. In this case, however, the tribe was to function as an additional welfare state.

This, then, is the context that surrounded the idea of a tribal corporation – or, more properly, this is the context that led Ngāi Tahu towards the adoption of a corporate model as the flagship for its development and move to modernity.

By the late 1980s and early 1990s, the relationship of corporations and tribal development was well and truly subject to debate within rural communities, among urban Māori and, at the national level, in Parliament (Hill 2009). The debate at the time was lively, fierce and confrontational. What was clear among tribal leaders was that if the tribe was to function in the future, the traditional structures that operated within small village communities would not be adequate to the task of managing the new assets and cash the Crown was about to transfer.

It has now been well over a decade since the Ngāi Tahu claim was settled in 1998. Now, the question that needs to be asked is not so much concerned with whether the approach was right or wrong, but what the fundamental strengths and weaknesses of the proposed model were, and has the classic neo-liberal economic approach served the tribe as well as it could.

Iwi and Tribal Corporations

The most surprising aspect of the Māori economy is that until 1996, tribes or *iwi* simply did not exist in legislation. In fact, the early New Zealand settler government actively set about stamping out tribal entities by legislation. Yet in the face of this quite significant political hurdle that denied any legal status to tribal bodies, Māori persisted in their tribal affiliations. This is itself instructive, because this chapter essentially argues that Māori and their traditional tribal values are intrinsic to the manner in which they organize themselves. The primary institution used by the settler government to undermine tribal values and social cohesion was the Native Land Court, which was established in 1862 under the Native Lands Act. As Stuart Banner has argued in a series of articles examining the decapitalization of Māori in the nineteenth century, the Native Land Court was established for the systematic transfer of land from Māori to the British Empire. In drawing to a conclusion, Banner wrote:

> *By the end of the century, the Māori no longer had most of their land,*
> *and they no longer had their system of property either. One way of*
> *organizing rights in land had been superseded by another. The*
> *British, with the military and technological superiority to establish a*
> *government and pronounce the rules by which land would be owned*
> *and transferred, had been able to force Māori to reconceptualize*
> *land as composed of geographic spaces rather than as use rights. The*
> *colonization of land, the physical substance, could not have proceeded*
> *without the simultaneous colonization of property, the mental structure*
> *for organizing rights to land.*
>
> *(Banner 1999)*

While Banner may have overestimated the capacity of the settlers to force
Māori to reconceptualize their approach to land, he was right in the sense that
the settlers had introduced a new system of organizing the land, which saw the
Native Land Court and individual title gain ascendancy over the traditional
mechanisms of customary rights regulated by *whanau* (extended family), *hapu*
and *iwi* relationships. The core idea in not recognizing tribal entities in statute
was essentially based on the premise that tribal entities acted as the collective
body that held authority over the land. In the 1840s–50s, it was becoming clear
that tribal leaders were becoming more and more reluctant to sell land, and this
posed a problem for the settler government – whose interest was, of course,
centred on land acquisition. As the nineteenth-century New Zealand politician
Henry Sewell explained:

> *The object of the Native Land Act [1865] was twofold: to bring the*
> *great bulk of the lands of the Northern Island which belonged to the*
> *natives … within the reach of colonization. The other great object was,*
> *the detribalization of the natives – to destroy if possible, the principle*
> *of communism which ran through the whole of their institutions, upon*
> *which their social system was based, and which stood as a barrier in the*
> *way of all attempts to amalgamate the Native race into our own social*
> *and political system. It was hoped that by the individualization of titles*
> *to land, giving them the same individual ownership that we possess*
> *ourselves … their social status would become assimilated to our own.*
> *(New Zealand Parliamentary Debates 1877: 254)*

In order to destroy tribal entities, land was individualized in 1865. From this
period onwards, *iwi* were reduced to 'shadow' organizations, with the Crown
always attempting to provide an alternative mechanism to the tribal entity.

Yet there is also good reason to believe that the move towards de-tribalizing Māori was also due to the nature of the tribal economy, which definitely had advantages over the individualized nature of the settler economy. Lady Mary Ann Martin, the wife of Sir William Martin, the first Chief Justice of New Zealand, wrote in 1847:

> *Everywhere large tracts of wheat were grown, and the natives contributed largely towards the erection of mills. Many bought cows, and friends of ours travelling through the country a year or two later were pleasantly surprised to find home-baked bread and fresh milk offered to them in the villages, instead of potatoes only. This general stir throughout the country made us acquainted with the tribes that lived in the interior, near to the hot springs and lake district on the East Coast. The soil was not favourable for wheat-growing, but they brought scraped flax and Indian corn to Auckland. To do this they had to buy cutters or schooners. There were one or two good harbours near. It was wonderful to see the amount of patience and self-denial exercised by these wild people. No one man could obtain money enough to buy a vessel. It must be a tribal purchase, and become tribal property. Whole villages – men, women, and children – worked for months, scraping flax, till the money was raised.*
>
> (Martin 1884: 54)

Similar observations can be found throughout the nineteenth-century literature. The underlying theme that occurs throughout all records is the collective nature of labour, property and tribal assets or capital, which cuts across the Hobbesian tradition of self-interest as the core motivation for economic activity. Likewise, in 1852, an article in the *Daily Southern Cross* newspaper made a number of insightful observations about the economy of the Auckland market:

> *The provision trade, of which we now treat, may be emphatically termed native …. Of the live and dead stock, brought into the Auckland market, they convey no idea; nor could any one, except those familiar with the patient, plodding, money-loving habits of the native tribes, form the remotest conjecture of the immense quantities of pigs, poultry, potatoes, onions, turnips, carrots, maize, wheat, and other articles of their own producing, which are back and canoe borne from distant places into Auckland; nor could a stranger conceive the large amount of coin which these indefatigable native husbandmen expend in the purchase of vessels, agricultural implements, horses, clothing, and the*

other appliances of necessity, convenience, or comfort, which a rapidly
increasing civilization has taught them to appreciate, and a persevering
industry has enabled them to acquire.

('*The Auckland Provision Trade*' 1852: 3)

By the middle of the nineteenth century, Māori had a solid grasp of how the market worked and where land featured in this economy. While the Treaty gave the Crown the right of pre-emption, or the right to be sole purchaser of Māori land, which it could then sell on at a much higher price to *Pakeha* (British) settlers, Māori also saw that they too could control the market for selling land. Māori could collectively decide not to sell their land – and this is the option they chose in Taranaki. As the Waitangi Tribunal shows in its Taranaki Report, Māori collectively decided against selling land to settlers (Waitangi Tribunal 1996).[3] Both in terms of market and land purchasing, Māori acted as a collective. Whether it be conducting land transactions or trading with the settler community, more often than not that collective was the *hapu* within the *iwi*.

By taking these observations into account, and acknowledging the fact that by the 1860s tribal authorities wanted to restrict the unregulated sale of land to the Crown and *Pakeha* settlers, the 1865 Native Land Act – which sought to de-tribalize the natives – may be more clearly understood. De-tribalizing the natives was a way of undermining the collective forum in which Māori operated to organize and manage their economic and political influence. The 1865 Native Land Act is therefore the historic reference point for *iwi* corporations today, and in particular the basis for which the 1996 Te Runanga o Ngāi Tahu Act is its intellectual counterpoint. The 1865 Native Land Act sought to undermine tribal entities, whereas the 1996 Te Runanga o Ngāi Tahu Act re-established the tribal group as the principal entity for managing Māori capital assets, and consequently heralded the evolving tribal economies of New Zealand in the twenty-first century.

Between 1865 and 1996, tribal groups had no legal standing in New Zealand, and therefore could not function as corporate entities. What Māori had during this era were a series of Crown-created agencies that attempted to represent Māori interests, while ultimate responsibility rested with the Crown

---

3 The Waitangi Tribunal pointed out there was no cartel of Māori that acted against land selling, and the idea of such a cartel was a figment of the settler/Crown imagination. However, the Tribunal did note there was a growing policy against land sales among Māori (Waitangi Tribunal 1996).

(Hill 2004: 247–65, Hill 2009: 247–74). The best example of this was the plethora of Trust Boards that emerged with the Labour government in the 1930s. The Trust Boards were typical micro-management Crown creations, where board members were accountable to the Minister of Māori Affairs for the expenditure of their own monies to the degree that, by the 1980s, ministerial permission was still required for any expenditure over NZ$200.[4] By the 1980s, however, Māori had tired of these organizations and it was quite clear that regardless of Crown legislation, Māori were still fundamentally tribal. The tribal nature of Māori was obvious when they needed to mobilize on a national level, whether with the Māori Battalion of the Second World War or to help organize the Te Māori exhibition of the 1980s. What, then, forced the Crown to change a well-established policy of not dealing with *iwi*, to recognizing the collective nature of *iwi* and establishing *iwi* as corporate bodies under New Zealand law?

Historians have attempted to explain this change by referring to a combination of factors, none of which seem convincing enough to wholly explain the huge transfer of assets from Crown to Māori.[5] Over the years, many Māori had slowly been moving to large towns and cities, and by the 1980s, 80 per cent of the Maori population was urban. Previously, Māori had largely dominated rural sectors, and even then they were not politically dominant because their vote was limited to the traditional four Māori seats. Furthermore, their political capacity was always in question, simply because the general electorate for the settler population was numerically overwhelming. The settler government created the Māori electoral seats in 1868 to provide dedicated political representation for Māori. This system lasted until 1996, when another seat was added, and then an additional two Māori seats were created for the 2008 general election (Hill 2009). With the shift of younger Māori into urban centres, Māori political influence was no longer limited to the electoral seats set aside for the Māori vote. In the 1970s and 1980s, they were influencing the wider political scene by voting in the general urban electorates, particularly in Auckland, where most of the Māori population was to be found. Consequently, Māori became more politically active. The 1975 Land March was heavily influenced by Martin Luther King's civil rights march on Washington in 1963 and Gandhi's 1930 salt march. Yet none of these factors seem enough to explain why there was such a massive transfer of assets from the Crown to Māori after

---

4   The requirement to gain ministerial approval for any expenditure over NZ$200 was eventually removed in the 1980s (*New Zealand Parliamentary Debates* 1996).

5   Academic and writer Dr Ranginui Walker saw the strengthening of *kaupapa* Māori as a result of activism from the 1970s and 1980s (Walker 1990). For more discussion on this topic, see also Belgrave, Kawharu and Williams (2005).

the Ngāi Tahu settlement. Urbanization and the Māori protest movement were easily handled by the governments of the day (Kelsey 2005: 81–104).

The most significant factor that led to the growth of the Māori economy and tribal corporations was the economic change that fundamentally transformed New Zealand society: Rogernomics. Rogernomics takes its name from Roger Douglas, the fourth Labour government's Minister of Finance (1984–87), who deregulated the New Zealand economy in the same way the United States had been deregulated in the Reagan era. Rogernomics was New Zealand's variation on the neo-liberal economic policies that stemmed from the ideas of Frederick Hayek and Milton Friedman. In quite simple terms, at the time New Zealand's economic situation was dire. The government's response was to place critical state assets into state corporations that would act with the intention of producing a profit for the government, which was the shareholder (Ward 1999, Hill 2009). This was implemented by means of the 1986 State-Owned Enterprises Act.

However, the stumbling point for the government's plan was the claims to the principal capital assets, land, fisheries and minerals, made by Māori under the Treaty of Waitangi. Māori won a substantial victory in 1986 when the Court of Appeal sought enforcement of Section 9 of the State Owned Enterprises Act, which declared: 'Nothing in this Act shall permit the Crown to act in a manner that is inconsistent with the principles of the Treaty of Waitangi.' The Court of Appeal established several principles that affect us today. What is often neglected in analysis of New Zealand's financial crisis of the 1980s is the fact that the Crown's capacity to sell its assets was impeded until claims by Māori were to be resolved by the Waitangi Tribunal. The Waitangi Tribunal had been established in 1975 under the Treaty of Waitangi Act. The Tribunal was given the powers to investigate breaches of the Treaty of Waitangi from 1975 onwards. While the Treaty of Waitangi Act was significant in a symbolic sense, the political and legal capacity of the Tribunal was limited simply because it only had powers to make recommendations to government and it could only investigate 'alleged' Treaty breaches after 1975. Māori were quick to criticize the terms of the Act, arguing that by 1975 most of the land had already been taken because the Treaty of Waitangi had never been honoured (Walker 1990: 253–5). Māori hopes for a more just application of the Treaty were further enhanced in 1985, when the fourth Labour government passed new legislation giving the Tribunal retrospective powers to investigate breaches of the Treaty of Waitangi dating back to 1840, when it was signed.

This legislation was a significant step, although the Tribunal still only had powers of recommendation. However, in 1987 a Court of Appeal decision included the opinion of Chief Justice Cooke that the Crown had a duty to remedy past breaches of the Treaty and that the Tribunal's recommendations should be acted upon unless there were very exceptional circumstances:

> *In the sense that if the Waitangi Tribunal finds merit in a claim and recommends redress, the Crown should grant at least some form of redress, unless there are grounds justifying a reasonable Treaty partner in withholding it – which would be only in very special circumstances, if ever.*
>
> *(New Zealand Māori Council v. Attorney-General [1987])*

While the Tribunal still only had the powers to recommend, this decision certainly put weight behind its recommendations. With the political and judicial powers leaning towards Māori, the Crown's financial base was less than secure. The Crown needed revenue. Māori were a significant bloc. The easiest solution was to negotiate a transfer of assets from the Crown to Māori, leaving the Crown with a significant revenue stream to cover its debt. We need to be quite clear: the Crown was cash-strapped. Regardless of claims of goodwill between the races, the Māori economy which is now emerging rests on a combination of neo-liberal economic policy and litigation through the judicial system. Political goodwill from the Crown was due to its own economic mismanagement, moral failings and judicial losses (Richards 2010: 298–9).[6]

The problem, however, was that Māori were simply not prepared in any structural sense to receive the expected assets. Now we take the idea of a tribal corporation for granted, but in the 1980s and early 1990s, no Ngāi Tahu village council would have held cash that amounted to more than NZ$10,000. While the Crown prepared itself to devolve assets to Māori, a range of non-tribal entities arose to claim them – among them the Churches, urban Māori groups, the Māori Women's Welfare League and even national gang organizations, such as Black Power. That *iwi* would receive these assets was by no means a certainty (Hill 2009: 221–46).

---

6   The political background to this is outlined by Raymond Richards in his biography of former New Zealand politician and Prime Minister Geoffrey Palmer (Richards 2010: 298–9). Richards explains how, after the State Owned Enterprises decision by the Court of Appeal in 1987, the Labour government passed the Treaty of Waitangi (State Enterprises) Act 1988, which permitted Crown assets to be sold, but then obliged the Crown to purchase the assets back and return them to Māori if ordered to do so by the Waitangi Tribunal.

The possibility of a corporation being a representative structure for our tribe seemed obvious enough. After all, corporations were legal personalities, and there was no reason why a tribe called Ngāi Tahu could not also be a legal personality. Consequently, in 1996 Ngāi Tahu became the first tribe in New Zealand to actually exist in statute. The legislation was standard, in the sense that Section 6 of the Act declared that Te Runanga o Ngāi Tahu has 'perpetual succession and a common seal, with power to purchase, accept, hold, transfer and lease property, and to sue and be sued, and having all the rights, powers, and privileges of a natural person' (*Te Runanga o Ngāi Tahu Act 1996*, s. 6). Ngāi Tahu was now structurally sound enough to hold, purchase, transfer and lease property as a legally recognized entity. In 1998, Te Runanga o Ngāi Tahu received from the Crown a NZ$170 million cash settlement and capital assets, such as land and forests, which were valued at approximately NZ$270 million.

However, while Ngāi Tahu had created a corporate body that could hold its assets, it was less clear how it would manage and grow these assets. To this end, Te Runanga o Ngāi Tahu's 2009 Charter made the following declaration which separates Ngāi Tahu from a standard corporation. The Charter requires Te Runanga o Ngāi Tahu directors to adhere to two principles:

> *(i) to use prudently the assets allocated to it and to prudently administer them and its liabilities by operating profitable and efficient businesses; and*

> *(ii) to pursue in an efficient manner such social and cultural development and natural environment objectives as may from time to time be approved by Te Rūnanga in its capacity as Trustee in so far as the social and cultural development and natural environment objectives so approved fall within the charitable objects of the Charitable Trust.*
>
> *(Te Runanga o Ngāi Tahu 2009)*

Our original model for development completely reflected the trickle-down theory that was evident in the 1980s. However, the Charter clearly embeds corporate social responsibility into the business and economic management practices of the tribe as a corporation. Structurally, Ngāi Tahu separated itself into two sections that would sit under the tribal council (see Figure 6.1).

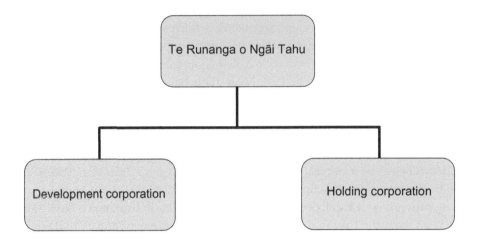

Figure 6.1   **Ngāi Tahu tribal structure**

The underlying principle was that the holding corporation was to hold and manage our assets, and the development corporation would meet the second objective of social and cultural development. The holding corporation was essentially the commercial part of the company that created, managed and produced a profit, while the development corporation operated with the intention of meeting the social and cultural needs of tribal members. The revenue supply would be driven by Ngāi Tahu holdings, and the dividend would then be delivered to the development corporation – trickle-down theory in a nutshell. Our needs for education, health and cultural development would be defined and targeted within the framework of Rogernomics.

What we found, however, is that this was a fundamental mistake – and one we have not fully resolved – because the basic premise of Ngāi Tahu's corporate structure simply reflected a situation all New Zealanders would recognize. New Zealanders, since the first Labour government of 1935, are essentially committed to a welfare state, and this ideal was reflected in our distribution model. In the main, economic policy in welfare states is primarily about welfare distribution, as opposed to wealth generation. The Ngāi Tahu development corporation soon found it was faced with the politics of distribution and the questions that go with it:

- Who receives a distribution of wealth – the young for education, or the elderly for their health?

- Why focus on tertiary education when so many of our young fail in secondary schools?

- Why not simply distribute the annual dividend equally among all members of the tribe, or should the distribution be allocated only to those who live within their tribal domain? After all, why should a tribal member whose family has lived in the UK for five generations receive a dividend?

From 1998 to 2005, the tribe wrestled with these questions in a largely ad hoc manner and without any real theoretical base, other than one where social and cultural development was defined by neo-liberal economic theory. However, by 2004 the tribe had developed into a top-heavy corporation in which we soon found ourselves spending NZ$5 to distribute NZ$1 to tribal members. In the main, that dollar primarily came out in the form of a quarterly tribal magazine. It was clear that urgent action was required.

In 2005, Te Runanga o Ngāi Tahu made the decision to remove the development corporation and replace it with a groundbreaking initiative called Whai Rawa (Te Runanga o Ngāi Tahu 2006: 18–19). Whai Rawa was essentially based on the economic ideas of Hernando de Soto, who argued that capitalism essentially rests on capital (de Soto 2000). Unless tribal members have capital, they will never be able to generate wealth. The basic premise was that Ngāi Tahu would set up bank accounts for all members of the tribe, and every year an annual distribution of approximately NZ$100 would be allocated to their account. If tribal members managed to save NZ$100, the tribe would allocate the same amount. On that basis, each member could save NZ$300 per annum. The key point here is that the Whai Rawa savings plan was for all tribal members, whose savings added to the available interest for distribution. Withdrawals from this account could only be made by tribal members, for three reasons which fitted the Whai Rawa goal of building three capital assets among *whanau* (family) and individual tribal members. The three important areas of capital assets were defined as knowledge capital (education), social and business capital, and personal capital (superannuation and a retirement plan). It was expected that by the age of 18 years, a tribal member would have saved enough to pay NZ$12,000 towards their tertiary education. This was their knowledge capital. By the age of 35 years, a tribal member would have enough for a NZ$28,000 deposit on a house, and by retirement they would have saved approximately NZ$193,000. The direct link with de Soto was the deposit for a house, because de Soto learnt that in the Western world, small businesses are built on families mortgaging their homes.[7] Although it was never explicitly said, our view was that a tribal member could sell their house to finance their company. The Whai Rawa initiative was the first step Ngāi Tahu took towards building individual capital assets among its members. It was the first step we took towards the idea of developing a distinct modern tribal economy. New Zealanders will be aware that this was a forerunner to the Kiwisaver scheme the Labour government introduced in 2007.

In developing a tribal saving scheme that built individual capital from a collective base, there was also an opportunity to develop similar schemes among other tribal groups in New Zealand. Māori generally have more than one tribal affiliation, so it is not unreasonable to expect a member affiliated to other similar tribal schemes to have three similar but separate accounts – thereby creating substantial core capital amongst Māori that is not fragmented by the politics of distribution or annual dividends. This has yet to occur.

Conclusion

So where does this leave Ngāi Tahu for the twenty-first century? Ngāi Tahu is a reflection of its tribal heritage and values as much as it is a reflection of the neo-liberal economic theory of the 1980s. At a superficial level, it is a tribal entity that functions to service tribal members. In that sense, it is an indigenous corporation. Yet at a deeper level, it is a modern adaptation of the settler economy, with *Pakeha* workers dominating the holding corporation. In 2006, the staff ratio for the holding corporation was less than 20 per cent Ngāi Tahu. It is, of course, impossible for the descendants of the settlers to ever represent tribal values and beliefs. Rather than reflecting tribal development, it could be argued that the corporate model has been a victory for colonial hegemony. Te Runanga o Ngāi Tahu's commercial origins are certainly Western, but its political origins are very much Māori. The irony is that the wealth – from which all present profits stem – can be traced back to tribal values and beliefs, which of course underpinned the Ngāi Tahu claim and search for justice. Equally, however, the huge financial and capital transfer of wealth could only have occurred with the changes in the global economy of the 1980s.

The challenge is whether similar tribal corporations can indigenize corporation models to fully benefit collective tribal communities, rather than

---

7   Te Runanga o Ngāi Tahu (2004). 'A Concept Document: He Ara Whai Rawa Mo Ngāi Tahu
     Whānui' (unpublished). Financial projections in this report were base assumptions.

individual staff. What we know from the Ngāi Tahu story is that Whai Rawa offers a glimpse into an alternative economic framework that has yet to be fully realized.

References

Banner, S. 1999. 'Two properties, one land: Law and space in nineteenth-century New Zealand'. *Law & Social Inquiry*, 24(4), 807–52, doi: 10.1111/j.1747-4469.1999.tb00406.x.

Banner, S. 2000. 'Conquest by contract: Wealth transfer and land market structure in colonial New Zealand'. *Law & Society Review*, 34, 47–96.

Belgrave, M., Kawharu, M. and Williams, D. (eds). 2005. *Waitangi Revisited: Perspectives on the Treaty of Waitangi*. Melbourne: Oxford University Press.

de Soto, H. 2000. *The Mystery of Capital: Why Capitalism Triumphs in the West and Fails Everywhere Else*. New York: Basic Books.

Evison, H.C. 1988. *The Treaty of Waitangi and the Ngāi Tahu Claim: A Summary*. Christchurch: Ngāi Tahu Māori Trust Board.

Evison, H.C. 1997. *The Long Dispute: Māori Land Rights and European Colonisation in Southern New Zealand*. Christchurch: Canterbury University Press.

Goldfinch, S. and Malpass, D. 2007. 'The Polish shipyard: Myth, economic history and economic policy reform in New Zealand'. *Australian Journal of Politics and History*, 53(1), 118–37, doi: 10.1111/j.1467-8497.2007.00446.x.

Hill, R.S. 2004. *State Authority/Indigenous Autonomy: Crown–Māori Relationships in New Zealand/Aotearoa 1900–1950*. Wellington: Victoria University Press.

Hill, R.S. 2009. *Māori and the State: Crown–Māori Relations in New Zealand/Aotearoa 1950–2000*. Wellington: Victoria University Press.

Kawharu, I.H. (ed.). 1989. *Waitangi: Māori and Pakeha Perspectives of the Treaty of Waitangi*. Auckland: Oxford University Press.

Kelsey, J. 1990. *A Question of Honour? Labour and the Treaty, 1984–1989*. Wellington: Allen & Unwin.

Kelsey, J. 2005. 'Māori, Te Tiriti and globalisation: The invisible hand of the colonial state', in *Waitangi Revisited: Perspectives on the Treaty of Waitangi*, ed. M. Belgrave, M. Kawharu and D. Williams. Melbourne: Oxford University Press, 81–104.

Martin, M.A. (Lady Martin). 1884. *Our Māoris*. London: Society for Promoting Christian Knowledge, http://www.enzb.auckland.ac.nz/document?wid=656, accessed 26 March 2012.

New Zealand Māori Council v. Attorney-General [1987]. *New Zealand Law Reports*, 1, 664–5.

New Zealand Parliamentary Debates. 1877. 24, 254.

New Zealand Parliamentary Debates (Hansard). 1996. 16–18 April, 11,948–50.

Ngāi Tahu Māori Trust Board. 1993. *Annual Report.*

Richards, R. 2010. *Palmer: The Parliamentary Years.* Christchurch: Canterbury University Press.

Sorrenson, M.P.K. 1989. 'Towards a radical re-interpretation of New Zealand history: The role of the Waitangi Tribunal', in *Waitangi: Māori and Pakeha Perspectives of the Treaty of Waitangi*, ed. I.H. Kawharu. Auckland: Oxford University Press, 158–79.

State-Owned Enterprises Act 1986, http://www.legislation.govt.nz/act/public/ 1986/0124/22.0/ DLM97377.html, accessed 26 March 2012.

Stokes, E. 1980. *Tauranga Moana: A Study of the Impact of Urban Growth on Rural Māori Communities.* Hamilton: Centre for Māori Studies and Research, University of Waikato.

Te Runanga o Ngāi Tahu. 1997. *Te Karaka (Special Edition): Crown Settlement Offer Consultation Document from the Ngāi Tahu Negotiating Group*, Christchurch: Ngāi Tahu.

Te Runanga o Ngāi Tahu. 2004. 'A Concept Document: He Ara Whai Rawa Mo Ngāi Tahu Whānui' (unpublished).

Te Runanga o Ngāi Tahu. 2006. *Meeting Papers, 18–19 March.* Ngāi Tahu Holdings Group of Companies Human Resources Statistics, 8 March, 14/14, Christchurch: Ngāi Tahu.

Te Runanga o Ngāi Tahu. 2009. *Charter of Te Runanga o Ngāi Tahu*, Christchurch: Ngāi Tahu, http://www.ngaitahu.iwi.nz/Publications/Governance/Charter2009. pdf, accessed 26 March 2012.

Te Runanga o Ngāi Tahu Act 1996, http://www.legislation.govt.nz/act/private/ 1996/0001/latest/DLM117218.html, accessed 26 March 2012.

'The Auckland Provision Trade'. 1852. *Daily Southern Cross*, VII(471), 2 January, 3, http://paperspast.natlib.govt.nz/cgi-bin/paperspast?a=d&d=DSC18520102. 2.10, accessed 26 March 2012.

Waitangi Tribunal. 1991. *Ngāi Tahu Land Report*, http://www.waitangi-tribunal. govt.nz/reports/viewchapter.asp?reportID=D5D84302-EB22-4A52-BE78- 16AF39F71D91&chapter=30, accessed 26 March 2012.

Waitangi Tribunal. 1996. *The Taranaki Report: Kaupapa Tuatahi*, http://www. waitangi-tribunal.govt.nz/reports/summary.asp?reportid={3FECC540- D049-4DE6-A7F0-C26BCCDAB345}, accessed 26 March 2012.

Waitangi Tribunal. 1999. *The Wananga Capital Establishment Report.* Wellington: GP Publications, http://www.waitangi-tribunal.govt.nz/reports/viewchapter.asp? reportID=39E13093-2F4D-4971-ACA0-28E811572755&chapter=2, accessed 26 March 2012.

Walker, R. 1990. *Ka Whawhai Tonu Matou: Struggle Without End*. Auckland: Penguin.

Ward, A. 1999. *An Unsettled History: Treaty Claims in New Zealand Today*. Wellington: Bridget Williams Books.

PART III
Creating Ethical Leadership

7

Navigating the Tension between Global and Local: A Communication Perspective

Colleen Mills

Introduction

The twentieth century witnessed extraordinary changes in the way business was conducted. These changes largely came on the back of technological advances which created opportunities to do business in different ways (Aggarwal 2008) and global conflicts which, by thrusting countries and their peoples into alliances as well as armed opposition, expanded individuals' sense of their place and space in the world. The wide-ranging consequences of these changes have encouraged people to reposition themselves – both psychologically and in many cases physically – as global citizens. Furthermore, the technological advances and global conflicts have made the boundaries between societies increasingly permeable and supported rapid globalization of both labour markets and economies. This has introduced a raft of culturally related complexities that challenge organizations (Bachmann 2006: 722). The implications for management in the twenty-first century are huge. According to McLean and Lewis (2010: 30):

> The march of globalisation has turned conventional management on its head, making the management task a more difficult and challenging one. Moreover, as many business decisions have become globalised, managers' roles have become intertwined with issues of cultural adaptation and conflicts in communication exacerbated by cultural diversity.
>
> (Xie et al. 2008)

The twenty-first-century manager must operate in business and organizational environments that are simultaneously shaped by the homogenizing effects of new communication technologies, market conditions, international corporate structures (Gimenez 2002: 323) and national boundary permeability, along with the cultural diversity that accompanies these globalizing influences. In this chapter, I grapple with the question of how twenty-first-century managers can define their practice and navigate this tension between the increasingly standardized management practices that accompany globalization and the subjectivities that distinguish the local and personal worlds of those they encounter in their management roles. I do this by focusing on communication, which I define as the collaborative process of constructing shared meaning.[1] It is my contention that management is essentially a communication function, so such a communication perspective offers the manager the necessary insights and tools to understand and resolve this tension.

The chapter starts by considering some of the effects of globalization before addressing some often taken-for-granted and poorly understood features of communication, in particular that it is a highly contingent and collaborative process that, in my view, is best understood from a relational perspective. I use this discussion to develop a series of communication principles that encourage inclusive 'we-ness' thinking and authenticity. These principles are offered here as a framework for effectively addressing the tensions between global and local and the 'consensus–diversity dilemma' (Argote and McGrath 1993: 336), which Bachmann (2006: 721) somewhat euphemistically labels the 'melting pot or tossed salad' question, and which twenty-first-century managers increasingly must resolve. It is my view that the principles I present in this chapter can provide the philosophical foundations from which authentic and sustainable management practices can be synthesized.

---

1   There is no consensus on the definition of communication, and there is unlikely to ever be one (Miller 2005: 11). By defining communication as a collaborative process of creating shared meaning, I am being consistent with the constitutive model of communication, which proposes that communication is the primary social process whereby psychological, social, cultural and economic realities are created. For an excellent discussion, which contrasts this model with the simpler and more common everyday transmission model of communication that proposes communication as the consequence of a process of sending and receiving messages, see Craig (1999).

The Effects and Challenges of Globalization

Globalization, a term that sits very comfortably in our vocabulary, is widely understood in terms of its economic definition, which, according to Van Der Bly (2005: 875), is:

> *international economic integration that can be pursued through policies of 'openness', the liberalization of trade, investment and finance, leading to an 'open economy'.*[2]

However, Van Der Bly (2005: 876) also points out that from a sociological perspective, the meaning of globalization is more ambiguous. She observes that this ambiguity is founded in three dialectics: globalization as a process versus globalization as a condition; globalization as reality versus globalization as futurology and one-dimensional globalization versus multi-dimensional globalization. It seems that, according to Van Der Bly (2005: 876), a rather confusing literature has resulted from scholars' unwillingness to explicitly position their work in relation to these dialectics.

This confusion is less evident in the management literature, where globalization has largely been viewed from the macro-economic perspective, and this perspective has been used to explain why the tempo, substance and complexity of management have changed. As a consequence, there has been relatively little acknowledgement that at both the local and global level, the changes attributed to globalization have hardly been uniform. This means that claims about management beginning with 'globalization has ...' need to be approached with considerable caution. Certainly, markets and corporations have moved from being local to international and then to global, aided by technologies that have facilitated transnational and global communication, and this has produced convergence in some managerial practices (Barnet and Cavanaugh 1995), but in other respects convergence has not occurred (Hoecklin 1995: 4). It seems that while economically, globalization has created a single entity commonly referred to as the global market or marketplace (for example, Chadraba and O'Keefe 2011, Natale and Sora 2009), at the inter- and intra-organizational levels, where people experience business life, there is considerable plurality. While some organizations operate in an environment of 'business as usual' where 'usual' means the dominant local way of operating, others are faced with competing practices – a consequence of 'the local' and 'the global' ways operating concurrently (Hofstede 1997). This creates major

---

2   See, for example, Khor 2001: 7, World Bank 2002: 23.

challenges for those managers in these organizations who must navigate the interactional complexities created by such duality. They must reconcile local ways of interacting with those of their business partners who may be anywhere in the world. Furthermore, in addition to these external interactions, most large organizations today, especially the multinational corporations, have employees from, and in many cases in, a wide range of different cultural settings. Employees from different cultures will interpret the way an organization runs in different ways (Trompenaars 1993: 13). This means that competing values, beliefs and practices must be reconciled internally as well.

Not surprisingly, there is no single simple recipe for addressing and reconciling competing management practices. This is because the values, attitudes and beliefs upon which management practices are founded are often taken for granted and not readily available for critical evaluation. They are also aligned with and reinforced to varying degrees by the social, cultural, economic, bureaucratic and political environments in which they emerged. The consequence is that the interface between local management practices and practices that have emerged as Western companies have spread globally can be approached differently according to the setting and organization. For instance, Heenan and Perlmutter (1979) use the terms 'ethnocentric' and 'geocentric' to distinguish between two different types of corporate communication that can occur in multinationals. Ethnocentric multinational corporations have tight communication structures, low tolerance for difference and a high concentration of power with relatively small amounts of communication. In contrast, geocentric multinational corporations have a loose communication structure, high tolerance for difference and a low concentration of power, but large amounts of communication. Neither are necessarily consequences of a corporation succumbing to standardized or global ways of operating. In fact, it could be argued, the capacity of a geocentric approach to communication to accommodate competing ways of communicating would be of considerable advantage to companies that operate in global markets with diverse customers and workforces. Muratbekova-Touron (2008) provides a case study which supports this argument. She shows how adopting a geocentric operating style was necessary in a French multinational in order to cope with day-to-day operations in its Anglo-Saxon multinational acquisitions. The French corporation's approach, which was essentially the local French approach and fundamentally ethnocentric, was found to be ineffectual in these acquisitions, and this prompted a process of radical restructuring to establish a more geocentric way of operating that could accommodate the Anglo-Saxon way of operating. This case highlights the need to manage in ways that accommodate divergent organizational cultures rather than standardizing them, and provides empirical evidence consistent with the proposition that the geocentric approach, specifically in this case with regard to international human resource management (IHRM), allows the global integration–local adaptation dilemma to be resolved (Bartlett and Ghoshal 1988).

Such solutions encouraged Gimenez (2002: 324) to conclude that claims of conflation of local and global practices, which have been used as evidence of a global culture, may be largely 'an optical illusion'. Hoecklin (1995) supports this. She suggests that internationalization has merely produced superficial behavioural convergence. She cites research that suggests that instead of bringing a global way of operating to organizations that overrides local practices, internationalization has led to cultural differences being accentuated. For example, Hoecklin (1995: 4) describes a study of an American multinational which revealed that rather than embracing a standardized – that is, global – way of behaving, this company's French, German and British managers 'had values and behaviours *more French, more German and more British* than those of their compatriots working for local, domestic companies' (Laurent 1983; author's emphasis). Hoecklin (1995: 5) goes on to liken globalization to colonization in order to argue that local cultural resilience[3] rather than cultural replacement occurs in the face of both internally and externally imposed change. Certainly, globalization can precipitate localization,[4] which can take the form of some sort of anti-globalization backlash (Kim 2009: 46).

What this means is that in large multicultural organizations, one of the key challenges for managers is to identify competing practices, both internally and externally, and to establish an appropriate response. This response may entail developing standard company practices – that is, apply a consensus approach – but such practices can be difficult to institute and sustain. What we do know is that when different practices and the values that underpin them are not reconciled, problems occur. For instance, in a pilot study of foreign companies in Thailand, Sriussadaporn (2006) found communication problems between expatriate managers and their Thai employees that were clearly a result of unresolved differences in cultural values between the two parties. Overall, the problems were attributed by the managers to culturally different mentalities and concepts of accountability, task assignments, time management, language deficiencies and personal/work relationships (Sriussadaporn 2006: 333). For instance, according to the German, Hungarian and American expatriate

---

3   This refers to the ability of cultural practices to persist in the face of alternative practices. The most resilient cultures are able to sustain their values, beliefs and practices in the face of actions designed to modify or replace them (that is, cultural replacement).

4   This is the process of favouring local values, beliefs and practices over foreign ones.

managers, their Thai employees lacked accountability. This was displayed in the way they did not disclose important personal information to their managers and did not speak up about things that should be done. The expatriate managers attributed this lack of accountability to an inability of Thai employees to think proactively, analytically and systematically. However, the Thai managers, while recognizing this issue of accountability, attributed it to the inexperience of young Thai employees and their culturally different way of prioritizing compared to their expatriate managers. Sriussadaporn (2006: 334), on the other hand, suggests such differences can be attributed to Thai cultural communicative norms such as conflict avoidance, emotional control and politeness.

The same study found that Japanese, German, Hungarian and American expatriates assumed that Thai employees' unwillingness to seek help or to say that they could not do a task or give a task completion time were signs of a lack of commitment to work tasks. In contrast, the Thai managers attributed these communication patterns to the cultural value of *kreng jai*,[5] which leads Thai people to rarely refuse to undertake tasks requested by their managers. This value means that Thai workers have trouble expressing themselves to their managers even when they are uncertain they can complete a task.

Such research shows us that competing practices are not only a challenge because of the conflict they can cause, but also because any solutions are complicated by the different ways individuals and cultural groups account for the cause of such practices. Clearly, we should not lose sight of the fact that the ways people account for the behaviour of others (that is, their attributions) are informed by culturally based values too.

It could be argued such challenges would be less significant in local companies that do not have operations in any other country. On the surface, this may be true, as such companies would be able to be more ethnocentric than multinationals in their practices, given that they are likely to experience less pressure to look beyond local social mores and management traditions. However, in reality, even when operations are localized, twenty-first-century companies are confronted with consumer and employment markets that are increasingly culturally heterogeneous as a result of rising immigration, tourism and the international connectivity available through the Internet and new media. Such rising heterogeneity presents challenges to 'the local way', which in many multicultural societies has always been contested and

---

5   *Kreng jai* refers to Thai people's reluctance to upset another by 'refusing requests, accepting
     assistance, showing disagreement, giving direct criticism, challenging authority or confronting
     a conflict situation' (Sriussadaporn 2006: 343).

pluralistic at some level. Current globalization[6] has simply added the possibility of further cultural diversity, more variable cultural dynamics and a higher speed and saturation of cultural development to the situations managers have always had to navigate. In particular, it has heightened the challenges faced by those managers endeavouring to sustain the consensus approach to management that characterizes ethnocentric corporations.

It is becoming increasingly clear that if an organization wants to be successful, it cannot afford to overlook the opportunities and challenges presented by the cultural diversity in both its local employment market and its external environment. As Lewis notes:

> *Cultural diversity is not something that is going to go away tomorrow, enabling us to plan our strategies on the assumption of mutual understanding. It is in itself a phenomenon with its own riches, the exploration of which could yield incalculable benefits for us, both in terms of wider vision and more profitable policies and activity.*
>
> *(Lewis 1999: 2)*

To grapple successfully with cultural diversity's opportunities and challenges, however, requires knowledge of how cultures vary, as it cannot be assumed that managerial practices grounded in the values and beliefs of one cultural perspective can be fairly applied to people operating from another (Hoecklin 1995: 8–9, Trompenaars 1993: 4–5). Managers need to have the cultural knowledge necessary to appreciate other perspectives and how these shape behaviour, expectations and the way behaviour is interpreted. Otherwise, according to Gudykunst and Kim (1997: 41), if we use our culturally based habitual ways of thinking and behaving to guide our behaviour in new situations (for example, in situations involving people from unfamiliar cultures), our ability to appreciate the behavioural choices available is constrained. They propose effective intercultural communication requires not only an awareness of other perspectives, but also an openness to new information and the ability to create new and specific categories to accommodate this information. These are the characteristics that Langer (1989) uses to define 'mindfulness'. According to Gudykunst and Kim (1997: 42–3), when people are mindful of the process of communication in an intercultural setting, actively seek to understand how others are interpreting the situation and have the skills to seek this understanding and appropriately categorize it, then communication

---

6   Globalization is not a new phenomenon. History shows us that human society has experienced repeated waves of globalization.

effectiveness is enhanced. The following section explores some of the helpful cultural frameworks which can be used to frame this mindfulness.

Dimensions of Cultural Diversity

Many scholars have sought to delineate the dimensions across which the behaviour of cultural groups varies (for example, Gudykunst and Kim 1997, Hall 1976, Hofstede 1980, Hofstede 1984, House et al. 2004, Lewis 1999, Schwartz 1999, Ting-Toomey 1988, Ting-Toomey and Kurogi 1998, Triandis 1994, Triandis 2000, Trompenaars 1993). Without doubt, the most influential has been Hofstede (1980, 1997, 2005), whose study of employees across the large multinational IBM gave rise to a framework of work-related values,[7] with each value presented as a continuum between two opposite poles. These bipolar value dimensions are briefly described in Table 7.1.

Table 7.1   **Summary of Hofstede's cultural dimensions**[8]

Dimension	Explanation
Individualism–collectivism	This refers to the degree to which personal goals prevail over collective goals. In individualistic cultures, personal goals have priority over those of the in-group. In collectivistic cultures, group goals have primacy, with interdependence being valued over independence.
Uncertainty avoidance	This refers to the tendency to avoid ambiguity and uncertainty. Cultural groups with high uncertainty avoidance have a greater dependence on rules and structure than those with low uncertainty avoidance.
Power distance	This refers to the degree to which members of a cultural group accept that power is distributed unevenly. Status and power differences are accepted much more in a cultural setting with high power distance than one with a low power distance.
Masculinity–femininity	Masculinity is characterized by overt signs of power and status and direct goal-seeking communication, while femininity is characterized by more modesty and less direct, face-saving communication.
Long–short-term orientation	A long-term orientation is characterized by values of persistence and personal adaptability, ordering relationships by status, thrift and having a sense of shame: values that are oriented towards the future. In contrast, the short-term orientation is characterized by a desire for quick results, personal steadiness and stability, saving face, respect for tradition, spending and the reciprocation of greetings, favours and gifts: all values that are oriented towards the present and the past.

7   Initially, Hofstede (1984) identified four value dimensions. These were subsequently extended to five. The fifth dimension is attributed in the first instance to Michael Harris Bond and his associates.

8   For the story of the development and subsequent evolution of these dimensions, see Minkov and Hofstede (2011).

While both ends of each dimension exist to some extent in all cultural groups, it seems that many cultural groups tend to favour one end of each continuum over the other (for example, Chinese culture typically has a much stronger long-term focus than New Zealand's dominant *Pakeha*[9] culture). Such comparisons of national cultures reveal that dominant Western societies, such as the United States, Britain and Germany, are distinctively different from rising economic and political powers such as India, China and Korea. These Western cultures are strongly individualistic, which, according to intercultural communication scholar Ting-Toomey (1988), means they exhibit direct and self-focused interactional strategies that encourage confrontation, domination and compromise. However, less individualistic societies, like India, China and Korea, show a preference for less direct approaches to conflict, such as obliging the other party or avoiding conflict altogether. Given this contrast, it is easy to see how, at a societal level, Western operating styles might cause problems for Western companies when interacting with groups from India, China and Korea.

How do twenty-first-century managers accommodate such polarities operationally, both internally and in their dealings with customers, suppliers, government agencies and other external stakeholders? The answer to this question is complicated by the fact that value-based frameworks such as Hofstede's are focused at the national level, which means that they do not provide a totally reliable basis for comparing the cultural differences at the level of the individual (Leung et al. 2002: 287, Bond et al. 2004: 177–8), with the possible exception of Hofstede's individualism–collectivism dimension, which applies at both the cultural and individual level (Falkheimer and Heide 2006: 183).

Edward T. Hall's (1976) work, with its focus on communication, provides a useful way of linking individual behaviour to cultural dimensions. He proposes that communication can be understood by considering the code (that is, the words) employed, the interactional context (that is, the relationships, roles and rules of engagement) and the meaning that the interaction has for interactants (Baldwin, Perry and Moffitt 2004: 159). Individuals' cultural experiences shape the degree to which they privilege context versus code. In what Hall calls 'high-context' cultures, individuals give precedence to meanings they infer from the relationships, roles and rules of engagement (that is, context) associated with a situation. In contrast, in a 'low-context' culture, relatively more meaning is inferred from the spoken words (that is, the coded message). According to

---

9   *Pakeha* is a term used by Maori, the indigenous people of New Zealand, to refer to the European settlers and their descendants. It is commonly used by both Maori and non-Maori.

Ting-Toomey (1988, Ting-Toomey and Kurogi 1998), individualistic cultures and low-context communication styles go hand in hand, as do collectivistic cultures and high-context communication. Ting-Toomey (1988) predicts that people from individualistic cultures will have a different focus, mode of operation, face needs and preferred conflict style compared with people from collectivistic cultures. She suggests that people from individualistic cultures will be more likely to focus on their own needs as opposed to other people's needs, to use a direct communication strategy, to have a need for autonomy (a negative face dimension) and to exhibit a dominating or collaborating conflict management style (Baldwin, Perry and Moffitt 2004: 162). This supports the proposition that individualism–collectivism, which in the first instance is a cultural dimension, does gain expression in how individuals interact.

Regardless of the extent to which cultural differences impact on individual behaviour, there is no doubt that managers must work with considerable diversity, both in their internal and external activities, as a result of globalization and its associated effects. To do this requires a sound management philosophy, one that informs management practices in ways that support ethical, equitable and sustainable processes and outcomes. The following section makes a case for embracing a management philosophy that is founded on the assumption that management is essentially a communication process.

Management: A Highly Contingent Communication Process

Management is ultimately about the co-ordination of human and physical resources in order to achieve goals (Inkson and Kolb 2000: 6), regardless of whether these goals are societal, business or personal. Irrespective of where management occurs or what is being managed, this co-ordination is a social process. This means that communication is inevitably at the heart of management, as it is both the means and a consequence of co-ordinated social action, and as such is a fundamental part of organizational life (Mills 2009: 370).

While it would be convenient to have standard ways of communicating, even in most routine organizational or business situations, the reality is that how people communicate is contingent upon who is interacting, why they are communicating, the resources they have available to engage with each other, and the physical, social and psychological context in which this engagement is occurring. In other words, the nature of communication is contingent upon the 'who', 'why', 'how' and 'where' of the situation.

This gives all communication a degree of subjectivity which must be managed in order to optimize the likelihood of achieving acceptable outcomes. Effective communication management and management in general require recognizing the fundamentally contingent nature of communication and possessing the knowledge and skills to anticipate this subjectivity and work with it. The enormity of what this requires in practice can only be appreciated if we stop to consider the myriad different dimensions that contribute to the 'who', 'why', 'how' and 'where' of communication. No one can ever expect to acquire all the necessary knowledge and skills to anticipate and operate effectively in every communication situation. What is achievable, though, is an appreciation that communication is inevitably a subjective process, and a desire to translate this appreciation into constructive action. Thus, it can be argued, the principle that all communication is contingent is a good starting point from which to derive a foundation for authentic and sustainable management principles in an increasingly global world.

Our communication practices are grounded in the cultural settings in which they emerged and continue to be used. Little wonder, then, that much has been written on the particular communication practices that prevail in different cultures – for example, Lewis (1999) provides an excellent guide for intercultural managers. These cultural differences in communication practice have been theorized by a wide range of scholars. Of particular prominence is Hall's (1976) theory of high- and low-context communication mentioned earlier in this chapter, which can be used to differentiate between the ways communication occurs in different cultural settings. Hall (1976) proposes that high-context communication is characterized by a high level of information being coded in the elements of the non-verbal context or contained within the interactants, while low-context communication is characterized by considerably more information being coded in the linguistic code and a much lower reliance on tacit information. This means that low-context communication is more explicit, direct and speaker-centred. Much less is left for the receiver to infer. When people interact with others who do not approach communication with the same level of contextual sensitivity, the risk of miscommunication and conflict is high. For example, it is very easy for those who rely heavily on the spoken code to ignore unspoken protocols and symbolic acts such as how a business delegation is constituted or how a location is chosen for a meeting. In high-context cultures like Japan, these are likely to have been decided with careful consideration of culturally based norms. The choices made would be laced with meanings that could go unnoticed in a society where low-context communication is the norm, or merely acknowledged as others' ways of doing things. Conversely, the heavy reliance on explicit verbalization that typically prevails in low-context societies could be perceived as condescending in a high-context society (Hall, cited in Korac-Kakabadse et al. 2001: 7–8).

The globalization of the employment market and economies has brought 'others' from high- and low-context cultures to 'us' at both the corporate and personal levels, and has added considerably more complexity to the already subjective nature of communication. Managers are increasingly confronted with the need to be much more culturally aware and cross-culturally competent than previously because increasingly, the 'others' are sufficiently different in terms of their communication style to make it impossible to anticipate their behaviour accurately. This inability to accurately predict another person's behaviour is the basis of the discomfort we experience when communicating with strangers (Gudykunst and Kim 1997: 32).

Scholars such as Hofstede (1980, 1997), Trompenaars (1993), Gudykunst and Kim (1997) and Hall (1976) alert us to ways of thinking about cultural differences that provide a foundation for addressing behavioural diversity. However, because not all people from a particular culture think or behave in the same way, these need to be used in conjunction with data on particular individuals' behaviour if they are to be useful. As Treven, Mulej and Lynn (2008: 28) note: 'Sometimes there is greater variation within single cultures than across cultures.' The increased population mobility of modern times means that this observation is becoming even more valid. More than ever before, people are exposed to the world beyond their doorstep, either directly through travel, overseas education and employment opportunities, or virtually through the plethora of media[10] available. Compatriots are becoming increasingly diverse in terms of their cultural values and experiences and how these shape their self-identities, frames of reference and behaviours. This means that while we must recognize that national cultures shape how managers and individuals generally conceptualize 'human nature, relationships to nature, work, time, relationships, space and language' (Gopalan and Thomson 2003: 313), we cannot afford to base management decisions upon cultural stereotypes. Every individual's behaviour will be shaped by their unique mix of cultural values and experiences. Managers need to have strategies for gathering data on this behavioural diversity at the level of the individual so that they can be 'other'-

---

10 Here I am referring to all types of media but need to acknowledge that new media, especially social media such as Facebook, have contributed significantly to our increased ability to experience other worlds beyond our doorstep without physically venturing into them.

or audience-centred – a key prerequisite for creating constructive communication environments.

Gathering feedback through regular communication audits (Hargie and Tourish 2009: xv–xvi) is one way to ensure that the subjectivities of individuals' predispositions and preferences can be detected. Communication audits involve actively and systematically soliciting information about communication practices. They can be carried out in a variety of ways, including questionnaires, interviews and focus groups. When done well, such audits allow managers to tap into the experiences of individuals and detect the level of diversity that exists in terms of their communication expectations, preferences and experiences. The collected data allow managers to measure how cohesive and constructive the communication environment they are managing is.

Cohesiveness – that sense of togetherness or 'we-ness' we experience in groups that are working well together – provides the foundation for a sense of being an insider and a member of a community. As such, it is an important dimension in the creation of constructive communication environments. The following section puts forward the case for focusing on cohesiveness and the sense of solidarity it engenders in order to create authentic and sustainable management practices.

Moving from 'Other' to 'Us' and Outsider to Insider

One of our most 'hard-wired' approaches to understanding our world is the use of binary oppositions. We understand a phenomenon by contrasting it with what it is not. Hot is understood by contrasting it with cold, light with dark, small with large, and so on. Social cognition is no different. Psychologists confirm that we define ourselves by making social comparisons (Smith, Bond and Kağçibaşi 2006: 222) between the groups we belong to and those we do not (that is, our social identity), and between ourselves and other individuals. We identify ourselves by stressing what we are opposed to (Burke 1973) and the groups we do not belong to (Abrams and Hogg 1990, Hogg and Abrams 1988, Tajfel and Turner 1986). What is more, we do this in a way which enhances our positive self-regard (Augoustinos, Walker and Donaghue 2009: 31). When taken to the extreme, we create strongly negative profiles for members of groups we do not belong to. This spawns stereotypes which, when negative and resistant to contrary information, provide the foundations for prejudice and discrimination.

Group prejudice is not a sound basis for constructive communication management, or management in general. It allows stereotypes rather than situations and person-specific information to provide the basis for social action. Not surprisingly, the results are frequently unfortunate. A much more constructive strategy is to realize that we are all outsiders (that is, a member of someone else's out-groups) in some circumstances. When we reflect on our own experiences of being confined to an out-group, we can start to appreciate the consequences of placing others in the 'outsider' category. When this appreciation breeds empathy, we have a valuable foundation for managing communication with people we judge to be different from ourselves (Natale and Sora 2009). No one likes to be considered an outsider or to be marginalized, so reflecting on what this feels like helps us to appreciate the desirability of behaving inclusively. An inclusive orientation encourages actions that facilitate both our own and others' transitions from outsider to insider, and is fundamental to developing sustainable positive relationships and operating in a changing global environment: it fosters rapport (Senseing 2009). Rapport is important in business as it is positively linked to customer satisfaction and word of mouth in the professional services context (Macintosh 2009).

Furthermore, rapport is the lifeblood of fulfilling relationships. Such relationships can, in turn, be conceived to be the essence of our sense of positive self-regard and the lifeblood of co-ordinated action and sustainable organizations (Gergen 2009). Instead of conceiving of organizations as collections of individuals applying individual skills, Gergen (2009) proposes that we should reconceptualize organizations as being a consequence of relational processes:

> It is through relational coordination that the organization comes to life. Organizations live or die in the swarm of daily interchange – in complimenting and criticizing, passing and retaining information, smiling and frowning, asking and answering, demanding and resisting, controlling and consenting.
>
> (Gergen 2009: 312)

Managers and the processes they manage are intrinsically communicative, so managerial effectiveness – if we accept Gergen's view – is measured in terms of the quality of the relationships that are created by and supportive of this communication. When we communicate in ways that move out-group members into our in-groups, this generates a sense of shared identity –

the basis of inclusiveness – which arguably increases the likelihood of rapport and understanding.

This relational perspective can be applied at a more macro level to guide how we understand and operate at an organizational, cultural and societal level. As Gergen notes:

> A relational perspective invites us to expand our vision. It is not the well-being of single organizations that is at stake, but the broader relational flows that sustain and vitalize not only our cultures, but the conditions of global existence generally. The challenge, then, is to facilitate the co-active process in which the very borders between inside and outside are blurred.
>
> (Gergen 2009: 345)

When an organization, culture or society builds relationships that allow outsiders' voices to come inside, be heard and integrated, then the foundation for the 'them and us' dichotomy is weakened because differences can be explained and mutual understanding enhanced. In other words, 'they' can be appreciated and collective discourses, based on a sense of 'we' and 'us', can emerge – see Mills (2006) for a strategy for doing this in academe.

Communication: A Process of Collaboratively Creating Shared Meaning

One of the most persistent misconceptions about communication, especially management communication, is that it is a one-way dissemination process that simply involves passing and receiving messages between individuals or collectives (Crossman, Bordia and Mills 2011: 267). This stems from the early days of communication theory, when the Shannon–Weaver transmission model (Weaver and Shannon 1963) prevailed as the primary way in which communication was conceived. Communication theory has moved a long way since then, but the 'sender, receiver, channel, message encoding and decoding' thinking at the heart of the Shannon–Weaver model is still used extensively to structure corporate thinking about communication and communication management. Much miscommunication and many poor business outcomes can be attributed to this mechanistic and simplistic way of representing what is, in reality, a dynamic and complex social process. Reducing communication to a process of passing messages coded by a sender to a receiver who then decodes the encoded message tends to direct the focus away from the communicating parties and the subjectivities they bring to bear on the process in order to collaborate in creating mutual understanding. Instead, it focuses attention on the messages that are being passed between the parties and the mechanisms for achieving this exchange. This is despite the fact that it is not until meaning is created in response to a message that communication can be said to have occurred.

The extant literature is littered with case studies addressing instances where there has been a failure to ensure that a mutually agreed meaning has been achieved and the consequences of these failures. The advent of a range of new media (for example, email, social networking sites, texting and weblogs) which enhance our ability to disseminate messages to ever wider and often unknown audiences is reinforcing this dissemination thinking by making us focus even more strongly on messages and mechanisms for sending them. Calls to ensure that feedback is gained to establish whether the meaning given to a message by its recipients is consistent with the sender's intended meaning are more salient than ever given the dissemination possibilities such technologies present. It seems that our enthusiasm for the carrying capacity and superficial connectivity new media provide is obscuring the costs incurred by not being readily able to appreciate the subjectivities of our audiences and the dangers of not being present to assess impacts and confirm shared meaning. Brewer (2010) reports on a multi-case study of the factors virtual workers consider to cause miscommunication in international virtual workplaces. Respondents were most likely to attribute miscommunication to (in order) language, technology, information sharing and culture. They 'seldom shifted into metacommunicative mode to consider how such factors as ethos, rank and context might be contributing to day-to-day problems' (Brewer 2010: 343). These findings suggest a predisposition to focus on message content (for example, lack of detail, missing information), technology and stereotypical cultural behaviours to explain miscommunication in the virtual workplace, rather than personal communication preferences and the nature of social engagement and how these impact on the effective co-construction of meaning. The participants did not mention the fundamental building blocks of relationship development that encourage rapport and relationship-building. Nor did they appreciate the layers of collaboration and contextual interplays that come together to create a communication event and (hopefully) shared meaning. The following section provides an explanation for why this can happen.

Meaning Is In People, Not Messages

The unquestioned acceptance of the dissemination model of communication predisposes people to talk about communication (and attribute miscommunication) in terms of messages rather than shared meaning (Miller 2005: 12). Messages, however, are merely stimuli that can prompt attention and meaning-making activity in others, but the precise nature of the resultant attention and meaning is never certain. This is because both the attention generated and the meaning that is ascribed to a message are products of many things, most notably, according to Schulz von Thun (1981), the nature of the message, the nature of the relationship between communicating parties, the sort of appeal the receiver infers from the message and what the sender discloses to the receiver about him or herself in the process of transmitting the message. In other words, it is what people do in response to messages and the relational context in which they find themselves rather than just the messages themselves that determine meaning.

To influence the meaning-making process of others is, arguably, fundamental to the process of management. It requires self-awareness on the part of the manager, as well as audience and relationship knowledge – not simply an appreciation of what it is that needs to be said (the message). This is because the process of meaning-making is inevitably a social process that happens in the relationship created between interacting parties (Weick 1995, Gergen 2009). When these interacting parties have little knowledge of themselves and/or the others involved, then achieving effective communication is at best a matter of chance, and at worst likely to be problematic. The absence of 'self' and 'other' knowledge predisposes interactants to rely on assumptions about the other parties and the nature of the relationships between parties. These assumptions are typically self- and in-group-referenced. If the interacting parties do not share a common cultural background, then interaction is much harder to understand and manage, as such assumptions may well be inappropriate.

Scholars who examine intercultural communication stress the need for mutual understanding, but emphasize different elements that need to be understood and reconciled. Trompenaars (1993), for example, proposes that there are five value orientations that shape behaviour when relating to others: (1) the extent to which rules prevail over relationships; (2) the degree to which the group is valued over the individual; (3) the range of feelings that are expressed; (4) the range of involvement that is appropriate, and (5) how status is ascribed. The particular positions of organizational leaders and employees in relation to these value orientations will shape an organization's culture (Trompenaars 1993: 138) and determine whether its ways of operating are at odds with or consistent with the prevailing societal culture in which it is operating.

Trompenaars (1993) intersects two bipolar dimensions to define a four-quadrant typology of corporate cultures: equality–hierarchy and person orientation–task orientations. The four corporate cultures created (that is, the family, the Eiffel Tower, the guided missile and the incubator) can all be distinguished in terms of the relationship between employees, attitude to authority, ways of thinking and learning, attitudes to people, ways of changing, ways of motivating and rewarding, and approaches to criticism and conflict resolution. When global meets local, as is the case in multi-national companies and local companies with culturally diverse workforces, the challenge is to reconcile differences between corporate culture and the prevailing local culture in terms of these dimensions. This is not simple. Even when employee relationships, attitudes to authority and reward systems seem consistent, their meaning to individuals from different cultures can vary considerably (Hoecklin 1995: 3). At some level, there will always be diversity. What is more, this diversity – cultural or otherwise – is not a static condition. It is highly dynamic.

What we can take from all this is that managers are confronted with diverse and dynamic ways of thinking and behaving that shape organizational life in complicated ways that are obscured if communication, which is at the heart of organized activity, is simply treated as an exchange of messages. An understanding of oneself and others and a commitment to understanding both and forging inclusive relationships need to underpin managerial behaviour if it is to be effective in an age where local and global constantly interact.

Authentic Communication: The Overarching Goal of Effective Communication

In recent times, communication thinking and the quest for principles of effective communication have spawned a range of theoretical perspectives. Among these are perspectives that advocate two-way dialogic and symmetric communication between parties. In so doing, they emphasize the interdependence between organizations and their communities and provide the potential for corporate communication to be community-building and communitarian. Such perspectives propose that organizations should be relationship-oriented and behave as responsible members of their communities. These theoretical perspectives converge around and provide the theoretical underpinning for the ten principles of authenticity in communication proposed and examined by Bishop (2006). Communication should be truthful, consistent, comprehensive, receptive to feedback, clear, caring, accessible, fundamental, relevant and timely. The dilemma in settings characterized by marked levels of diversity is that these principles are not uniformly understood. They are open to different interpretations. What may be considered clear in one cultural setting, for example, may be far from clear in another setting. There is the whole issue of tacit knowledge, expectations and interpretive frameworks rooted in the beliefs, assumptions and norms that constitute the essence of culture (Bachmann 2006: 724). People cannot be assumed to bring the same frames of reference to a particular collaboration. For such a set of principles to be of any value, they need to be interpreted and the implications for communication in a given situation need to be made explicit. They need to be made sense of in a way that facilitates mutual understanding so that they can be enacted appropriately. This highlights the importance of those in management and leadership positions actively taking on sense-giving (Gioia and Chittipeddi 1991: 442)[11] roles – that is, taking responsibility for helping subordinates to make common sense of principles of engagement such as Bishop's (2006) principles. Thayer suggests:

> *A leader at work is one who gives others a different form, a different 'face', in the same way that a painter or sculptor or poet gives those who follow him (or her) a different way of 'seeing' – and therefore saying and doing and knowing in the world …. The leader is a sense-giver.*
>
> *(Thayer 1988: 250–54)*

Cultural diversity at all levels (local, international and global) brings with it a bounty of resources and opportunities, but also challenges that are most clearly manifested in multicultural workgroups. Here, different perspectives and understandings rub up against each other and need to be integrated in order to allow productive collaborations to occur. A measure of consensus is needed on what is likely to work (Bachmann 2006: 722), but at the same time, the benefits diversity brings need to be preserved. This tension is referred to as the 'diversity–consensus dilemma' (Argote and McGrath 1993: 336), the 'accuracy–cohesion trade-off' (Weick 1987: 23) or the 'melting pot or tossed salad' question (Bachmann 2006: 721). A communication perspective suggests that managers and leaders should take responsibility for creating conversations that make

---

11 Gioia and Chittipeddi (1991: 442) define sense-giving as the 'process of attempting to influence sensemaking and meaning construction of others towards a preferred redefinition of organizational reality'.

sense of this tension, particularly in ways that allow a diversity–consensus balance to be achieved that satisfies the contingencies of specific situations. It is my view that there are some fundamental communication principles that provide a valuable underpinning for this sense-giving process. I have been introducing these principles, which grapple more specifically with diversity than those proposed by Bishop, in various ways throughout this chapter. I will now bring them together and summarize them in the following section.

Resolving the Tension between Local and Global

We now have the basis for a framework to manage the tension between local and global in contemporary business which is grounded in principles derived from an understanding of the nature of communication. The features of this framework are given in Table 7.2.

Table 7.2   **Communication-based principles for effective contemporary management**

Principle	Explanation
Be data-driven and mindful	When people are data-driven, their reliance on assumptions and stereotypes gives way to empirically supported conclusions, which provide a much more reliable basis for meaning-making. Data about others are best gathered firsthand in the 'act' of interaction, which requires participants to be mindful (that is, present) and to attend to the contingencies and processes of mutual meaning-creation.
Be authentic	Bishop (2006) proposes that authentic communication should be truthful, consistent, comprehensive, receptive to feedback, clear, caring, accessible, fundamental, relevant and timely. However, what these principles mean in practice may vary in different cultural settings. What is also needed is a sense of oneself and others so that these principles can be applied in ways that take into account the people communicating and the relationships between them.
Enact a meaning rather than message orientation	This involves moving away from a dissemination model of communication and embracing a constitutive model. Such a shift enhances the likelihood of achieving constructive communication rather than just information dissemination.
Think relationally	When the focus is on creating mutual understanding, the relationship rather than the individual has pre-eminence. Management can be viewed both as a process of nurturing relationships and a consequence of them.
See diversity as the norm	Everyone is unique at some level. Constructive relationships and effective communication require this diversity to be accepted, understood and responded to in a way that generates rapport and a sense of inclusion ('we-ness').

Recognize that all social action is contingent	Social action is dialectically related to the psychological, social and physical circumstances in which it occurs. It changes according to these circumstances, and in turn shapes them.
Be responsive and flexible	The contingent and dynamic nature of social activity means that we need to be flexible. Standardized responses limit the degree to which we can respond to contingencies and continuous change.
See management as a sense-giving role	Effective management is about well-co-ordinated action. This can only be achieved when the diversity–consensus dilemma is resolved. Managers are responsible for ensuring a common sense emerges, either by shaping the relationships in which sense is made or by providing the sense that allows this resolution to occur.

If these principles were used to inform managerial practice, then local and global ways of operating could become more receptive to, informed about and, hopefully, appreciative of each other. If, as suggested, diversity were seen as inevitable and something all individuals contribute to as a consequence of their own uniqueness rather than something 'others' have that needs to be confronted, controlled or overcome, then this receptivity would be enhanced and constructive. Most importantly, if diversity is uncoupled from group and cultural stereotypes, then communication and the personal relationships and circumstances in which it occurs could take centre stage. With communication competence as the ultimate goal, our propensity to focus on message-sharing would be supplanted by the pursuit of shared meaning and the creation of a sense of cohesion – or, in other words, 'we-ness'.

Applying a relational perspective would promote a shift from thinking about management in terms of inter-group (for example, national cultural groups) processes to thinking about inter-individual interaction. At the inter-individual level, stereotypes would have less influence as interaction at this level occurs much more on the basis of the interactants' personal qualities rather than their social identities (Augoustinos, Walker and Donaghue 2009: 26), so the basis for discrimination (that is, actions founded on social group prejudices) would be eroded. The key point is that a relational approach such as that described here (re-)locates diversity at an individual level rather than a cultural level. This could be construed as consistent with an individualistic orientation, but in fact, operationally it sits most comfortably with a more collectivistic world view – one where interconnectivity and collective action are valued over individual action and achievement (Hofstede 1997: 50).

The communication perspective of the challenges of twenty-first-century management presented in this chapter leads us to reflect on the role of relationships and what Gergen (2009) terms 'relational being'. Gergen (2009) proposes that a sustainable future, both locally and globally, requires placing relationships at the forefront of our thinking and practices. Relationships emerge over time and require ongoing attention to survive. A relational perspective also encourages a longer-term view of the consequences of co-ordinated action, and in so doing improves the chances of business sustainability. This applies at both intra- and inter-organizational levels. Not only will the application of the communication principles addressed in this chapter enhance the likelihood of authentic and sustainable inter-organizational processes, by managing intra-organizational processes from a relational rather than resource or message perspective employees are more likely to feel included, understood and a valued part of their organization.

Conclusion

In this chapter I have explored challenges to contemporary management posed by globalization from a communication management perspective and proposed a set of core communication principles that, I argue, are well-placed to provide the philosophical foundations from which authentic and sustainable management practices can be synthesized. I believe that practices grounded on these communication principles and a commitment to inclusiveness would enable twenty-first-century managers to grapple in a constructive way with the dynamic tension between the homogenizing effects of globalization, increased diversity and reactive localization they are likely to encounter. It has not been my intention to deny the all-pervasive and often unconscious influence of culture and cultural values, but by proposing that management is ultimately a communication process that occurs between individuals, my intention has been to (re-)locate management in the space created by interpersonal interaction – in the realm of relationships. The result is a case for taking a relational rather than the more prevalent information dissemination approach to management communication in order to navigate the consensus–diversity dilemma that poses increasingly complex and demanding challenges for the twenty-first century manager.

References

Abrams, D. and Hogg, M.A. (eds) 1990. *Social Identity Theory: Constructive and Critical Advances*. Hemel Hempstead: Harvester Wheatsheaf.

Aggarwal, R. 2008. 'Globalization of the world economy: Implications for the business school'. *American Journal of Business*, 23(2), 5–12.

Argote, L. and McGrath, J.E. 1993. 'Group processes in organizations: Continuity and change', in *International Review of Industrial and Organizational Psychology*, ed. C.L. Cooper and T.I. Robertson. Oxford: Wiley & Sons, 333–89.

Augoustinos, M., Walker I. and Donaghue, N. 2009. *Social Cognition: An Integrated Introduction*. London: Sage.

Bachmann, A.S. 2006. 'Melting pot or tossed salad? Implications for designing effective multicultural workgroups'. *Management International Review*, 26(6), 721–47.

Baldwin, J.R., Perry, S.D. and Moffitt, M.A. 2004. *Communication Theories for Everyday Life*. Boston, MA: Pearson.

Barnet, R.J. and Cavanaugh, J. 1995. *Global Dreams: Imperial Corporations and the New World Order*. New York: Simon and Schuster.

Bartlett, C.A. and Ghoshal, S. 1988. 'Organizing for worldwide effectiveness: The transnational solution'. *California Management Review*, 31(1), 54–75.

Bishop, B. 2006. 'Theory and practice converge: A proposed set of corporate communication principles'. *Corporate Communications: An International Journal*, 11(3), 214–31.

Bond, M.H., Leung, K., Au, A., Tong, K-K. and Chemonges-Nielson, Z. 2004. 'Combining social axioms with values in predicting social behaviours'. *European Journal of Personality*, 18, 177–91.

Brewer, P.E. 2010. 'Miscommunication in international virtual workplaces: A report on a multicase study'. *IEEE Transactions on Professional Communication*, 53(4), 329–45.

Burke, K. 1973. 'The rhetorical situation', in *Communication: Ethical and Moral Issues*, ed. L. Thayer. New York: Gordon and Breach, 263–75.

Chadraba, P.G. and O'Keefe, R.D. 2011. 'Human resources: Interculturation as an asset in the global marketplace'. *Journal of International Business and Cultural Studies*, 4(1), 1–13.

Craig, R.T. 1999. 'Communication theory as a field'. *Communication Theory*, 9(2), 119–61.

Crossman, J., Bordia, S. and Mills, C.E. 2011. *Business Communication for the Global Age*. Sydney: McGraw-Hill.

Falkheimer, J. and Heide, M. 2006. 'Multicultural crisis communication: Towards a social constructionist perspective'. *Journal of Contingencies and Crisis Management*, 14(4), 180–89.

Gergen, K.J. 2009. *Relational Being: Beyond Self and Community*. New York: Oxford University Press.

Gimenez, J.C. 2002. 'New media and conflicting realities in multinational corporate communication: A case study'. *International Review of Applied Linguistics in Language Teaching*, 40(4), 323–43.

Gioia, D. and Chittipeddi, K. 1991. 'Sensemaking and sensegiving in strategic change initiation'. *Strategic Management Journal*, 12, 433–48.

Gopalan, S. and Thomson, N. 2003. 'Information searching behaviours and the attribution process of cross-national managers: A conceptual framework'. *Teaching Business Ethics*, 7(3), 313–28.

Gudykunst W.B. and Kim, Y.Y. 1997. *Communicating with Strangers: An Approach to Intercultural Communication*. 3rd edn, Boston, MA: McGraw-Hill.

Hall, E.T. 1976. *Beyond Culture*. New York: Doubleday.

Hargie, O. and Tourish, D. (eds) 2009. *Auditing Organizational Communication: A Handbook of Research, Theory and Practice*. London: Routledge.

Heenan, D.A. and Perlmutter, H.V. 1979. *Multinational Organization Development*. Reading: Addison-Wesley.

Hoecklin, L. 1995. *Managing Cultural Differences: Strategies for Competitive Advantage*. Wokingham: Addison-Wesley.

Hofstede, G. 1980. *Culture's Consequences: International Differences in Work-related Values*. Beverly Hills, CA: Sage.

Hofstede, G. 1984. *Culture's Consequences: International Differences in Work-related Values*. Abridged version, Beverly Hills, CA: Sage.

Hofstede, G. 1997. *Cultures and Organizations: Software of the Mind*. London: McGraw-Hill.

Hofstede, G. 2005. *Cultures and Organizations: Software of the Mind*. Revised and expanded 2nd edn, New York: McGraw-Hill.

Hogg, M.A. and Abrams, D. 1988. *Social Identifications: A Social Psychology of Intergroup Relations and Group Processes*. London: Routledge.

House, R., Hanges, P., Javidan, M., Dorfman, P. and Gupta, V. (eds). 2004. *Culture, Leadership and Organizations: The GLOBE Study of 62 Societies*. Thousand Oaks, CA: Sage.

Inkson, K. and Kolb, D. 2000. *Management: Perspectives for New Zealand*. Auckland: Pearson Education.

Kim, S.S. 2009. 'China and globalization: Confronting myriad challenges and opportunities'. *Asian Perspective*, 33(3), 41–80.

Korac-Kakabadse, N., Kouzmin, A., Korac-Kakabadse, A. and Savery, L. 2001. 'Low and high context communication patterns: Towards mapping cross-cultural encounters'. *Cross-cultural Management*, 8(2), 3–24.

Langer, E. 1989. *Mindfulness*. Reading: Addison-Wesley.

Leung, K., Bond, M.H., Reimel de Carrasquel, S., Muñoz, C., Hernández, M., Murakami, F., Yamaguchi, S., Bierbrauer, G. and Singelis, T.M. 2002.

'Social axioms: The search for universal dimensions of general beliefs about how the world functions'. *Journal of Cross-cultural Psychology*, 33(3), 286–302.

Lewis, R.D. 1999. *When Cultures Collide: Managing Successfully Across Cultures.* London: Nicholas Brealey.

Macintosh, G. 2009. 'The role of rapport in professional services: Antecedents and outcomes'. *Journal of Services Marketing*, 23(2), 71–9.

McLean, J.E. and Lewis, R.D. 2010. 'Communicating across cultures: Management matters'. *British Journal of Administrative Management*, Summer, 30–31.

Miller, K. 2005. *Communication Theories: Perspectives, Processes and Contexts.* Boston, MA: McGraw-Hill.

Mills, C.E. 2006. 'Penetrating discourses: The key to empowerment and collaborative action'. *Australian Journal of Communication*, 33(2, 3), 1–6.

Mills, C.E. 2009. 'A case of making sense of organisational communication', in *Auditing Organizational Communication*, ed. O. Hargie and D. Tourish. Hove: Routledge, 370–90.

Minkov, M. and Hofstede, G. 2011. 'The evolution of Hofstede's doctrine'. *Cross Cultural Management: An International Journal*, 18(1), 10–20.

Muratbekova-Touron, M. 2008. 'From ethnocentric to a geocentric approach to IHRM: The case of a French multinational company'. *Cross Cultural Management: An International Journal*, 15(4), 335–52.

Natale, S.M. and Sora, S.A. 2009. 'Ethics in strategic thinking: Business processes and the global market collapse'. *Journal of Business Ethics*, 94, 309–16.

Schulz von Thun, F. 1981. *Miteinander Reden 1. Störungen und Klärungen. Allgemeine Psychologie der Kommunikation*. Hamburg: Rowohlt Taschenbuch.

Schwartz, S.H. 1999. 'A theory of cultural values and some implications for work'. *Applied Psychology: An International Review*, 48(1), 23–47.

Senseing, K. 2009. 'The five essential skills for a global marketplace'. *Employment Relations Today*, 36(1), 27.

Smith, P.B., Bond, M.H. and Kağçibaşi, Ç. 2006. *Understanding Social Psychology Across Culture: Living and Working in a Changing World*. London: Sage.

Sriussadaporn, R. 2006. 'Managing international business communications at work: A pilot study in foreign companies in Thailand'. *Cross-cultural Management*, 13(4), 330–44.

Tajfel, H. and Turner, J.C. 1986. 'The social identity theory of intergroup relations', in *Psychology of Intergroup Relations*, ed. S. Worchel and W.G. Austin. Monterey, CA: Brooks Cole, 7–24.

Thayer, L. 1988. 'Leadership/communication: A critical review and a modest proposal', in *Handbook of Organizational Communication*, ed. G. Goldhaber and G.A. Barnett. Norwood, NJ: Ablex, 231–263.

Ting-Toomey, S. 1988. 'Intercultural conflict styles: A face-negotiation theory', in *Theories in Intercultural Communication*, ed. Y.Y. Kim and W.G. Gudykunst. Newbury Park, CA: Sage, 213–35.

Ting-Toomey, S. and Kurogi, A. 1998. 'Facework, competence in intercultural conflict: An updated face-negotiation theory'. *International Journal of Intercultural Relations*, 22, 187–225.

Treven, S., Mulej, M. and Lynn, M. 2008. 'The impact of culture on organizational behavior'. *Management*, 13(2), 27–39.

Triandis, H. 1994. 'Culture and social behaviour', in *Psychology and Culture*, ed. W. Lonner and R. Malpass. Boston, MA: Allyn and Bacon, 169–73.

Triandis, H. 2000. 'Culture and conflict'. *Journal of Psychology*, 35(2), 145–52.

Trompenaars, F. 1993. *Riding the Waves of Culture: Understanding Diversity in Global Business*. New York: Irwin.

Van Der Bly, M.C.E. 2005. 'Globalization: A triumph of ambiguity'. *Current Sociology*, 53(6), 875–93.

Weaver, W. and Shannon, C.E. 1963. *The Mathematical Theory of Communication*. Urbana, IL: University of Illinois Press.

Weick, K.E. 1987. 'Perspectives in action in organizations', in *Handbook of Organizational Behavior*, ed. J.W. Lorsch. Englewood Cliffs, NJ: Prentice Hall, 10–28.

Weick, K.E. 1995. *Sensemaking in Organizations*. Thousand Oaks, CA: Sage.

8

Vocational Calling and the Search for a New Approach to Business Leadership

Peter Cammock

Introduction: The Global Financial Crisis – a Failure of Leadership?

In the latter part of 2008, the world was rocked by an economic shockwave that decimated finance houses in New York and London and precipitated a global financial crisis (hereafter referred to as the GFC) which, at the time of writing, still looms as a major threat to the economies of the West. The economic policies of successive US administrations and the undisciplined behaviour of Western consumers all contributed to the GFC. But perhaps even more significant were the practices of a managerial elite who exploited the legislative deficiencies of their economies to reap huge profits and then walked away with millions, while their organizations lay in tatters and the taxpayers picked up the bill.

In the early stages of the GFC, the arrogance, greed, and in a number of cases criminality, of prominent financial leaders raised disturbing questions about the capability and integrity of Western business leadership. Given that many of the leaders at the centre of the GFC held Masters of Business Administration (MBA) degrees from Ivy League business schools, serious questions have been asked about the educational processes that have helped to develop them. Business commentators and educators alike have begun to question the ethics and motivation of business school students themselves.

This chapter suggests that the GFC is indicative of a widespread failure of leadership. It argues that part of the rehabilitation of business leadership would involve a fundamental reassessment of the values and motivations of business leaders and would-be leaders. In particular, it discusses the age-old concept of 'calling', and suggests that calling could be a powerful and positive foundation for business leadership.

Bellah et al. (1985) suggest that calling is one of three orientations that people can bring to their work. The first is that of the 'job', where the orientation is entirely instrumental and work is seen strictly as the provider of material benefits for the pursuit of security and enjoyment outside the workplace. The second orientation involves a deeper investment in work, and is that of 'career'. Money is still important, but there is an added desire to advance within the corporate or professional hierarchy. In contrast to the first two orientations, work pursued as a calling (while not devoid of concerns with money and recognition) is primarily pursued for the fulfilment it provides and the social contribution it makes. It seems reasonable to conclude that the self-interest evident in the behaviour of many business leaders associated with the GFC was driven by a career orientation rather than any sense of calling.

In this chapter, I provide a detailed description of the origins and nature of calling, draw on New Zealand case study research to describe the concept in greater detail and to discuss the benefits of a calling orientation for leaders, and examine some of the limitations of the concept of calling, both within Western culture and when engaging with non-Western cultures (in this case, with Pacific communities). In reaffirming its potential benefits, this chapter confirms that calling is not a concept to be taken lightly. The finding and pursuit of a calling is no weekend venture. It requires great personal discernment, courage and sacrifice – and when pursued in such a spirit, the orientation of calling has great potential as a foundation for business leadership.

Leadership and the MBA

WEAKNESSES IN BUSINESS SCHOOL EDUCATION

In 2010, I attended two international conferences of MBA directors. In both conferences, participants raised the possibility that the MBA degree itself may have been a contributor to the GFC. This was an issue worthy of attention. While the drivers of the GFC are complex and systemic, the attitudes fostered by the business school community have probably not been helpful.

Since the reforms of the 1950s, business schools have generally placed a much stronger emphasis on bottom-line rationality, quantitative analysis and profit-maximization than they have on responsible leadership and community contribution. Neither have they done an adequate job of exploring or challenging the motivations of the students who enter their programmes. In the great majority of cases, MBA programmes are marketed as – and understood by applicants to be – a means to career advancement. A comment made by an MBA student, included on a business school brochure, highlights this point: 'It was about career progression. I wanted to go to that next management level and all the people I was competing against had MBAs, so it seemed like the right thing to do.'

While there is nothing wrong *per se* with such motivations, they would ideally be balanced with a genuine interest in a managerial career and a desire to make a contribution. The average MBA selection process does little to explore applicant motivations regarding social contribution, and neither does it enquire much into values or character. If such issues are raised in the selection process, they are likely to take second place to the measurement of academic capability and business acumen. The failure of business schools in these areas is illustrated by a widely reported survey of 5,300 students, covering the years 2002–2004, in which an incredible 56 per cent of MBA respondents admitted to cheating regularly during their course of study (Sachar 2006).

CHANGES IN THE BUSINESS SCHOOLS

The GFC has certainly gained the attention of business school educators. There is now widespread agreement that they have a responsibility to address not only the competency, but also the deeper motivations and mindsets of their students. In line with this thinking, Rakesh Khurana, Professor of Leadership Development at Harvard Business School, argues that the basic tenets of business education need to be readdressed. 'MBA graduates', he suggests, 'need to enter (or re-enter) the business world with a different mindset – one that says, "I will create value rather than extract value", rather than, "I'll give back to society after I make a lot of money"' (Krell 2010: 4).

The changes Khurana advocates may already be under way. In the wake of the GFC, calls for business school curricula to place greater emphasis on topics such as risk management are being supplemented with widespread appeals for increased attention to ethics and social responsibility. There are also signs of a shift in the orientations of the business school students themselves. The MBA

Oath, developed by the Harvard MBA class of 2009, is one example. The oath is a commitment to 'create value responsibly and ethically'. Outside Harvard, there are a growing number of MBA programmes with a social responsibility and sustainability focus.

Alongside the shift toward greater social responsibility, there are articles reporting students making comments such as, 'I'm not exclusively interested in money. I want to do something that I'm really passionate about and to find a situation where I can make a difference' (Krell 2010: 5). This last statement is particularly interesting in that it recalls the definition of calling given by Presbyterian theologian Frederick Buechner, who asserts:

> *The [calling] for you is the one in which your deep gladness and the world's deep hunger meet. When you are doing what you are happiest doing, it must be something that not only makes you happy but that the world needs to have done.*
>
> *(Buechner 1973: 95)*

Comments like these suggest that the future may see more business leaders motivated by the desire to make a contribution. This, of course, is not to advocate for a solely philanthropic approach to business. The generation of profit is a vital part of any commercial enterprise. There is a difference however, between a business orientation that is entirely focused on profit-maximization and one that balances shareholder returns with the needs of other stakeholders, such as staff, customers and the broader community. Indeed, there are indications that organizations that have a more balanced stakeholder focus may be more rather than less profitable over the medium term (Kotter and Hesketh 1992, Collins and Porras 1994).

The same principle can be applied to business leaders. There is nothing wrong *per se* with ambition, achievement and income. The need is not for such motivational drivers to be removed from the leadership mix, but rather for them to be leavened with a genuine passion for the work itself and a desire to make a meaningful contribution in the leader's sphere of influence. The hope is that such leaders would not only bring a greater benefit to their staff, customers and communities, but also that their organizations would ultimately yield better financial returns as well. With these possibilities in mind, the next few sections explore the nature of calling more fully, and lay the ground for consideration of its relevance to business leadership.

The Nature of Calling

RELIGIOUS FOUNDATIONS

The word 'calling' derives from the Greek *klesis* and the Latin *vocatio*, both of which point to a call or invitation to a particular type of vocation, life or destiny. The concept of calling dates back to antiquity. In the Jewish tradition, we find Moses called into leadership from the burning bush on Mount Sinai, and a succession of prophets and kings called and anointed by divine decree. In early Christianity, the original apostles were called directly by Jesus the Christ, and later, Paul's calling was inspired by divine revelation on the road to Damascus.

Outside Judeo-Christian tradition, following the birth of Prince Siddhartha Gautama, an astrologer predicted he would be called either to be a great king or a holy man. At the age of 29, Siddhartha began a path of material renunciation that would lead him to become the Buddha. In the Middle East, Mohammed was called to prophetic office by the angel Gabriel. Thereafter, he wrote the words of the Quran and began the spread of Islam.

During the Protestant Reformation, the concept of calling, which had been largely confined to a call to religious life, found application in the world of secular work. Martin Luther taught his followers to make the best of their immediate situation, asserting that any work done with a sense of duty could be transformed into a divine calling as long as it contributed to the 'general welfare of humankind' (Hardy 1990). In a collection of sermons published after his death in 1564, John Calvin (1574) taught that a calling was not simply a matter of fulfilling one's duty in whatever station one happened to occupy, but rather flowed from a unique set of God-given talents that lay at the core of every individual human being and that required expression in a particular task or vocation.

In the Calvinist conception, a calling involves the application of a person's unique talents in a type of work that contributes to the well-being of others. Calvin asserted that it was each person's 'solemn duty to discover and embrace' their particular talents and to find work in which those talents might be employed in the service of others. 'For as God bestows any ability or gift upon any of us, he binds us to such as have need of us and as we are able to help' (Calvin 1574: 307).

In short, Calvinist doctrine suggests the individual's duty is to discover both their unique talents and the setting in which they might be most usefully applied. Calvin suggests that this is a universal duty: 'For everyone without exception God's Providence has prepared a calling, which he should profess and in which he should labour. And this calling is ... God's commandment to the individual to work for the divine glory' (Calvin 1574: 106).

TWO STRANDS OF CALLING

Bunderson and Thompson (2009) refer to the Protestant conception of calling as 'classical', and note that 'calling is that place within the world of productive work that one was created, designed, or destined to fill by virtue of God-given gifts and talents and the opportunities presented by one's station in life' (Bunderson and Thompson 2009: 37). As discussed above, classical definitions of calling contain two discrete strands. The first involves the discovery of one's unique 'gifts and talents', and the second the recognition of invitations to deploy those gifts and talents in the service of others. The first element opens the path to personal fulfilment and avocation. The second reveals the path of public duty, a path in which a particular social need and invitation provides a context in which our unique gifts and talents are offered to the world.

This two-stranded understanding of calling remains a key feature of many academic definitions. Bellah et al., for example, define calling as 'work performed for its own sake, for the personal meaning and value associated with it' (Bellah et al. 1985: 6), but which people also believe has a positive impact on society. Wrzesniewski et al. define calling as work people 'love', which simultaneously 'contributes to making the world a better place' (Wrzesniewski et al. 1997: 22). In their forthcoming paper, Wrzesniewski, Tosti and Landman again emphasize the dual aspects of personal fulfilment and duty when they suggest that 'a person with a calling works for the fulfilment gained by doing the work and the sense that the work makes the world a better place'. Bunderson and Thompson found that the zookeepers in their study experienced their calling to work with animals as both 'a source of transcendent meaning, identity, and significance' and an 'offering to society ... they feel obligated to make because of their particular gifts and society's need' (Bunderson and Thompson 2009: 38).

The two strands of calling in which the personal talents, passions and preferences of the individual are deployed in some form of public service or duty provide an important balance in understanding calling. This balanced perspective is not always apparent, however, either in the literature or in practice. Western consumer societies tend to over-emphasize the personal passion and benefits of calling and underplay the importance of duty and contribution. In other cultural traditions, the dictates and requirements of the community tend to overshadow personal passion and preferences. These distinctions are not insignificant in their implications for leadership, and are discussed in greater detail later in the chapter.

THE BENEFITS OF CALLING

Recent research suggests that a sense of calling confers many advantages. People who regard their work as a calling are more satisfied with their organizations, their work and their lives in general than those with a job or career orientation (Wrzesniewski et al. 1997, Duffy and Sedlacek 2007). They also express a stronger identification with their work units, along with higher trust/confidence in their managers, stronger commitment to their organizations, less conflict, better relationships with their peers and higher satisfaction with their specific work tasks (Cameron 2008). People who experience their work as a calling are less likely to experience stress, depression and conflict between work and personal life, and are more resilient in the face of career choices for which they express regret (Cameron 2008).

Unsurprisingly, there is a strong association between the experience of work as a calling and the sense that the work is meaningful. Grant (2008) found that the stronger the experience of work as a calling, the stronger the sense that the work is meaningful. Other scholars have suggested the experience of calling may provide the 'deepest' and most 'extreme' path to meaningful work (Hall and Chandler 2005). The experience of meaningful work has been associated with reduced stress, depression, turnover, absenteeism, dissatisfaction and cynicism – and increased commitment, effort, engagement, empowerment, happiness, satisfaction, fulfilment, performance and productivity (Cameron 2008).

While these benefits are significant and positive, there is also need for a little caution. The intentional introduction of meaning into the work experience brings with it the possibility of manipulation. Marxist writers have long been suspicious of managerial attempts to widen the range of employee motivations addressed in the workplace. In the Marxist perspective, workers that once had to offer bodies and minds to the workplace may (as the work experience is manipulated to be more meaningful) be required to offer their souls. Charismatic leaders are masters of manipulating their followers' emotions and creating a sense of meaning. In some cases, the invocation of meaning leads to positive outcomes – for example, in the case of Winston Churchill's leadership. In other cases – for example, under the leadership of Adolf Hitler or Jim Jones – the results have been tragic. The difference between 'genuine' and 'manufactured' meaningfulness needs to be included in considerations of the benefits of calling.

CALLING AND DESTINY

The research on calling and meaning touches on a significant dimension of calling that receives considerably less emphasis in the more recent literature. In Calvinist theology, the coming together of a deeply fulfilling avocation and the summons to public service is no trivial thing. It brings with it a sense of destiny, and a sacred duty for an individual to find their calling and to make the sacrifices required to fulfil it for the benefit of the community and for the glory of God.

The Calvinist conception of calling reflects early Protestant theology in which God and destiny perform a critical unifying role in bringing personal fulfilment and public duty together. Concepts of personal fulfilment and public duty are merely different sides of the same coin, with both deriving from a deeper field of destiny moved and motivated by God's will. In this setting, even the most profound sacrifices can be personally fulfilling in that they may invoke not only the satisfactions of public contribution, but also the personal peace and fulfilment of the grace of God.

Webster's *Third New International Dictionary* (1976: 615) defines destiny as 'that to which any person or thing is destined ... the predetermined course of events often conceived as a resistless power or agency'. Curiously, destiny finds a place in the lives of many famous leaders. Joan of Arc was called to drive out the English by no less than Saint Michael, Saint Catherine and Saint Margaret. And Napoleon Bonaparte said:

> *All my life I have sacrificed everything – comfort, self-interest, happiness – to my destiny .... I feel myself driven towards an end that I do not know. As soon as I have reached it, as I shall become unnecessary, an atom will suffice to shatter me. Until then, not all the forces of mankind can do anything against me.*
>
> *(Campbell 1949: 72)*

Winston Churchill (1948) wrote: 'I felt as if I were walking with destiny, and that all my past life had been but a preparation for this hour and this trial' (Churchill 1948: 38). Martin Luther King, speaking in Memphis Tennessee in 1968, said: 'I just want to do God's will. And He's allowed me to go to the mountain. And I've looked over, and I've seen the promised land!' In 2008, *Rolling Stone* magazine described Barack Obama as 'destiny's child' and wrote of his conviction that his presidential campaign had been spurred on by a 'call' from the masses of people who supported him.

The statements of such leaders find a ready parallel in a variety of writing. In *Man's Search for Meaning*, Viktor Frankl (1984) writes:

> One should not search for an abstract meaning of life. Everyone has his own specific vocation or mission in life to carry out a concrete assignment which demands fulfilment. Therein he cannot be replaced, nor can his life be repeated. Thus, everyone's task is as unique as is his specific opportunity to implement it.
>
> *(Frankl 1984: 131)*

Psychologist James Hillman expresses a similar sentiment when he states: 'Each person enters the world called …. A calling may be postponed, avoided, intermittently missed. It may also possess you completely. Whatever; eventually it will out. It makes its claim. [It] does not go away' (Hillman 1996: 6–7).

Joseph Jaworski (1996) reflects:

> I believe that everyone is born with a destiny or purpose, and the journey is to find it. The ultimate aim of the servant leader, the quest, is to find the resources of character to meet his or her destiny, and to find the wisdom and power to serve life that way …. This is the call to service that most of us deny throughout our whole life … this call to give ourselves to something larger than ourselves, and to become what we were meant to become.
>
> *(Jaworski 1996: 223)*

The thread of destiny can also be discerned in recent academic writing on calling. Duffy and Sedlacek (2007: 591) define calling as 'a transcendent summons' to take up a specific 'life role'. The zookeepers in the Bunderson and Thompson (2009) study experienced a similar sense of 'summons' and destiny. They described a feeling of being 'led' or 'pushed' into the 'right places', with their work being 'pre-determined by their idiosyncratic "wiring" and apparent in the unfolding of their lives'. In this sense, their responsibility was 'not to decide, but to discover and dutifully embrace' their work (Bunderson and Thompson 2009: 33).

The concept of balance discussed above remains important here. As we have seen, a calling involves a coming together of specific personal talents and preferences with particular community needs. In a similar fashion, the call of destiny is invariably in line with distinctive individual capabilities. The invitation is not to pointless self-sacrifice, but to the deployment of particular talents in a way that will be simultaneously fulfilling for the individual and of service to the community. It is also important to note that the concept of calling presented above derives from a predominantly Western (specifically Anglo-American and European tradition). As is discussed below, the orientation of non-Western cultures to the idea of calling can be very different. The reader may also find it of interest to compare the definitions of calling discussed in this chapter with those of dharma, as described by Nilakant and Lips-Wiersma in Chapter 4.

Calling in Action: A New Zealand Study

In the previous sections, calling emerges as a threefold combination of personal talents, passions and preferences, deployed (by invitation) in some form of social service, with both the personal passion and the social service being guided by a deeper sense of invitation and destiny. The opening section of this chapter suggests that such an orientation may have been in short supply in the world of business leadership, particularly in the case of the leaders involved in the GFC.

In *The Spirit of Leadership* (Cammock 2009), I employed a case study methodology to tell the stories of 16 New Zealanders who have transformed their lives and made a vibrant contribution to their communities by finding and following a passionately held vocational calling. The study did not involve any large-scale corporate business leaders, but did include a number of people who were self-employed and/or running their own small businesses. The respondent group comprised sports car manufacturer Neil Fraser, willow-basket maker Mike Gillooly, historian and archaeologist Barry Brailsford, neuro-linguistic programming practitioner and trainer Richard Bolstad, organic market gardeners Tony and Lynette Mallard, psycho-dramatist Max Clayton, conservationist Hugh Wilson, therapists Lynn Timpany and

Sara Crane, community leader Margaret Jefferies, midwife Bronwen Pelvin, writer Fiona Farrell, smallholder Jane Chetwynd, artist Sally Hope, mother of six Lee Ball and theatre owner Rodney Cook.

Consistent with the definitions given above, all of the respondents described their experience of calling in terms of three key elements: first, an 'internal call', manifested as a particular passion identified in early childhood; second, a vivid experience of 'external calling' or 'invitation' that led them to direct their passion into a particular type of work, and third, an underlying sense of destiny, connection and/or divinity that they experienced as a guiding force in following their calling. It is important to note that this sense of destiny was a central theme of the participants' experience, despite their wide variety of spiritual beliefs. It emerged as a unifying theme of connection and 'oneness' that seemed to transcend their individual religious (and non-religious) orientations. Together, their stories provide a rich description of the three elements of calling as they operated in the lives of a cross-section of New Zealanders. Their experiences are discussed in greater detail below.

PASSION AND THE INTERNAL CALL

All the respondents described a particular interest or passion that provided a powerful internal guide towards their future work.

The first interview was with sports car maker Neil Fraser, who was asked: 'Where did this interest start and how did it develop into a full-time business?' Neil immediately identified the source of his interest as what I later described as a passionately experienced 'internal call'. He responded:

> *Well, it's not something you wake up one day and say, 'I think I'd like to make cars,' and draw up the strategic plan, borrow the money, buy all this new plant and open the doors one day as a carmaker. You have to kind of accidentally grow into it with some sort of strong force driving you that you are not even aware of really. There is some other thing going on and I suppose it is a passion really, because there are many, many obstacles that something has to get you over, to carry on. What happened for me, to take that particular route was that I was always a passionate car person, child really. I took great pride that I was able to drive my grandfather's tractor at some silly young age and had my licence four days after I turned 15. I was just a car nutter.*
>
> (Cammock 2009: 84)

Like Neil, every one of the respondents spoke of a passion that informed, and, at times discomforted, their lives and provided the first guiding impulse towards their future calling. In all cases except one, the passion was present from childhood. Historian and archaeologist Barry Brailsford grew up with a strong sense of social justice and a love for the land and 'the mystery of its past'. Fiona Farrell wrote from when she 'was very little'. Conservationist Hugh Wilson spent his formative years 'doodling and designing nature reserves', while mother of six Lee Ball remembered her 'visions as a child' of wanting to 'be a mother [and] have a family'. Artist Sally Hope recalled being fascinated with 'the light shining on things' as a very young girl, and theatre owner Rodney Cook remembered being 'fascinated by movies' as a boy. Richard Bolstad noted 'the things that I'm doing in my life began very, very early', and market gardener Tony Mallard recalled he 'always loved seeing things grow right from the time I was very small' (Cammock 2009).

The experiences of the respondents conform to previous academic definitions of calling in that they clearly have found work they love that is personally fulfilling. They also conform to the second aspect of calling in that they all responded to a sense of invitation from the broader community.

INVITATIONS AND THE EXTERNAL CALL

As discussed above, Buechner's definition suggests that a calling emerges from the meeting of our own 'deep gladness and the world's deep hunger' (Buechner 1973: 95). The calling, he continues 'must be something that not only makes you happy but that the world needs to have done' (Buechner 1973: 95). In the lives of the respondents in the New Zealand study, the world's need was announced by a distinct sense of external call or invitation that they remembered vividly years later. This invitation generally involved some form of external stimulus, but it was also deeply personal in that the answering response was invariably guided by the values and images of the internal call.

Barry Brailsford's deep-seated 'sense of social justice' developed into a project in which he was sending young student teachers up to predominantly Māori schools, on the East Coast of New Zealand's North Island. This project required him to visit his students – and on one of these visits he found himself in the remote and 'fascinating little village' of Te Kaha:

> *I had to spend the night at the Te Kaha pub. And about 5 o'clock I went down and they were playing pool [and] this Maori Elder came over,*

this old, old, guy. And he was good. We probably held the table for an hour and a half. It was all laughter, hilarious. Anyway I was going to play a really difficult shot and as I was going to play he said in my ear, 'Mr Bloody Professor, what are you doing for young Maori?' He said it in a big voice, sharp. And he just put his cue down, pushed all the balls aside. End of game and gave up the table. I was absolutely stunned. This voice had cut through everything. I'd been hit from the side with a king hit. I sat down [and] back comes [the Elder] with a half gee, puts his jug down, takes two glasses and he pours me a beer. He's looking at me with tears in his eyes, weeping. He said, 'I weep for my children. I weep for my grandchildren.' He said, 'I can do nothing about it.' Then he looked at me, 'What are you going to do?' It's what's called a dart in your heart, that's how the Elders describe it. He threw it. 'What are you going to do?' 'You can do something, I can't.' He showed his pain. He put everything out, no facade. So we talked, you know. And that moment changed my life.

(Cammock 2009: 129)

Neil Fraser's passion for cars and his 'twenty-five years of daydreaming' about making his own sports car led him to a classic moment of calling. He was at a racing track when he saw an imported Caterham sports car and had an almost revelatory 'flash of an eye' experience, in which he realized he could (and should) make a car of the same design. Jane Chetwynd's life changed dramatically when she responded to an advertisement in her local newspaper for a 'house on 155 acres': 'I can't tell you it was a very logical decision, it was more a gut feeling. It was a sense of rightness. A very strong gut feeling. And it's rewarded me.' Richard Bolstad went to a training seminar in energy work and had a 'visual and kinaesthetic experience of what was going on there. Life had been knocking on my door for a long time but that was when I noticed.' Lee Ball saw her future husband for the first time and felt 'just a jolt of like, that's him'. Sara Crane attended her first counselling session and knew 'this is absolutely what I want to do!', while midwife Bronwen Pelvin's first home birth was 'a real higher experience, a real "ah ha" experience'. Basket-maker Mike Gillooly's 'little heart leapt' the first time he saw cattle eating out of a woven basket in a library book, and Max Clayton's life began to change when he chanced on an article on psychodrama on a 'little table' at his dentist (Cammock 2009: 130–35).

The respondents' experiences are illustrative of the second strand of calling, which is the invitation to pursue a personal preference in the context of a broader social invitation and need. In the respondents' experience, the coming together of these two strands did not occur in isolation, but took place in the context of a broader sense of destiny and/or connection.

CALLING AND DESTINY

The great English poet William Blake spoke of 'forces grander than any individual human life' that sit beneath the visible surfaces of human experience and act 'like a kind of permanent gravity field, the currents ... acting and pulling upon us according to our particular heft and weight' (cited in Whyte 2002: 8). As discussed above, respondents in the Bunderson and Thompson (2009) study mirrored Blake's 'grand forces' when they spoke of a sense of 'summons' and 'destiny' that attended their calling as zookeepers.

This same sense of destiny, along with an intimation of a deeper connection and spiritual support, was very much present in the stories of respondents in the New Zealand study. Barry Brailsford described his perspective thus:

> *People think that this world of consumerism, debts, bills you can't pay and mortgages, is the real world. But that's rubbish, that's an illusion. The real world is totally different. It's a world of spirit, of wairua moving, of power, of healing and nature that's amazing. It's absolutely incredible.*
>
> *(Cammock 2009: 170)*

Bronwen Pelvin spoke of 'collectiveness' and a 'good and beneficent universe', Fiona Farrell of being 'linked' to 'some energy which could be called God', Jane Chetwynd of 'a very strong spiritual feeling' about her farm that acted as a 'guiding force', and Mike Gillooly of 'divine energy'. At one point during the interview, Neil Fraser stopped the conversation and said: 'Just one more thing on that. You could never plan that ... and ... I do believe [God] had something to do with all of those bits falling into place.' Max Clayton said simply: 'I'm sure none of these things that have happened to me, happened by chance.' Therapist Lynn Timpany suggested: 'We're all God and we're all kind of resting in an element of that that's also the whole.' Richard Bolstad spoke of 'spiritual reality behind this reality', while Rodney Cook reflected: 'It's definitely destiny from when I was young.' Sara Crane referred to 'the Christ within', and Sally Hope concluded her interview by stating: '[It's the] relationship with God, isn't it. All of this isn't it' (Cammock 2009: 170–73).

Even Tony Mallard, who was the least inclined to spiritual explanations of any of the respondents, spoke of the deep connection with their property, noting that it's 'almost as much a part of us as the family is in a way, all inseparable'. He went on to describe how:

> We suddenly found we didn't need [chemical sprays]. It was quite incredible really. The soil just wiped out every aphid. It's quite bizarre. We can't understand it, we can't explain it. It just became natural. We'd be putting [no fertilizer] on and the stuff would be looking good. Crazy. It's quite dramatic. It's hard to explain. [It's] mighty satisfying. Yeah, there's a certain peace about it isn't there, that it's doing this for us. As far as I'm concerned we've been blessed really.
>
> (Cammock 2009: 183)

SACRIFICES AND GIFTS

One final aspect of calling is worth mentioning before we close the discussion of the New Zealand study. The zookeepers in the Bunderson and Thompson study experienced their work as both 'a source of transcendent meaning, identity, and significance as well as unbending duty, sacrifice, and vigilance' (Bunderson and Thompson 2009: 50). While they clearly experienced their work as highly meaningful, they were also obliged to work for little pay, in frequently unpleasant conditions, with little opportunity for career advancement or social acknowledgement.

The respondents in the New Zealand study also experienced major trials and had to make significant sacrifices in the pursuit of their callings. Barry Brailsford, for example, recalled:

> I did on one occasion go outside and scream at the universe. 'To hell with this, I can't do it! I'm just taking too much, too many blows.' And I do believe it carved into my health. The stress of it was utterly incredible at times …. [Pure] determination kept [me going] but there was more than that. I knew that this was bigger than me. That in fact, I suppose in the end, it was worth giving my life for.
>
> (Cammock 2009: 145)

The respondents' stories make it clear that their pursuit of calling required sacrifice. They also referred frequently to a need to commit and 'surrender' to the process. Bronwen Pelvin came to see herself as a kind of servant of a process that was finally 'going to happen by itself'; Fiona Farrell spoke 'of a leaping off'; Lee Ball recalled the 'lovely' feeling of surrendering to a deeper unfolding in her life, and Richard Bolstad learnt to trust whatever 'life is doing with me' (Cammock 2009: 149).

These sentiments are very much aligned with the processes of surrender, trust and service that Senge argues are the essence of great leadership:

> The fundamental choice that enables true leadership in all situations (including, but not limited to hierarchical leadership) is the choice to serve life … in a deep sense, my capacity as a leader comes from my choice to allow life to unfold through me. This choice results in a type of leadership that we've known very rarely, or that we associate exclusively with extraordinary individuals like Gandhi or King. In fact, this domain of leadership is available to us all, and may indeed be crucial for our future.
>
> (Senge, as cited in Jaworski 1996: 2)

In the poem 'The Swan', translated by Robert Bly, Rainer Maria Rilke describes the choice 'to serve life' as a form of 'dying', a dying that involves 'letting go of the ground we stand on and cling to every day' (Rilke 1981). It is this 'letting go', this surrender, this movement from the known to the unknown that constitutes the core of the leadership journeys of each of the respondents in the study. Each step requires a departure from the known way and a more and more wholehearted commitment to a less than clearly defined future life. This approach to life and leadership is seldom referenced in the literature, but has tended to be associated with ideas of calling into traditional forms of religious life. However, this broader experience of calling and leadership may be heard of with much greater frequency, and increasingly in the corporate and business worlds, as new conceptions of leadership unfold.

In all cases, the respondents' commitment and sacrifice was rewarded with moments of inspiration and a variety of 'gifts'. At one point during our interview I asked Sally Hope what it was like for her at the moment when she captured what she called 'that spark of liveliness coming out' of the faces of the people she paints. Sally thought for some time and finally said simply, 'It's awe' – and wept at the thought of it:

> It's awe, really. That's right it's an awe. Oh, it makes me feel sad. I don't know that I could say any more about that. It's an awe of beauty.

Wouldn't it be nice to be able to express love. To paint love, wouldn't it be magic. Imagine that. Wow, when that's in their faces, and the light shining on them, through them and I think, 'Oh, isn't it amazing. Ah, what peace.' Yeah, and there's the awe thing again. Awe [and] beauty.

(Cammock 2009: 182)

Just as Bunderson and Thompson's (2009) zookeepers experienced moments of transcendence, so did the respondents in the New Zealand study enjoy the specific gifts that came into their lives as a direct consequence of their vocational journeys. They spoke variously of being 'blessed', of the satisfaction of having performed at their best, of leaving a legacy, of 'belonging', 'abundance', 'familiarity', 'grounded[ness]', 'joy', 'love' and 'awe'. In many of their stories, these gifts were accompanied by a profound sense of being 'at home' in their lives and vocations. Indeed, of all the gifts described by the people in this study, it was this quiet sense of groundedness and home-coming that left the strongest impression.

Calling in Action: Some Experiences with Pacific Leaders

Following publication of *The Spirit of Leadership*, I became involved (through a combined initiative between the University of Canterbury and New Zealand's Ministry of Health) in leadership development work with a group of talented Pacific health leaders resident in New Zealand. This chapter has already highlighted the Western (European and Anglo-American) origins of calling, and it was fascinating to work with the concept within a Pacific cultural perspective. My engagement with the Pacific leaders took place over three years, in three one- and two-day workshops in which leadership and calling were the key points of focus.

In the definitions discussed above, calling emerged as a combination of personal talent/passion and community need. In general, Western conceptions of calling tend to place a greater emphasis on the individual satisfactions of finding and following a calling, and less on the path of duty and contribution (Bunderson and Thompson 2009). They also make it clear that it is the individual's responsibility to discover their particular talents and to determine the means whereby they might offer them to the community. In this sense, although calling involves an offering of community service, the process at core is highly individualistic.

By contrast, the Pacific participants in the leadership workshops clearly came from cultures where community responsibility was considered more important than individual preference. One of the older Tongan leaders dismissed the Western concept of calling out of hand. He argued that in Pacific culture, personal inspiration and passion were irrelevant because individual direction was determined by community needs as interpreted by parents and elders. In his view, calling was entirely a matter of duty and of submission to the needs of the family and the village. His perspective left little room for personal preference or for the self-directed development of individual talents and preferences.

I was intrigued by the discussion, and in late 2010 took the opportunity to interview a young Pacific leader in depth. She acknowledged that the Tongan participant was 'right to some extent, particularly for those still living in the Islands'. She reaffirmed that 'families and communities are a big part of life in the Pacific' and that this has significant implications for the ways in which young people in particular think about their future work.

It is expected that young people will be respectful of their elders and try to help their families and communities to do better. If they come from a poor background and have a chance to be educated, they won't have the opportunity to find themselves. They will be told by their parents what career they will pursue. Often, it will be medicine or law. The sense of trying to find what you love, what you are good at, is a Western thing. In terms of finding a calling, a majority of Pacific people are not given the opportunity when they are younger because they live in a culture that is communal. Until your parents give you the freedom, you will not have the chance.

The sense of duty to family and community was clearly present among participants in the leadership workshops. For them, the external call and the invitations of family and community outweighed the passions and intimations of the internal call. This perspective was not without its conflicts, especially for the younger New Zealand-born participants. The young Pacific leader quoted above was very aware of this conflict, and also noted the confusion that can result from the clash between the expectations of the different cultures:

> Within Pacific culture parents feel it is their responsibility to guide
> their children. Though it's not always guiding, sometimes it's telling.
> A lot of the conflict comes from the influence of Western society.
> Pacific parents tell [their children] what they have to do. Then they see

[their Palangi peers] doing what they want to do and they feel they can't
[make their own choices].

The young leader suggested that when the opportunity to make their own choices arises (with or without permission), it can be a real challenge for some of the young Pacific people. They can find themselves caught between two cultures and lose direction:

Sometimes a Pacific student will fail at law or medicine and their families will say, 'Well, do what you want to do'. Then trying to find what you love can be an ongoing problem. Or sometimes they get influenced by the feeling of, 'What about what I want to do?' They don't listen to their parents, they don't have that direction. Then they fail because they don't have [parental or personal] direction.

Fortunately, the young leader interviewed experienced no such lack of direction. After failing to get into medical school, she recalled: 'I was able to do my own thing and I feel I've found what I was supposed to do.' She had clearly found her calling. Given this, I asked her whether it was still beneficial for some families and communities to impose the choice of work onto their young people. 'Is it a good thing?', she asked rhetorically:

If the goal is to bring people out of poverty it's a good thing. But I wouldn't have been happy doing medicine. I wouldn't have felt any freedom. But it depends on your definition of happiness. If being given the opportunity to do what you want makes us happier or not I can't say.

My meetings with the Pacific leaders provided a different understanding of calling, one that is weighed much more in favour of community-dictated contribution than those that have emerged in the West. The Pacific orientation is a far cry from the narrow self-interest that was so evident in the period before the GFC, and it presents an interesting contrast with the Western conceptions presented earlier in this chapter. As the world becomes more and more globalized and interconnected, more of these kinds of differing perspectives will emerge. Hopefully, this will ultimately yield greater understanding, insight and acceptance, rather than rigidity and conflict.

Calling and Leadership

This chapter began with reference to the GFC and the careerism and greed of many of the business leaders involved. As an alternative to the self-interest of such leaders, it has explored the orientation of calling. So many of the world's most destructive leadership episodes have been as a result of leaders whose motivations were based on personal career advancement and self-interest rather than any sense of calling and contribution. One can only wonder at what might result if a larger percentage of the world's business leaders took up their roles with the types of motivation exhibited by the respondents in the New Zealand study of calling, or with some of the sense of community present in Pacific culture. It would certainly be of tremendous social benefit if the GFC were to precipitate sufficient introspection in business schools and among would-be business leaders to significantly increase the number of corporate leaders who experienced their work as a genuine and passionately held calling.

The calling orientation clearly brings a greater sense of personal alignment and enjoyment, along with a heightened desire to contribute and make a difference in the world. The leadership requirements go further, however. In the past, effective leadership was seen as a straightforward product of skilled task performance, the more rapidly performed the better. In the latter part of the twentieth century, it became clear that purely task-focused approaches to leadership are insufficient to meet the challenges of our time. We now live in a hyper-kinetic world in which the potential is unprecedented and the challenges are complex, interdependent, and potentially apocalyptic. The innovation and creativity demanded of leaders in the global economy involves much more than solid intellect and competent task performance. Neither can the need for such creative requirements be addressed by simply working harder, longer or faster. Speed can never be a substitute for imagination, and the complex challenges of the global economy will not be addressed by simply driving the outmoded paradigms harder.

For the first time in modern organizational history, there is a call for leadership that has a certain flow and economy of means – leadership that not only performs all of the rational tasks of traditional organizational leadership, but is also underscored by personal qualities such as creativity, passion, vitality, spirit and soul. This type of leadership cannot emerge from a job or career orientation. It requires a vitality that can only derive from a kind of ongoing conversation with Blake's 'grander, more eternal, more essential parts of ourselves' (cited in Whyte 2002: 8) This type of conversation is a rarity in corporate life, and is increasingly at risk in a world of superficiality, haste and consumerism. It is nevertheless at the core of the leadership that is now required not only in the business world, but also in a broader world that stands on the brink of chaos.

This chapter advocates business leadership that is experienced as a calling and that fits the concept of calling, as described above. Neither is the concept limited to business leadership. It seems possible that we all have a calling that is unique to us, and Senge's 'choice to serve life' (Senge, cited in Jaworski 1996) is made as we discover that calling and find a way to live it out in the world. Such callings are not necessarily limited to major corporate roles, and neither are we limited to one calling per life. At any given time in our lives, however, there will be intimations from within us – and from the external world – as to what our particular role is to be. To go against these intimations is to deny both our core identity and the leadership we might offer to the world. To follow them is to lay the foundations of great leadership, be it quiet and unrecognized or highly public and acclaimed.

Effective, ethical and responsible business leadership nevertheless remains critical, and the concept of calling has profound implications for this domain of leadership. As suggested above, the intensity, complexity and competitive nature of the global environment not only demand immense skill, but also creativity, vision, vitality, passion and soul. Such qualities cannot be developed on a weekend workshop or even in an extended course of academic study. The central precept of this chapter is that they require an orientation in which leadership is experienced as a deeply aligned calling that allows the leader 'to feel that what [they] do is right for themselves and good for the world at exactly the same time' (Whyte 2002: 8).

The fostering of this type of orientation would require a profound shift in the practices of business education. As discussed at the beginning of this chapter, there are already positive changes occurring in business schools, particularly with the development of courses such as ethics, social responsibility and sustainability. The development of large numbers of business leaders with a genuine sense of calling and contribution, however, cannot be achieved by adding on a few courses. It is time for a radical change in the teaching and practice of business leadership. The drivers of the current malaise go much deeper, and must be addressed at a foundational level. The concept of calling offers a step in the establishment of such a foundation.

Conclusion: Some Final Caveats and Paradoxes

WESTERN INTERPRETATIONS OF CALLING

In its description of calling, this chapter has emphasized the balance of self-fulfilment and public duty, and the possibility of sacrificing short-term self-interest to a broader sense of destiny. This is no lightweight concept. Calling has a long history, and requires deep attention, discernment and sacrifice to find and follow. In the Western definitions of calling, that sense of depth and balance is not always apparent.

For example, Bunderson and Thompson's (2009) review noted that 'modern conceptualizations [of calling] tend to be more self-focused, emphasizing "duty to the self" … and the importance of self-knowledge, identity, self-fulfilment, and the pursuit of (personal) happiness …. Calling in this self-directed view', they argue, 'is really about finding work in which one can thrive and be fulfilled, about finding one's bliss at work.' They go on to say that while those with a calling may espouse 'the belief that the work contributes to the greater good, this belief is more of a benefit than a duty' (Bunderson and Thompson 2009: 33). Their assertions are generally borne out by a literature that makes little reference to the deeply sacrificial submission to destiny and public duty that marked the call to service of many saints and leaders of the past.

The danger here is that a demanding but ultimately transforming process, with deeply spiritual origins, is turned into a watered-down concept stripped of its real power. The West is no stranger to 'fast-food' approaches to spiritual matters. At worst, the same impulses towards self-interest that drove the GFC could undermine a process that could be transformative for business leadership. The hope, however, is that there is sufficient understanding of the calling process and enough genuine desire for positive change for an authentic shift in business leadership to occur.

THE PARADOX OF CALLING

While the movement towards self-interest in Western definitions of calling are concerning, it is less easy to question the more community-orientated understanding of calling advocated by some Pacific leaders. Whether Pacific conceptions of calling retain their strength as engagement with Western society is intensified remains to be seen. On the other hand, the West could certainly benefit from more of the community-focused perspectives present in

Pacific culture. The experiences of the respondents in the New Zealand study, however, raise the interesting possibility that the distinction between personal preference and community may be an artificial one.

It was of interest that the process of sacrifice, commitment and surrender discussed above paradoxically led the respondents to a vocational place in which they seemed to be doing exactly the work they loved to do. They used terms such as 'awe', 'love', 'pleasure' and 'pride' in describing their lives and work. The paradox here is that the very letting go that underscored their commitment seemed to bring them to exactly the place in which their personal needs were met. Perhaps at this deep level of commitment, when the drivers of ambition and ego are replaced by the images and invitations of the call, our 'own sweet will is', just as the poet Yeats asserts in 'A Prayer for My Daughter', 'Heaven's will'. In this place, our deepest personal desires and those that 'life' – and ideally, our community – holds for us become one and the same.

The second paradox is that in pursuing their own highly individualized vocational journeys, many of the respondents came to a place of deep connection and oneness. Again, as discussed above, respondent after respondent in *The Spirit of Leadership* spoke of 'oneness' and 'collectiveness', and referred variously to 'a collective unconscious', 'something living through me', 'a path laid out', 'the whole universe', 'divine synchronicity', 'life', 'divinity' and 'God'. For many of the respondents, the very individuality of their quest seemed, paradoxically, to provide the seeds for their connection with others and with the 'Other'.

There was a sense that attending to their own highly idiosyncratic creative images led directly to their participation in a broader emergence. Lynn Timpany described this as pursuing her personal vision while simultaneously 'resting in an element that's also the whole'. Here the respondents' experiences lend weight to mythologist Joseph Campbell's paradoxical claim:

> We have not even to risk the adventure alone, for the heroes of all time have gone before us ... we have only to follow the thread of the hero path .... And where ... we had thought to be alone we shall be with all the world.
> (Campbell 1949: 25)

The final paradox builds on the first two and suggests that we can be of most service to the world when we are most attentive to ourselves. The therapist Sara Crane referred to this paradox when she said: 'If you are truly serving your own person in yourself then you are serving life and the community.

If you are absolutely true to your calling, well then you will be serving the community' (Cammock 2009: 195). The sense here is that our attention to what physicist David Bohm (1996) might call our own 'unfolding' might well place us in touch with a much deeper and more widespread unfolding, or *Zeitgeist*, that is simultaneously moving many other people.

In the context of this emerging whole, the apparently idiosyncratic images and invitations we experience as individuals – described above as the internal and external call – may have profound implications for global leadership. As we commit to our own highly localized images and sense of calling, we may well be contributing to, and co-creating, an unfolding whole that is changing the world. According to Senge et al., we now:

> *Have a new systems axiom … what is most systemic is most local. The deepest systems we enact are woven into the fabric of everyday life ….* *This is so important for us to understand. We, everyone of us, may be able to change the world, but only as we experience more and more of the whole in the present.*
>
> *(Senge et al. 2004: 234)*

'And only', adds his co-author Scharmer, 'as we learn to use ourselves as instruments for something larger than ourselves to emerge' (Senge et al. 2004: 235). If these ideas hold true, it may well be that the ultimate gift of a calling – and of the kind of leadership journeys described in this chapter – is that of participation in the co-creation of a better world.

References

Bellah, R.N., Madsen R., Sullivan, W.M, Swidler, A. and Tipton, S.M. 1985. *Habits of the Heart: Individualism and Commitment in American Life*. Los Angeles, CA: University of California Press.

Bohm, D. 1996. *Unfolding Meaning: A Weekend of Dialogue*. London: Routledge.

Buechner, F. 1973. *Wishful Thinking: A Theological ABC*. New York: Harper & Row.

Bunderson, S. and Thompson, J.A. 2009. 'The call of the wild: Zookeepers, callings, and the double-edged sword of deeply meaningful work'. *Administrative Science Quarterly*, 54(1), 32–57.

Calvin, J. 1574. *Sermons of M. John Calvin upon the Epistle of Saint Paul to the Galatians*. London: Lucas Harison and George Bishop.

Cameron, K.S. 2008. *Positive Leadership: Strategies for Extraordinary Performance*. San Francisco, CA: Berrett-Koehler.

Cammock, P. 2009. *The Spirit of Leadership: Exploring the Personal Foundations of Extraordinary Leadership*. Christchurch: Leadership Press.

Campbell, J. 1949. *The Hero with a Thousand Faces*. Princeton, NJ: Princeton University Press.

Churchill, W. 1948. *The Second World War, Volume I: The Gathering Storm*. Boston, MA: Houghton Mifflin.

Collins, J. and Porras, J. 1994. *Built to Last*. New York: HarperCollins.

Duffy, R.D. and Sedlacek, W.E. 2007. 'The presence of and search for a calling: Connections to career development'. *Journal of Vocational Behavior*, 70, 590–601.

Frankl V.E. 1984. *Man's Search for Meaning*. New York: Pocket Books.

Grant, A.M. 2008. 'Employees without a cause: The motivational effects of prosocial impact in public service'. *International Public Management Journal*, 11(1), 48–66.

Hall, D.T. and Chandler, D.E. 2005. 'Psychological success: When the career is a calling'. *Journal of Organizational Behavior*, 26(2), 155–76.

Hardy, L. 1990. *The Fabric of This World: Inquiries into Calling, Career Choice, and the Design of Human Work*. Grand Rapids, MI: William B. Eerdmans.

Hillman, J. 1996. *The Soul's Code: In Search of Character and Calling*. New York: Random House.

Jaworski, J. 1996. *Synchronicity: The Inner Path of Leadership*. San Francisco, CA: Berrett-Koehler.

Kotter, J.P. and Hesketh, J.L. 1992. *Corporate Culture and Performance*. New York: Free Press.

Krell, E. 2010. 'Why character is destiny for business schools – and the MBAs they groom'. *Baylor Business Review*, 28(2).

Rilke, R.M. 1981. 'The Swan', from *Selected Poems of Rainer Maria Rilke*, trans. Robert Bly. New York: Harper Perennial.

Sachar, E. 2006. 'MBA students cheat more than other grad students, study finds', *Bloomberg Business and Financial News*, http://www.bloomberg.com/apps/news?pid=newsarchive&sid=aw7s9m0BmcBo, accessed 26 March 2012.

Senge, P.M., Scharmer, C.O., Jaworski, J. and Flowers, B.S. 2004. *Presence*. New York: Doubleday.

Weber, M. 1905 (trans. 1930). *The Protestant Ethic and the Spirit of Capitalism*, trans. Talcott Parsons. London: Routledge Classics.

Whyte, D. 2002. *Crossing the Unknown Sea: Work as a Pilgrimage of Identity*. New York: Riverhead Books.

Wrzesniewski, A., McCauley, C.R., Rozin, P. and Schwartz, B. 1997. 'Jobs, careers and callings: People's relations to their work'. *Journal of Research in Personality*, 31, 21–33.

Wrzesniewski, A., Tosti, J. and Landman, J. 'If I could turn back time: Occupational regret and its consequences for work and life'. *Personality and Social Psychology Bulletin* (under review).

9

Cultivating Character: The Challenge of Business Ethics Education

John Alexander

Introduction

In the wake of global financial crisis and repeated instances of fraud and corruption by business executives in recent years, the call for a value-based business education has intensified. People have come to believe that the type of education imparted in business schools has not only contributed to the systemic failure of leadership in the corporate world, but continues to promote self-interested and unethical graduates (Podolny 2009, Krishnan 2008). In a way, this assessment seems justified, because many business schools have thus far ignored the teaching of ethics, maintaining that it is not a subject of inquiry for traditional functional areas of business studies.[1] Even the business schools that teach ethics courses do so ineffectively, either because the teaching concentrates on imparting some ethical knowledge divorced from the actual business world or because ethics is not well infused and integrated into the whole curriculum. Educators often overlook the fact that the role of any school should be to prepare its students for a lifetime of learning from experience. However one might want to intensify efforts in ethical training, most education

---

1 In India, there are about 1,680 business schools. Of these, only a handful teach business ethics as part of their programme. Only recently, after the Dalai Lama visited the Indian Institute of Management (IIM) in Ahmedabad in January 2008, have IIMs incorporated Business Ethics courses into the curriculum. This indifference to or isolation from business ethics education is a cause for concern, particularly because the top corporate organizations in India and other countries are increasingly moving towards ethically conscious business, social responsibility and value-based management. Companies are also increasingly expecting a high level of soft skills with regard to social and environmental accountability in management trainees.

in business ethics – as in all other business capabilities – will occur in the actual workplaces where people spend most of their lives.

In recent years, in order to attract more able students and stay competitive when compared with similar institutions, many business schools have focused more on short-term performance drivers such as 'marketable skills', placements, and starting salary packages as measures of the value of their education. Long-term investments, such as cultivating the students' professional attitude, sense of social responsibility and development of powers of critical thinking and moral reasoning, have largely been neglected. It hardly needs to be emphasized that to succeed as a human being is no less important than to succeed as a business manager. Human qualities and business acumen should be harmonized to create a better atmosphere for life and work.

I propose that teachers and institutions that offer business education in India – and elsewhere in the world – should take business ethics education seriously. Such education should focus on the holistic development of character and responsible leadership, rather than just imparting technical skills and market-driven fragmented knowledge. This chapter develops this argument, first by highlighting how making good ethical decisions within the actual business scenario is deeply interwoven with the identity and character of the person involved. It then inquires into the relationship between individual and institutional ethics, pointing out the vital role that a positive corporate culture plays in shaping ethical sensibilities and contributing to the ongoing ethical training of individuals. Finally, on the basis of an evaluation of current business ethics education practices, it suggests some suitable pedagogical strategies.

The Role of Character in Business Decisions

Remarkably, Aristotle is one of the few thinkers who has engaged with the richness and complexity of moral reasoning and education (Hartman 2008, Curren 2007, Mintz 1996). His conception of moral education, which focuses on the development of virtues and practical wisdom, has enduring significance for the moral education of contemporary business leaders. It critiques the theory-application model of applied ethics which claims that people can make appropriate ethical decisions by applying ready-made theories and concepts to solve problems in a practical situation. To Aristotle, the character and disposition of the moral agents are as important as the knowledge they are able to assimilate and execute. Ethical decisions, whether in business or any other form of public life, are deeply interwoven with the character and identity of the decision-maker. Who I am, who we are or what the company is shapes and sets the tenor of the ethical future we want for our organizations and society.

At the end of Book I of the *Nicomachean Ethics*, Aristotle begins his account by making a distinction between the intellectual and moral virtues: 'Virtue ... is divided into classes .... Some virtues are called intellectual and others moral; [Practical] Wisdom and Understanding and Prudence are intellectual, Liberality and Temperance are moral virtues' (Aristotle 1978: 90). Aristotle's classification of virtues flows from and coincides with his concept of the division of the soul, or psyche. Moral virtues are identified with the desiring part of the soul – hence they are to be understood as tendencies to feel and be moved by our various desires and emotions – whereas intellectual virtues are identified with the rational part of the soul, and thus should be understood as capacities or powers of understanding, judgment and reasoning which are required to attain truth.

Having made this distinction between intellectual and moral virtues, Aristotle proceeds to comment on their uniqueness as well as their interdependencies in a way that seems appropriate for the task of business ethics education. He says:

> *Virtue, then, is of two kinds, intellectual and moral. Intellectual virtue owes both its inception and its growth chiefly to instruction, and for this very reason needs time and experience. Moral goodness, on the other hand, is the result of habit, from which it has got its name, being a slight modification of the word* ethos. *This fact makes it obvious that none of the moral virtues is engendered in us by nature.*
>
> *(Aristotle 1978: 91)*

Aristotle's claim here is that habit rather than mere heredity, nurture rather than mere nature, is the source of moral virtues.[2] The important lesson we should derive from this for business ethics education is that moral virtue is not a one-time event or something that can be taught through verbal instruction alone. On the contrary, it can only be brought about by proper upbringing and mentoring which concentrates on the good habits of doing the right things regularly and consistently:

---

2   In *Ethics* and *Politics*, Aristotle developed two ideas of nature: (1) nature as capacities given at birth, and (2) nature as the outcome of good habits and exercise of practical wisdom (Alexander 2005).

> *Anything that we have to learn to do we learn by the actual doing of it: people become builders by building and instrumentalists by playing instruments. Similarly we become just by performing just acts, temperate by performing temperate ones, brave by performing brave ones .... So it is a matter of no little importance what sort of habits we form from the earliest age – it makes a vast difference, or rather* all the difference *in the world.*
>
> (*Aristotle 1978: 91–92, emphasis mine*)

Aristotle's conception of moral learning, however, does not stop with his insistence on the importance of forming good habits. He goes on to assert the interdependence between moral virtue and the intellectual virtue of practical wisdom (*phronesis*). Aristotle is of the opinion that no one has true moral virtue without the intellectual virtue of practical wisdom. It is practical wisdom which enables people to perceive, discern and perform actions that pursue noble ends. Without practical wisdom – the ability to discern what is most important in a particular circumstance and the course of action to pursue – it is impossible for a person to successfully pursue noble ends. In Aristotle's scheme of moral education, practical wisdom thus both presupposes and completes moral virtue.

While Aristotle's approach emphasizes the importance and complexity of character education, in current industry and academic circles at least two other philosophies – moral intellectualism and determinism – offer an alternative view. Advocates of moral intellectualism believe being ethical mainly requires knowing the foundational ethical principles, and presume this knowledge will automatically translate into right actions. Moral intellectualists point out that to nurture the appropriate qualities to convert knowledge and awareness into actions is neither feasible nor desirable. Moral determinism can be identified in statements such as: 'Moral dispositions are shaped by family, religion and early schooling, long before people join a company or college' or: 'No one is going to teach me ethics at this point of my life – I know what I believe.' Determinists also believe there can be hardly any substantial changes to talents and basic dispositions acquired early in life and that whatever is learned early in life is sufficient to enable a person to function effectively.

Empirical evidence and research in developmental and educational psychology tend to support Aristotle's ideas rather than alternative theories (Jones 1990, Parks 1993, Gautschi and Jones 1998, Gardner 2007).[3] It is not too

---

3   Here are some results from a qualitative survey gauging the learning experiences of students in a two-year MBA programme business ethics course I taught: a majority of students,

strong to state that students and young executives in their twenties and thirties are, indeed, at a critical stage in the development of their perception about models of economic development, sustainability, globalization, social justice and appropriate solutions to ethical issues and dilemmas in business practice. It is a crucial period in which to develop the moral courage required to bridge the gap between knowing what is good and the capacity to actually do what is good. Often, executives and business leaders resort to unethical practices not because of lack of awareness and knowledge, because of lack of will and capacity to face the consequences.

Aristotle's philosophy reinforces and resonates quite well with some contemporary accounts of ethical behaviour in business. Educational psychologist Howard Gardner (2007), for example, advocates cultivation of the ethical mind in order to be able to make appropriate ethical decisions in the workplace and to live a satisfying life. As a result of his research into the behaviour of working professionals, he proposes that managers and executives should cultivate an ethical mind to develop and maintain high standards for themselves and their organizations:

> *An ethical mind broadens respect for others into something more abstract. A person with an ethical mind asks herself, 'What kind of a person, worker, and citizen do I want to be? If all workers in my profession adopted the mind-set I have, or if everyone did what I do, what would the world be like?'*
>
> *(Gardner 2007: 34)*

Gardner's idea of the ethical mind that focuses on obligations and responsibilities comes from his work in multiple intelligence that categorizes human cognitive capacities into five minds: the disciplined mind, synthesizing mind, creating mind, respectful mind and ethical mind (Gardner 2008). The disciplined mind is acquired by applying oneself in order to know something very well, to become an expert in an art, craft or profession. The synthesizing mind acknowledges the fact that we are flooded with information, and it is how we decide what to pay attention to, what to ignore, and how to put it together in a way that makes sense to us and others. The creating mind comes

---

approximately 92 per cent, thought the course was useful; 95 per cent of students, who had two to five years' work experience, believed the course was very important and useful, as it gave them the sense that ethical behaviour can truly be a tool for competitive advantage in industry; students who had no work experience – the freshers – reported that the course brought out possible dilemmas they might one day face and helped clarify the criteria they should use to make appropriate decisions when necessary.

up with new ideas that, in the course of time, affect other people. The respectful mind focuses on relationships with others – giving other people the benefit of the doubt, to know and understand them, not be too judgemental, and be capable of forgiveness. The ethical mind is the culmination and abstraction of the other four minds. It imbues a sense of purpose and meaning to our being and activities. It is the capacity to assume responsibility for oneself, others, our community and the environment. It is the basis for moral courage that impels people to go beyond their own experience and advantage, and face the consequences of their actions.

In an organizational setting, as Gardner (2008) illustrates, whistleblowers paradigmatically display ethical minds. Although many employees might notice an owner or top executive doing something wrong, they often prefer to ignore it or pretend not to notice, in order to avoid any consequences. Only the whistleblower is able to liberate themself from such narrow concerns and act courageously. The whistleblower acts ethically, even though it may cost in various ways – for example, losing a job, rejection by management and colleagues, and so on. In his research, Gardner outlines some of the salient qualities required of such individuals, which can be identified and cultivated (Gardner 2008: 127–51). These qualities are increasingly important, as more and more ethical situations and choices in the workplace are not just black and white, but are characterized by ambiguity, different viewpoints, competing claims, incomplete information and conflicting responsibilities. In such situations, moral assessments and decisions cannot be given to executives ready-made, but very much depend on the calibre and character of the decision-maker – and the experience, intelligence, integrity and process that person chooses to deploy.

Managers must cultivate the habit of checking their moral compass by using introspection and reflection; they must seek to be honest with themselves and others. This is particularly important in difficult circumstances. When everything is running smoothly, it is relatively easy to maintain ethical standards. Ethical fibre is really tested only when there are conflicting claims and pressures from different sides. Managers increase their chances of behaving ethically when, from time to time, they check and correct their moral compass to see if it is aligned with the purpose and objectives which they have adopted. Another way to monitor and enhance ethical behaviour is by developing the self-confidence to consider different opinions and seek advice from other people of integrity and experience. When a manager genuinely listens to counsel, from people both within and outside the organization, and tries to act on the basis of such advice, it is unlikely they will falter badly. Wise leaders know well that they do not have all the answers and are happy to submit their views to others before making a decision. Open discussion of problems rather than a dictatorial approach reveals hidden ethical dimensions and alternative points of view that should be taken into account. A highly moral and humane executive will undergo 'positive periodic inoculations' (Gardner 2008: 135–7) – that is, the capacity to draw lessons and inspirations from the experiences of other exemplary executives. An executive can be inoculated from the actions of some outstanding business leaders who are unwilling to compromise even in difficult times.

It is somewhat puzzling that educators in business institutions pay scant attention to the character education of their students, particularly when both ancient wisdom and contemporary findings emphasize the importance of character formation for business decision-making.[4] Business corporations, through defining their purpose solely in terms of economic profit-maximization, and colleges and universities in turn, through focusing narrowly on a set of saleable skills in the market, are in fact caught up in a vicious circle that undermines their own future.

The repercussions of this malaise are widely seen and felt. It may be true that character and personality cannot be moulded within a classroom, or during a business ethics course and a few years of business education. However, it is becoming clear that formal ethical training, done with care and with the active participation of students, enables students to confront their own assumptions and beliefs regarding real-life situations. When students are encouraged to express their viewpoints freely and the teacher leads the discussion in a sensitive way, a classroom can, in some sense, reflect the workplace, where multiple points of view need to be taken into account. If a business ethics classroom is an integral part of a student's introduction to the business world, it can lay solid foundations for a lifetime of learning. Experience shows us that people who have grappled with, thought about and discussed important ethical issues during their education and training are much better equipped to face issues that confront them later in life.

---

4   Although I have focused on Aristotle here, similar philosophies can be found in ancient Indian tradition as well (Kumar and Rao 1996, Mitra 2007). For a discussion of common good leadership in ancient India, particularly in Kautilya's *Arthashastra* and Emperor Ashoka's Edicts, see Alexander and Buckingham (2011).

Corporate Culture and Personal Ethics

French philosopher Paul Ricoeur offers a simple and yet profound definition of ethics. He says that ethics is 'aiming at the good life with and for others, in just institutions' (Ricoeur 1992: 172). This definition comprehensively includes the three dimensions of ethical reflection. The first dimension refers to the personal sphere, centred on aiming at the 'good life', or 'happiness' through virtuous actions. The second dimension refers to the interpersonal sphere, focused on matters of interaction and relationship with others found in family and other forms of informal relationships. The third dimension refers to the institutional sphere, understood as structures of living together in economic, social and political organizations. However, what must be underlined here is that the institutional dimension of ethics is irreducible to the interpersonal dimension, because its interactions are mediated through 'justice' and the 'ethos' of the respective organizations. This implies that ethics is as much an organizational issue as it is a personal or interpersonal matter. In practice, this also implies that managers or business executives who fail to provide ethical leadership and establish systems, policies and procedures that support ethical behaviour in their organizations share responsibility with those who knowingly indulge in malpractice.

In the previous section, I highlighted the urgent need for character education and ethical training in business schools for current and future executives. This objective can also be realized when the importance of business ethics education in the workplace is also acknowledged. Corporate institutions and organizations also have a role in shaping and refining an individual's attitudes and behaviour, and have a responsibility to ensure that executives establish and maintain high standards and a healthy corporate culture. Indeed, current business education needs to be restructured with a view to preparing students to acknowledge and assume greater responsibility for institutional ethics.

From teaching business ethics, I sometimes get the impression that some young people suffer from a sort of moral reductionism – a tendency that limits moral judgement of what is right and wrong only to the interpersonal sphere. The potential for organizations to influence individual behaviour and the responsibility of business leaders to establish and run ethical organizations are not exploited to the maximum (Parks 1993). Many tertiary students do tend to have a strong sense of interpersonal accountability in immediate personal relationships. They are conscious of the consequences of their actions on people with whom they interact on a regular basis. Yet what many of them fail to develop is an understanding of the systemic consequences caused by unjust and badly managed organizations. This oversight has serious implications, particularly because when young executives assume positions of responsibility in large organizations, they cannot plead ignorance of the institutional impact their decisions have on hundreds of people with whom they may or may not personally interact. When an organization is not managed by means of able leadership, fair rules and a positive vision, the power to cause harm to people and the environment can be far-reaching. By overlooking the institutional component of ethical intentionality, executives limit their moral imagination and shirk their larger responsibility to create a positive corporate culture.

In this context, it would be an incomplete assessment to conclude that the corporate fraud revealed at, for example, Satyam Systems or Enron were merely the acts of a few greedy senior executives (Paine 2003: 85–112). While the misdeeds and leadership failures of individuals should be acknowledged, it is no less important to stress that these instances of corporate collapse truly were an indictment of almost the entire corporate culture. This can also be said for morally praiseworthy conduct. Exemplary behaviour is often a reflection of a supportive organizational culture and philosophy, characterized by collective responsibility and accountability. In business ethics and leadership literature, it is often noted, for example, that Johnson & Johnson's resolution of the Tylenol crisis was possible due to the integrity and foresight of one individual – the then Chief Executive, James Burke. Yet, as Paine (2003: 91) rightly comments, even though the decision to conduct a nationwide recall of Tylenol capsules to avoid further loss of life must have originated with one individual, it would not have materialized if it were not supported by thousands of decisions made by other individuals at all levels of the organization. Therefore, it may be more appropriate to describe the Tylenol decision as an outcome not only of an individual's effort, but also the achievement of an organization's vibrant and healthy culture.

People can easily understand business corporations are organizations in which people influence one another to establish accepted values and ways of doing things. Yet the kind and degree of influence an organization can exert on its members often depends on the kind of purpose it espouses. A company that defines its purpose solely in terms of profit-maximization, and leaves ethics to chance or goodwill, influences its employees in that direction. On the other hand, a company that embraces a larger purpose than just profit-maximization and makes explicit efforts to be ethical in all its processes and outcomes shapes its employees quite differently. As Andrews puts it:

> *When they first come to work, individuals whose moral judgement may ultimately determine their company's ethical character enter a community whose values will influence their own. The economic function of the corporation is necessarily one of those values. But if it is the only value, ethical inquiry cannot flourish. If management believes that the invisible hand of the market adequately moderates the injury done by the pursuit of self-interest, ethical policy can be dismissed as irrelevant. And if what people see (while they are hearing about maximizing shareholder wealth) are managers dedicated to their own survival and compensation, they will naturally be more concerned about rewards than about fairness.*
>
> *(Andrews 2003: 73)*

Since the kind of institutional context and corporate culture in operation has a decisive role in what individuals will absorb and practise, it is an additional burden on senior managers and executives to understand and articulate that corporate success needs to go beyond profit-maximization. Not only do businesses that embrace broader objectives attract and retain better and more talented employees, but investors, suppliers and customers tend to be loyal to companies with a reputation for integrity and fairness. It is wrong for business leaders and managers to pit a company's shareholders' interests against the interests of other stakeholders, such as employees, customers and the community, and to think of successful management as making skilful trade-offs between the two. Just as a rising tide lifts all boats, it is becoming evident that the interests of all of a firm's major stakeholders usually rise and fall together. It is rarely the case that a company can keep its shareholders happy while other stakeholders are dissatisfied. Good managers consider their fiduciary responsibility not only in terms of maximizing profits for shareholders, but also in terms of the interests of other stakeholders, including the community and the environment. The degree and nature of the obligation towards various stakeholders would, of course, vary, but the best practices in the field indicate that willingness to view responsibility in a broader perspective will actually pay off in the long term. This implies that sometimes managers must be prepared to turn down profitable offers and lose money in the short term when such offers fail to pass ethical tests.

According to Collins and Porras (2002: 115–38), one of the reasons why companies such as IBM, Disney and Procter & Gamble came to be described as 'visionary' was because of their belief in the power of the organization to shape individuals' attitudes and abilities in line with the core ideologies of the company. As a result, these companies try to translate their core ideologies into a set of visible values, as well as putting mechanisms and procedures in place to actualize them in their business operations. They also undertake to educate and 'indoctrinate' their employees and other stakeholders so they fit in with the organization's culture. It is quite common to think that visionary companies are great places to work for everyone. But Collins and Porras's investigation has challenged this assumption. Visionary companies are great places to work, not for everyone, but *only* for those people who are able to absorb the company values and fit in with the company ethos. They found:

> Only those who 'fit' extremely well with the core ideology and demanding standards of a visionary company will find it a great place to work. If you go to work at a visionary company, you will either fit and flourish – probably couldn't be happier – or you will likely be expunged like a virus. It's binary. There is no middle ground. It's almost cult-like. Visionary companies are so clear about what they stand for and what they're trying to achieve that they simply don't have room for those unwilling or unable to fit their exacting standards.
>
> (Collins and Porras 2002: 9)

Here, terms like 'cult-like' and 'expunged like a virus' do not suggest that these organizations function like cults in the negative sense of the term. Instead, the point is to emphasize that these organizations have a much stronger corporate culture than other companies and have evolved policies, programmes and practices that preserve their core ideology in specific and concrete ways. Also, 'cult' in standard parlance means cult of personality, applying particularly to religious and social movements centred on a charismatic cult leader. In contrast, visionary companies are cult-like in their absolute focus on their core values and ideologies. Hence, when an organization is described as 'visionary' and 'a great place to work', it should not be thought of as soft, undisciplined and willing to accommodate anything and anyone. On the contrary, because visionary companies have such clarity about who they are, what they are about and what they are trying to achieve, they tend not to have much room for people unwilling, unsuited for or unable to adapt to their demanding standards.

Business educators should impress upon their students that responsible leadership involves creating a positive corporate culture that pays attention to not only profit-maximization, but also social obligations.

Paedagogical Strategies

If the objective of business ethics education, as argued in this chapter, is holistic character formation and not just teaching marketable skills, then careful consideration should be given to some paedagogical strategies and the importance of effective mentorship. It is essential to adopt teaching and learning methods that facilitate the development of intellectual capabilities and encourage maturity. To this end, case studies are proving to be one of the most effective ways of teaching business ethics. Case studies can be actual or hypothetical stories of situations in the business world where people are confronted with difficult ethical choices. Some may be presented in narrative forms, while others are structured into an analytical style in order to make moral dilemmas stand out clearly. Experience shows that teaching and analysing case studies enables students to become aware of the different moral issues involved and of the possible solutions to these issues (Hill and Stewart 1999, Watson 2003).[5] In comparison with lectures and other traditional paedagogical methods, case study is much more appealing and effective. It not only derives certain concepts and theories from real-life situations, but also makes students participate actively, challenging them to look for creative solutions to problems they face. A typical case analysis includes ascertaining the facts related to the case, identifying the major principles, rules and values involved, looking at the various options available for resolving the issues, and evaluating the decisions of the actors involved. For example, to teach about the value of justice and corporate social responsibility, rather than discussing these ideas in the abstract, it might be better to consider them by discussing an actual problem such as that created by the Special Economic Zones (SEZs) that are being set up in India. Thousands of SEZs are now established in the countryside, with the intention of attracting direct foreign investment and accelerating business growth and employment opportunities. And yet SEZs have displaced many poor farmers and communities because they use the vast areas of agricultural land on which their livelihoods depend. The unilateral ways in which the land has

---

5   Further results from the qualitative survey described in footnote 4 above showed that the students believed that the paedagogical methods used for teaching business ethics play a crucial role in generating interest in the subject and make a significant difference to learning outcomes. The students felt that the paedagogical methods must create awareness, rather than enforce particular ethical positions. Most of the students (96 per cent) thought the case study method was one of the best ways to teach business ethics since it can be used to bring about a multi-pronged way of looking at problems and help students come up with a holistic solution, where all stakeholders are satisfied. Case studies can also show that profits and ethics are not either/or options, but are strongly interlinked. Another learning method that was largely appreciated by the students was to use personal reflection: writing a short reflective journal on different problems and topics discussed in class.

been acquired and the inadequate compensation paid to displaced residents have become questionable. When students are presented with the dilemma of economic growth and employment opportunities on the one hand, and injustices to farmers and the poor on the other, it prompts them to think about what justice and corporate social responsibility actually means in a specific context, and what they can do about it.

Deploying stories and case studies is a good way to develop the moral imagination so crucial to the ethical training of people in responsible positions. As Werhane (1999: 93) puts it, moral imagination is 'the ability in particular circumstances to discover and evaluate possibilities not merely determined by that circumstance, or limited by its operative mental models, or merely framed by a set of rules or rule-governed concerns'. Being morally imaginative requires a combination of multiple capacities. It involves, at the outset, becoming aware of the actual situation, in all its dimensions and viewpoints. Moral imagination does not mean flight from reality, but getting deeply involved in reality. This implies that the executive perceives the situation and frames the problem correctly. Very often, mistakes can occur at the stage of ethical framing, especially when the person is careless or allows self-interest to take over. Furthermore, moral imagination also involves the ability to step back and disengage oneself from the situation, in order to evaluate it 'objectively', and the ability to come up with fresh solutions. It is true that our assessments and critiques are located in a particular culture, history, education and community. Nevertheless, only when we learn to devise ways of disengaging and stepping back will we be able to arrive at viable and achievable solutions to problems in corporate situations. A business ethics education that skilfully uses case studies and narratives from the corporate world has a better chance of cultivating the moral imagination of managers and executives.

Collaborative learning is another effective paedagogical strategy for business ethics education. Given the fact that education is a network of relationships not just between the teacher and students, but also among peers, business ethics education should value and adopt group processes and collaborative learning. Collaborative learning influences students in many ways, including building their self-esteem, leadership skills, intellectual performance, communication abilities and sensitivity to the needs of others. Collaborative learning methods often involve dividing students into teams for theoretical as well as practical projects. Emphasis here is on group discussions, group work, group responses and group reporting. As members of a team, participants take responsibility not only for their own learning, but also for the learning of others.

Somehow, it the idea has found its way into the business psyche and dominant models of business education that success in the corporate world requires individualistic intelligence and competitive work. But today, in the modern globalized knowledge economy, capacity for teamwork and collaboration with people from different background and cultures is as important as individual excellence and performance. Business enterprises and educational institutions that are unwilling to absorb this fact and reorient their focus will eventually become obsolete.

The benefits of collaborative learning are many. It makes the individual aware that, just as in the actual workplace and corporate setting, there can be multiple points of view on the issue at hand. One cannot simply hold a parochial view, saying that what he or she thinks is right. One should be able to give a reasonable justification for their own standpoint and be willing to listen to what others have to say. Individuals who have the responsibility of leading organizations and people should never fall into the complacent attitude of isolating themselves and refusing to listen to others. Collaborative learning also promotes a greater sense of community and serves as an excellent training ground for conflict management. In a collaborative project, individual success and group success is bound together; people are willing to accommodate and co-operate with each other. This does not, however, mean that there will not be disagreements. Conflicts of ideas and personalities are likely to occur in group processes and collaborative learning projects. As members of the team come from different backgrounds, upbringings and ideologies, it is only natural that there are conflicts of interests and interpretation. Learning to resolve them successfully through consensus and dialogue is important, as both young and experienced executives will sooner or later have to face situations of conflict.

The value and importance of continuous mentoring for business education, and particularly for ethical training, cannot be emphasized enough. People learn to do the right thing by observing good people and by copying what they do. What most attract and influence young minds are not sophisticated arguments and ethical theories, but everyday examples of courtesy, decency, fairness and goodness from the lives of successful people. The influence on young people will be even stronger and more enduring when such examples come not from remote and elevated heroes and saints, but from people who interact with them on a regular basis. Good role models and admirable examples of teachers and senior executives offer reliable standards of honesty, loyalty, integrity and compassion. They demonstrate why and how it is important to be ethical even under extreme pressure to do otherwise.

In a company or business school setting, this can take the form of at least two kinds of mentor–student relationship. The first is professional mentoring, wherein the concentration is on the development of vocational skills in order to improve the student's career opportunities. But educators are beginning to realize that professional mentoring needs to be supported by character mentoring – in which the mentor guides the mentee in cultivating a set of ethical attitudes and skills. In this approach, mentors serve not only as professional role models, but also as character role models. Even though theoretically it is possible to make a distinction between these two ways of guiding present and future professionals, effective mentoring is that which is able to combine both. A mentor who focuses only on professional mentoring and assists students with their career aspirations, but eventually fails to inspire people with a life of integrity, cannot exert a lasting influence.

Conclusion

Corporate leaders do not just occupy a position, but they are also expected to take a position on many different things that matter to both individuals and organizations. Taking a position often requires not only knowing what is right, but also having the capacity and moral courage to do what is right. It involves facilitating a positive corporate culture that encourages and recognizes ethical behaviour. At times, it may also require going against double standards and bogus corporate cultures that supposedly encourage individuals to display respect and integrity while encouraging them to compromise whenever it is expedient on the basis that 'everyone else does it'. Ethics is not merely doing what is feasible in the given situation, but changing the situation by doing what is right.

This chapter has pointed out that the capacities and courage required of a moral leader need to be cultivated deliberately through a character-focused business ethics education and through the practice of continuing mentorship in industry. It has also argued that business education needs to train both early career and experienced executives to uphold and promote high ethical standards and healthy corporate cultures. It is indeed a matter of urgency to realize that business ethics can no longer be left to goodwill or chance, simply because the cost of doing so will be huge for our future.

References

Alexander. J. 2005. 'Non-reductionist naturalism: Nussbaum between Aristotle and Hume'. *Res Publica: A Journal of Legal and Social Philosophy*, 11(2), 157–83.

Alexander, J. and Buckingham, J. 2011. 'Common good leadership in business management: An ethical model from the Indian tradition'. *Business Ethics: A European Review*, 20(4), 317–27.

Andrews, K.R. 2003. 'Ethics in practice', in *Harvard Business Review on Corporate Ethics*. Boston, MA: Harvard Business Press, 67–84.

Aristotle. 1978. *Ethics*, trans. J.A.K. Thomson, London: Penguin Books.

Badaracco, J.L. 2003. 'The discipline of building character', in *Harvard Business Review on Corporate Ethics*. Boston, MA: Harvard Business Press, 139–64.

Bowie, N.E. and Werhane, P.H. 2002. *Management Ethics*. Malden: Blackwell.

Collins, J. and Porras, J.I. 2002. *Built to Last*. New York: HarperCollins.

Curren, R. 2007. 'Cultivating the moral and intellectual virtues', in *Philosophy of Education: An Anthology*, ed. R. Curren. Malden: Blackwell, 507–16.

Gardner, H. 2007. 'The ethical mind'. *Harvard Business Review South Asia*, (March), 33–7.

Gardner, H. 2008. *Five Minds for the Future.* Boston, MA: Harvard Business Press.

Gautschi, F.H. and Jones, T.M. 1998. 'Enhancing the ability of business students to recognize ethical issues: An empirical assessment of the effectiveness of a course in business ethics'. *Journal of Business Ethics*, 17(2), 205–16.

Gellerman, S.W. 2003. 'Why "good" managers make bad ethical choices', in *Harvard Business Review on Corporate Ethics*. Boston, MA: Harvard Business Press, 49–66.

Hartman, E.M. 2008. 'Socratic questions and Aristotelian answers: A virtue-based approach to business ethics'. *Journal of Business Ethics*, 78, 313–28.

Hill, A. and Stewart, I. 1999. 'Character education in business schools: Pedagogical strategies'. *Teaching Business Ethics*, 3, 179–93.

Jones, T.M. 1990. 'Can business ethics be taught? Empirical evidence'. *Business and Professional Ethics Journal*, 8(2), 73–94.

Krishnan, V.R. 2008. 'Impact of MBA education on students' values: Two longitudinal studies'. *Journal of Business Ethics*, 83, 223–46.

Kumar, S.N. and Rao, U.S. 1996. 'Guidelines for value based management in Kautilya's Arthasastra'. *Journal of Business Ethics*, 15, 415–23.

Mintz, S.M. 1996. 'Aristotelian virtue and business ethics education'. *Journal of Business Ethics*, 15(8), 827–38.

Mitra, M. 2007. *It's Only Business! India's Corporate Responsiveness in a Globalized World*. New Delhi: Oxford University Press.

Paine, L.S. 2003. 'Managing for organizational integrity', in *Harvard Business Review on Corporate Ethics*. Boston, MA: Harvard Business Press, 85–112.

Parks, S.D. 1993. 'Is it too late? Young adults and formation of professional ethics', in *Can Ethics Be Taught? Perspectives, Challenges and Approaches*, ed. T.R. Piper et al. Boston, MA: Harvard Business Press, 13–72.

Podolny, J.M. 2009. 'The buck stops (and starts) at business school'. *Harvard Business Review South Asia*, June, 50–55.

Ricoeur, P. 1992. *Oneself As Another*, trans. K. Blamey. Chicago, IL: University of Chicago Press.

Watson, C.E. 2003. 'Using stories to teach business ethics'. *Teaching Business Ethics*, 7, 93–105.

Werhane, P. 1999. *Moral Imagination and Management Decision-Making*. New York: Oxford University Press.

10

Conclusion: New Directions in Corporate Social Responsibility

Jane Buckingham and Venkataraman Nilakant

Introduction

THE NEED FOR ALTERNATIVES

The persistence of the American model of the corporation into the twenty-first century is in part a result of the dominance of the American economy, particularly since 1945. However, as America weakens and global economies become increasingly driven by China, India, Brazil, Russia and Eastern Europe, the need to consider alternative ways of doing and managing business which include non-American and non-Western perspectives is becoming imperative. The chapters in this book all point to the need to reflect on the traditions of management, both Western and non-Western, which can contribute to the development of more equitable and sustainable economic practice both locally and globally. The rapid acceleration of globalization has made awareness of both non-Western and Western approaches to business critical to the success of corporations world-wide. China and India's economic acceleration is rapidly increasing their participation in a globalized business culture. At the same time, despite the high performance of a handful of companies, Japan's re-entry into economic prominence after a long period of economic stagnation is being hampered by a lack of flexibility and internationalization in management structures ('Japanese Corporate Performance' 2011). Globalization and awareness of non-Western approaches to management is no longer an optional extra in companies doing business with the non-Western world.

Managing Responsibly brings a range of non-Western responses to a global financial crisis and to a broader crisis in ethical management. It seizes this moment to stimulate debate. It urges all those participating in corporate management and in educating the next generation of participants in the global economy to seek more socially responsible alternatives to current models of 'self-interest maximization' business practice. This chapter emphasizes the historical specificity of the current model of the corporation and the challenge posed to its value base by new directions in contemporary economic analysis. Further, it takes up the challenges offered by Sen and Nussbaum to consider how current economic practice is based in fundamental injustices, marginalizing sections of the community – particularly the poor – and asks whether new approaches to measuring business success such as the 'capabilities approach' can help to resolve these injustices. By emphasizing that current notions of the corporation are relatively recent developments and historicizing the linkage of business management and social responsibility, this chapter challenges any assumption that the current economic order of things is natural, inevitable or impossible to change.

Non-sustainability of the Present Model

The present model of shareholder capitalism is simply unsustainable. According to the World Bank, the global GDP in 2010 was around US$63 trillion (World Bank 2010). According to management consultants McKinsey & Company, the value of global financial stock that includes equity market capitalization, outstanding bonds and loans in 2010 was around US$212 trillion (McKinsey & Company, *Capital Markets Up Date*, 2011). A 10 per cent increase on these financial assets of US$212 trillion translates to more than 30 per cent increase in the real economy of US$63 trillion. Such growth rates in the real economy are not only unsustainable, but unrealistic. The rise of financial stock has been fuelled by lowering interest rates in the United States which facilitated a property market bubble across the world that eventually led to the financial crisis of 2008. The plethora of books written on the global financial crisis point to some common themes as the underlying causes (Lewis 2010, Tett 2009, Sorkin 2009). Stagnant real wages in the United States since the 1980s widened the income gap and increased inequality. The only way for people in the lower strata of society to perceive improvements in their standard of living was through a debt-fuelled, consumption-oriented lifestyle. The US Federal Reserve, under Alan Greenspan, facilitated this lifestyle by lowering interest rates. Banks borrowed these low-interest funds and loaned them to people who lacked the wherewithal to pay back the loans with interest. Smart bankers with advanced quantitative skills created complex financial instruments such as collateralized debt obligations and sold them to other financial institutions to cover the credit risk. These well-intentioned efforts, instead of distributing risk, actually amplified it throughout the whole financial system, leading to the present crisis. Unlike the corporate equity and the commodity futures markets, the derivatives market was unregulated, relying instead on self-regulation. Unrestrained greed, masquerading as self-interest, provided the fuse that ignited the potent mix of toxic assets. While it is unfair to blame any individuals or groups for the current state of affairs, a naive belief in the ability of free markets to self-regulate and the hostility of the banks to external regulation stand out as the core themes.

The neo-liberal ideology that has promoted free-market capitalism as the panacea for the world's problems has had some unfortunate consequences. The most glaring of these is the way that in most countries, wealth is concentrated in the hands of a very few. As the 2011 'Occupy Wall Street' protestors pointed out, the top 1 per cent of the US population controls 40 per cent of the net worth in that country. Real wages in the United States have stagnated since the 1980s. The middle class, once seen as the vanguard of capitalism, has been impoverished. We are in a historical moment that calls for a re-examination of the current corporate model of governance and management. In this book, we have taken a tentative step in identifying alternative business models from other times and other parts of the world. We do not provide a substantive framework to replace the current self-interest-based model of corporate management. However, we do suggest that socially and economically sustainable alternative business approaches can be developed by implementing new approaches to measuring business success which include indices of human well-being broader than delivery of profit to a narrow band of shareholders. Further, we consider that any legitimate and sustainable alternative to current practice must be firmly rooted in an inclusive notion of justice. The optimism to seek an alternative to the present business models begins with recognition of the historical specificity of our economic and management practices and their vulnerability to change.

Historicizing the Corporation

In the Preface, we described a graph indicating the persistence of shareholder value as a management concept despite increased attention to CSR from the year 2000. The dichotomy represented in this graph reflects a long history of debate over the role of business in society. As this book suggests, the current concept of a corporation as 'a nexus of private contracts designed to enhance shareholder value' is neither universal nor inevitable as a business model (Banerjee 2007: 9). Rather, the modern corporation is the result of nineteenth-century legal changes which broke the dominance of earlier models of corporate entity that required incorporation under charter to the state. The East India Company, Vereenigde Oost-Indische Compagnie (United East India Company) and La Compagnie des Indes Orientales (French East India Company) which drove European expansion and provided the foundation of European colonial activity from the early seventeenth century were all constituted under state charter. Under American and European law, such chartered companies could lose their franchise if they were proven to have misused their powers or not acted in the public interest. The East India Company, for example, was systematically stripped of its trading powers in 1813 and 1833 as the terms of its charter were redefined by the British Parliament. On the grounds of recurrent bankruptcy and persistent disregard for both the British and the Indian public interest, Parliament transformed the company from a joint-stock company into an arm of the British colonial government in India (Robins 2006: 153–7, Peers 2006: 71–2). The degree to which this action was in the public interest of the Indian population is highly debatable (Banerjee 2007: 15). Within the late eighteenth- and early nineteenth-century rhetoric of utilitarianism and improvement, however, the British Parliament considered itself both legally entitled and morally justified to take such action, particularly when it was seen as of certain advantage to Britain (Robins 2006: 136–57).

While the East India Company was being dismantled as a joint-stock company, in America the subordination of the corporation to the state was being challenged. During the early nineteenth century, a series of laws gradually released American corporations from limitations on accumulation of wealth, property and the requirement to serve the public good – conditions of incorporation under state charter. The emergence of the new corporation was strongly contested in both private and public spheres. However, by the late nineteenth century, the involvement of the state in the formation of corporations in America had become redundant. The corporation was now a legal entity, in private ownership and possessing rights to private property. The reconfiguration of the corporation meant that it was no longer required to serve the public interest. The new model of the corporation was constituted at a specific historic moment principally to enable small, politically motivated interest groups to pursue the accumulation of private wealth with minimal restriction. As in the transformation of the East India Company into an arm of government, ideological support eased the transition. In the American case, emerging republican ideas of freedom and civic responsibility supported the economic structural change from chartered firm to corporate body (Banerjee 2007: 7–12).

Historicizing Corporate Social Responsibility

The long debate about the public responsibility of business which had driven the notion of the trading company and ideologies of free trade from the seventeenth century entered new territory with the creation of the corporation as a legal entity. By the early twentieth century, rather than accountability to the public interest mediated through state charter, a tension emerged between two ideas of the corporation: first, the assumption that the new corporate body was constituted to function primarily in the interest of its shareholders, and second, that it possessed a capacity, and indeed a duty, to operate on the basis of civic virtue. As with previous disputes over the role of corporations, the legal process of dispute-resolution continued to shape the character of the new corporation. Increasingly, legal judgments tended towards emphasizing the responsibility of the company's board of directors to maximize shareholder wealth over any exercise of civic virtue (Regan 1998: 294, Banerjee 2007: 13–14). In 1990, the American Bar Association clearly expressed the privileging of shareholder value in resolving legal disputes between shareholder and civic interest: 'While allowing directors to give consideration to the interests of others, the law compels them to find some reasonable relationship to the long-term interests of the shareholders when so doing' (cited in Banerjee 2007: 14).

The modern Western discourse of CSR has been configured as the effort to put a soul into the corporate body (Banerjee 2007: 15). However, it can be better, if less compellingly, understood as the continuation of the nineteenth-century debates over the relationship between business and society. As Chapters 4, 5 and 6 of this book indicate, this debate has by no means been limited to Western post-Enlightenment economies. The modern Western corporation has been maligned as a sociopathic individual acting purely in self-interest, without remorse and without regard for the safety of either itself or others (Patel 2009: 41–3). Contemporary managers do face real challenges in maintaining the profit needed to pay salaries as well as produce dividends within the rapidly changing market and currency conditions characteristic of the accelerated global economy (Regan 1998: 306). The problem is the degree to which profit is shareholder-orientated to the detriment of the broader stakeholders in the business, and with often catastrophic costs to environmental and social well-being (Patel 2009: 41–51).

From the 1950s, ideas of CSR developed as part of the struggle between the shareholder and civil society for the attentions of the corporation. However, the notion that acting out of social responsibility will be detrimental to the profitability of the firm remains a strong check on the attraction of CSR ideas to business (Regan 1998: 296). Moreover, there remain a plethora of ideologies and configurations of corporate social responsibility. One thing is clear; the ideologies of CSR are as susceptible as any other to changing economic conditions. The adoption in the 1980s of CSR as a strategy of business advantage – 'doing good to do well' – reflects an incorporation of this values approach into the robust 'greed is good' mentality of the 1980s (Banerjee 2007: 14, Vogel 2005). In the last two decades, however, economic crises have encouraged a more committed interest in CSR as supporting more economically sustainable business practices. Radical rethinking of the relationship between society and economy and the role of the corporation within that has emerged in a variety of economic fields.

Development Economics and Measurements of Human Well-being

Development economics has become a particularly rich field for economic critique. In the last few decades, development economics has diversified from its roots in welfare economics into a number of sub-fields, including economic theories of justice (Edwards and Pellé 2011: 336). Revised notions of economic justice have not remained confined to the realm of theory, but as economic downturn has followed the excesses of the 1980s, they have become embedded into measurements of human well-being. Most famously, Mahbub ul Haq and Amartya Sen's creation of a Human Development Index (HDI) to demonstrate the impact of economic conditions on human lives has moved the United Nations away from simple Gross National Product measures of income as measures of human well-being (Sen 2010: 226). The HDI and more recent calls for embedding human well-being into performance indicators for business and corporate activity reflect a growing recognition among not only International Monetary Fund and World Bank administrators but also ordinary citizens that human value cannot be subordinated to the demands of a profit margin.

Mismeasuring our Lives, the 2010 *Report by the Commission on the Measurement of Economic Performance and Social Progress* argued that despite the persistent orientation of economic measurements towards monetary values, ordinary people are not interested solely in income per capita and economic performance, but 'care about many dimensions of the quality of life' (Stiglitz, Sen and Fitoussi 2010: xx).

Contemporary economic analysis of 'quality of life' as a factor to include in business and corporate activity tends to be constructed in terms of a trade-off. Either 'quality of life' or profit are achievable, but not both. Reducing environmental damage by a mining company, for example, is seen as achievable only at a loss or reduction in economic value (Stiglitz, Sen and Fitoussi 2010: xx). The Commission argues that the dominant model of assessing quality of life in economic terms needs to be rethought, and a broader conceptualization of economic value as just one element of 'quality of life' needs to be developed (Stiglitz, Sen and Fitoussi 2010: xxii–xxvi).

These movements towards linking economic conditions to more realistic measurements of economic impact on human value reflect a deep intuitive understanding among ordinary people that the existing institutional models of economic valuation support business structures that are inherently unjust. The movement towards developing alternative economic measurements is driven by a desire to remove the 'clearly remediable injustices' embedded within economic practice (Sen 2010: vii). Underpinning our argument for alternative approaches to management is this deeper issue: the need to develop approaches to management and business practice that are recognizable as essentially just by people both in and outside the corporation.

Economic Justice

The notion of justice, like any philosophical position, has a long history and is culturally variable. From within the Western philosophical tradition, however, we can look at Anglo-American business ethics from a different perspective. We can see more clearly the importance and impact of notions of justice on economic theory and practice, and their implications for human welfare. There is a strong Western philosophical tradition of a contractual theory of social and economic relations and a range of contemporary versions of contractarianism. An underlying notion in this tradition is the idea that the motive of mutual advantage is at the core of economic and social relations (Nussbaum 2006: 50–54). These contractarian ideas broadly underpin the 'self-interest' philosophy discussed throughout this book as fundamental to current business practices. The Hobbesian tradition of contractarianism argues that humans act from positions of self-interest, and that 'maximizing self-interest' is at the core of all human action, including the decision to act morally or ethically towards weaker or more vulnerable members of society. As discussed in the first chapter of this book, it is this concept of self-interest-based contractarianism which dominates contemporary management culture. The Kantian tradition somewhat modifies Hobbesian ideas, arguing that as rational beings, we must recognize the ethical status of other human beings. Rather than the self-interest of the Hobbesian tradition, the Kantian approach posits that humans are motivated by commitment to a set of values which they believe they will be held to ('Contractarianism' 2007).

Although we may seem to function in some sort of 'neutral/commonsense' environment, both Hobbesian and Kantian notions of social contract underpin our everyday assumptions about life (Nussbaum 2006: 4). Moreover, they contribute to the way we understand economic relations and conceptualize ideas such as what constitutes a reasonable distribution of resources, including to those who are not economically powerful. Historically and practically, there is a strong hierarchy of political and economic power built into contractarianism. The economically strong, being the members of society wielding the greatest political authority, also have the opportunity to decide the shape of rights and the way notions of 'justice' are configured. The economically strong tend to be in the position to influence the way society is defined, even to decide who will be regarded as citizens and participants in political and economic opportunities and who will shape ethical and other decision-making (Nussbaum 2006: 9–95).

In modern contractarian theory, John Rawls fits more closely with the Kantian tradition, but even he finds it difficult to integrate some communities into broad theories of justice (Rawls 1999). Nussbaum argues that there are three groups which Rawls and other philosophers continue to neglect in their theories of justice: first, 'people with physical and mental impairments', second, 'all world citizens', and third, 'non-human animals' (Nussbaum 2006: 1–4). Leaving aside the non-human for this discussion, the categories of human beings identified by Nussbaum as neglected by existing theories of justice are the categories particularly susceptible to the impacts of the 'self-interest' models of globalized corporate activity. Nussbaum's contribution to the rethinking of justice has been her bringing of an Aristotelian approach together with insights from Amartya Sen's 'capability' approach to economic well-being into a reworking of Rawls's philosophy of justice (Nussbaum 2006). Based on the insights offered by Sen and Nussbaum, we suggest that a basis for rethinking approaches to business practice requires a radical repositioning of notions of justice not just to prioritize a small number of shareholders, but to include the groups typically excluded in theories of justice, particularly those with disabilities and the global poor. It is a lot to ask of companies to adjust their priorities while maintaining the profit which is the requirement of business activity.

However, the failure of Anglo-American business school approaches to business ethics and the spectacular economic and social breakdowns of recent decades indicate the need for such radical rethinking.

Capability Theory

Sen's approach to economic justice comes from development economics rather than corporate business models. As such, it does not prioritize shareholder value to the detriment of broader stakeholders, but focuses on the well-being of the wider community. It may appear strange to look for corporate approaches within development economics. However, as we have argued throughout this book, the evident failure of the existing models suggests that looking for alternatives outside the usual domain of business studies is a necessity. Sen's development perspective is a reminder that business transactions contribute not only to wealth-creation, but also to exacerbation of poverty in environmental and resource terms, as well as economic. Measurements of wealth such as mean increases in national or regional income per capita can hide other losses of local livelihoods and natural resources such as water supplies and forests. Sen's economics recognizes poverty as engaging broader aspects of human well-being than the purely monetary. He argues for the recognition of poverty as not simply an economic circumstance, but a condition of human rights deprivation.

For Sen, economic systems which generate poverty of opportunity – or, in other words, which limit human capability – are essentially unjust. Sen argues that poverty is not solely a matter of income, though income is a factor in poverty: from a capabilities perspective, 'poverty must be seen as the deprivation of basic capabilities rather than merely as lowness of incomes, which is the standard definition of poverty'. Low income can of course contribute to limitation of capabilities, but even high income can in some circumstances be inadequate for people with particular needs, such as those with a disability (Sen 2000: 90). A person who is unable to drive an ordinary car may be able to drive a specially adapted car. However, such a car would typically be more expensive than a standard model. Similarly, a person with little or no disposable income and who cannot afford an inexpensive crutch may be completely immobilized because they cannot gain the small additional portion of income needed. Capability in this context is tied closely to basic human rights – the capability to receive adequate nourishment, housing and education. However, the concept goes further than the basic needs for survival. According to the capability approach, the person's advantage is not based solely on their income or wealth, but on their capability or real opportunity to achieve the things of value to them, such as mobility, a social life and the opportunity to work.

The power of the capability approach lies in its contribution to the information base upon which a company's performance can be measured. Rather than measuring shareholder value, its focus is on a plurality of human functioning. The capability approach asks whether the company's performance will produce a profit in economic terms. But it also asks whether the company will contribute to the opportunity of its employees and suppliers to not only feed, clothe and shelter themselves and their dependents, but also educate their children and enjoy a social and cultural life that is meaningful to them. The capability approach is unique in embracing a plurality of concerns and not only accommodating provision of basic human needs for survival, but allowing for human aspirations such as developing new skills and opportunities, and enabling participation in cultural and community life. Essentially, it measures as successful not so much the means of living – the economic measurement of income – but the opportunity to live in a way that is valuable to the individual. In this sense, it focuses on the capability of people to live lives of value to themselves, rather than their acquisition of income or possessions as a measure of success (Sen 2010: 231–3). Sen's capability approach essentially offers alternative approaches to the assessment of human well-being which answer the needs posed in the *Report by the Commission on the Measurement of Economic Performance and Social Progress* discussed above (Stiglitz, Sen and Fitoussi 2010). It does not offer a blueprint for change, but includes a range of mechanisms which enable companies to be held more broadly accountable for their impact on human well-being at the local and global level.

Conclusion

The chapters in this book signal the viability of thinking about business in ways that, while maintaining the primary focus of business, do not give absolute priority to shareholder well-being and shareholder profit-maximization. Part II of this book – and indeed the earlier sections of this chapter – not only emphasize the historical particularity of the business models which currently dominate our globalized economy, but offer alternative historical and philosophical models for business practice. In Chapter 4, Nilakant and Lips-Wiersma suggest looking for alternative ethical business philosophies in Indian tradition. In the following chapter, Buckingham presents ancient Indian guild organizations as a practical example of viable integration of community needs and aspirations into business activity and profit-making. Turning to New Zealand in Chapter 6, Tau offers insights into the need to accommodate traditional Ngāi Tahu tribal ideals with the demands of contemporary corporate business despite the difficulties of such integration.

After examining non-Western historical and philosophical approaches to business and corporate governance, rethinking the way we measure business success is an important next step towards finding new approaches to doing business in a globalized future. In Chapter 3, Basu insists that the environmental and human health costs of doing business must be measured alongside profit in terms of loss and gain. We argue that the incorporation of broader measurements of human well-being into measurements of business success, as suggested by Sen's capability approach, will help to ensure that businesses cannot pursue profits while suppliers, customers and those living in the vicinity of business activity suffer. The recent 'blood minerals' case, for example, in which Congolese people work under slave conditions to supply rare earths for the electronics industry, is supported by measurements of business success that focus on profit rather than the broader human impact of business activities (Mason 2010).

It is naive to assume that businesses will easily embrace measurements that will potentially reduce their profit. However, some of the strategies suggested by Sanyal in Chapter 2, such as corporate governance laws, general legislation and competition, are powerful tools in persuading companies to take broader responsibility for their activities. After the United States passed legislation requiring transparency in supply chains, Nokia, for example, has joined a consortium working on 'supply chain due diligence' to ensure that mineral supply is not at the expense of human well-being ('EU vows' 2011, Nokia 2011). How effective such efforts will be and whether they will make for lasting change in the way business is done will not only be a matter of legislation. As discussed by Mills, Cammock and Alexander in Part III of our book, meaningful communication, a genuine interest in the just involvement of people in all aspects of business activity and the ongoing ethical education of corporate leaders will be necessary if any change in corporate culture is to gain traction.

Existing mechanisms for measuring economic health easily hide oppression, dehumanization and the political, social and economic exclusion of vast sectors of the global and local population. We hope that our book has opened a debate on how to rectify these manifest injustices. We argue that managing responsibly is more than managing the bottom line. It requires building notions of human well-being into business plans and taking responsibility for all aspects of business impact, not just the wealth of a few. As a starting point for rethinking business priorities, we suggest that integrating a 'capability approach' to measuring human well-being into corporate planning and practice offers a more equitable notion of economic justice upon which new business models, more broadly sustainable than 'self-interest maximization' shareholder models, can be developed. Hope for the future lies in such businesses, both voluntarily and legally regulated, and committed to high performance against a range of 'capability' indices, rather than a simple measurement of financial profit.

References

Banerjee, S.B. 2007. *Corporate Social Responsibility: The Good, the Bad and the Ugly.* Cheltenham: Edward Elgar.

'Contractarianism'. 2007. *Stanford Encyclopedia of Philosophy,* revised 4 April, http://plato.stanford.edu/entries/contractarianism/, accessed 26 March 2012.

Edwards, J.M. and Pellé, S. 2011. 'Capabilities for the miserable; happiness for the satisfied'. *Journal of the History of Economic Thought,* 33(3), 335–55.

'EU vows to tackle "blood minerals" in raw materials plan'. 2011. EurActive. com, 27 February, http://www.euractiv.com/sustainability/eu-vows-tackle-blood-minerals-raw-materials-plan-news-501117, accessed 26 March 2012.

Hansmann, H.B. 1980. 'The role of nonprofit enterprise'. *Yale Law Journal,* 89(5), 835–901.

'Japanese corporate performance: New against old'. 2011. *The Economist,* 10 February, http://www.economist.com/node/18114309, accessed 26 March 2012.

Lewis, M. 2010. *The Big Short: Inside the Doomsday Machine.* New York: W.W. Norton.

Mason, R. 2010. 'Pressure on mobile phone makers to stop using Congolese 'blood minerals'. *The Telegraph,* 12 September, http://www.telegraph.co.uk/finance/newsbysector/retailandconsumer/7997942/Pressure-on-mobile-phone-makers-to-stop-using-Congolese-blood-minerals.html, accessed 26 March 2012.

McKinsey & Company. 2011. *Capital Markets Up Date, 2011,* http://www.mckinsey.com/Insights/MGI/Research/Financial_Markets/Mapping_global_capital_markets_2011, accessed 21 May 2012.

Nokia. 2011. 'Nokia welcomes recent developments to fight conflict minerals'. 23 September, http://www.nokia.com/global/about-nokia/people-and-planet/news/news-article-1/, accessed 26 March 2012.

Nussbaum, M.C. 2006. *Frontiers of Justice: Disability, Nationality, Species Membership*. Cambridge, MA: Belnap Press.

Patel, R. 2009. *The Value of Nothing: How to Reshape Market Society and Redefine Democracy*. Melbourne: Black.

Peers, D.M. 2006. *India under Colonial Rule 1700–1885*. Harlow: Pearson Longman.

Rawls, J. 1999. *A Theory of Justice*. Cambridge, MA: Belnap Press.

Regan, M.C. 1998. 'Corporate speech and civic virtue', in A.L. Allen and M.C. Regan, *Debating Democracy's Discontent: Essays on American Politics, Law, and Public Philosophy*. Oxford: Oxford University Press, 289–375.

Robins, N. 2006. *The Corporation that Changed the World: How the East India Company Shaped the Modern Multinational*. London: Pluto Press.

Sen, A. 2000. *Development as Freedom*. New York: Anchor Books.

Sen, A. 2010. *The Idea of Justice*. Penguin.

Sorkin, A.R. 2009. *Too Big to Fail: The Inside Story of How Wall Street and Washington Fought to Save the Financial System – and Themselves*. New York: Viking Penguin.

Stiglitz, J.E., Sen, A. and Fitoussi, J. 2010. *Mismeasuring Our Lives: Why GDP Doesn't Add Up. The 2010 Report by the Commission on the Measurement of Economic Performance and Social Progress*. New York: The New Press.

Tett, G. 2009. *Fool's Gold: How the Bold Dream of a Small Tribe at J.P. Morgan Was Corrupted by Wall Street Greed and Unleashed a Catastrophe*. New York: Free Press.

Vogel, D. 2005. *The Market for Virtue: The Potential and Limits of Corporate Social Responsibility*. Washington, DC: Brookings Institution Press.

World Bank. 2010. *Gross Domestic Product 2010*, http://siteresources.worldbank.org/DATASTATISTICS/Resources/GDP.pdf, accessed 26 March 2012.

Index

Printed and bound by CPI Group (UK) Ltd, Croydon, CR0 4YY
08/05/2025
01864511-0007